Blood, Mud and Glory

THE INSIDE STORY
OF WIGAN'S YEAR

Blood, Mud and Glory

THE INSIDE STORY OF WIGAN'S YEAR

Neil Hanson

PELHAM BOOKS

To Lynn, who kept the candle burning
in the window facing the road home
from peerless Wigan . . .

PELHAM BOOKS

Published by the Penguin Group
27 Wrights Lane, London W8 5TZ, England
Viking Penguin, a division of Penguin Books USA Inc
375 Hudson Street, New York, New York, 10014, USA
Penguin Books Australia Ltd, Ringwood, Victoria, Australia
Penguin Books Canada Ltd, 10 Alcorn Avenue, Toronto, Ontario, Canada M4V 3B2
Penguin Books (NZ) Ltd, 182–190 Wairau Road, Auckland 10, New Zealand

Penguin Books Ltd, Registered Offices: Harmondsworth, Middlesex, England

First published 1991
1 3 5 7 9 10 8 6 4 2
Copyright © Neil Hanson 1991

Text and front jacket photographs © Graham Clay and Martin Robson 1991

ISBN 0 7207 1940 2

A CIP catalogue record for this book
is available from the British Library.

Typeset in 11½/13 pt Plantin Light
Printed in England by Clays Ltd, St Ives plc

CONTENTS

Acknowledgements

TO SEE a book through from conception to publication requires almost as large a team as Wigan need to win the Championship. In far-off southern parts, my thanks go to my agent Mark Lucas, for his wise and friendly advice, and to Roger Houghton and all his staff at Pelham Books, for making writing this book for him a genuine pleasure.

I was helped by so many people at Wigan that it is impossible to list them all. I have made a partial attempt in the *Dramatis Personae*, but my thanks and apologies to those I have inadvertently missed. The Wigan chairman, Maurice Lindsay, must be singled out, however, for granting me total access to Central Park. We have had our battles, as Maurice tried to protect his players from some of their, and sometimes my, indiscretions, but *Blood, Mud and Glory* literally could not have been written without his help.

Only one person refused his co-operation, the Wigan captain Ellery Hanley. His policy of not talking to the media has few exceptions and I was never likely to be one of them. Though he refused to be interviewed or directly quoted, he did allow his manager to comment on the first draft of the chapter on Hanley, *The Monarch of Central Park*. Parts of that chapter have been amended to reflect those comments. Until Hanley chooses to end his self-imposed media exile, it is perhaps as close to a statement from him as can be achieved.

With that exception, my thanks above all must go to the Wigan players, who have tolerated the presence of an interloper and, even worse, a Yorkshireman, throughout the highs and the lows of a memorable year. The Wigan players are remarkable athletes, skilled footballers and consummate professionals. What is most admirable about them though, is the fortitude and even diffidence with which they face the triumphs and the cruel disappointments, the painful injuries and the relentless pounding that they endure in training, and especially when playing professional rugby league.

To see at close quarters the battering that the players take in every game of the breath-taking, but ferociously demanding, high-speed collision sport that is modern rugby league, is to appreciate just how hard-earned is their money. This book is respectfully dedicated to them.

NEIL HANSON Ilkley, 1991

Introduction

IF OUTSIDERS think of Wigan at all, they are likely to do so in terms of smoky chimneys and terraced houses, coal mines and miners, flat caps, clogs and shawls, black puddings and pork pies. Wigan is a music hall joke, a land-locked town with a pier, the butt of comedians from Lands End to Leigh – the next town down the road from Wigan and as virulent in its attacks as next-door neighbours everywhere tend to be.

Wigan even managed to provoke John Wesley to a tirade against 'a town proverbially famous for all manner of wickedness'. Subsequent visitors were little kinder. William Dodd, writing in 1841, said he had never seen 'so much misery and wretchedness in such a small compass before', while the Reverend William Wickham, arriving to take over a parish in 1878, reported that the name of Wigan conjured up nothing but 'bad railway accidents, colliery explosions and monster strikes.'

The Industrial Revolution had fuelled Wigan's ferocious population growth as the twin industrial pillars of Victorian prosperity, coal and textiles, grew to dominate the town. One hundred years ago there were fifty collieries and half as many weaving and spinning mills in and around the town, now there is not a single colliery and the textile industry is reduced to a remnant. The principal employer in Wigan today is the Heinz factory, on the town outskirts.

Wigan's one, rather dubious, claim to twentieth-century fame is through George Orwell's *The Road to Wigan Pier*, a bitter attack on social deprivation in 1930s Britain, which has indelibly linked the town with poverty and slum housing. As a result, Orwell was reviled by Wiganers for giving the town a bad name. It is one of the more delicious ironies of Wigan's attempts to create a fledgling tourist trade that the pub in the Wigan Pier Centre, the socio-historical theme park created around the famous pier, is named the 'George Orwell'.

1

The Pier, an insignificant pimple on the canal bank from which the coal that made Wigan's fortune was loaded onto barges, is one of the three tourist attractions of the area, if the brown-painted road signs on the motorways around the town are to be believed. The others, Pennington Flash, a lake formed by mining subsidence, and the Three Sisters – 'Wigan's Alps' – three giant spoil heaps from the mining days, are also monuments to decline and industrial dereliction, recycled as bait for tourists on the trail of industrial heritage.

Apart from the Orwell-inspired infamy of its pre-war slum housing, however, Wigan has one other claim to twentieth-century fame; it is by far the greatest name in the sport of rugby league and has been so for nearly all of the game's ninety-five year existence. Champions a dozen times, Challenge Cup winners a dozen times, the club remains a dominant force in the British game, drawing an army of support from Wigan's 300,000 inhabitants.

The jokes that outsiders make about the town only serve to draw its community closer together. The Wigan Rugby League Football Club ground, Central Park, sits right in the centre of the town and the club is at the heart of Wigan. Soccer may be the national game in most other parts of Britain, but not in Wigan. When the conversation in the town's pubs turns, as it always does, to football, it is rugby league football, not the round ball game, that is under discussion.

At one time the collieries not only employed most of the adult male population, but also produced most of Wigan's rugby league players. Men hardened by tough physical work underground would emerge from the pits to don the famous cherry and white hooped shirts, earning a few extra pounds for their prowess on the field.

The appropriately-named Frank Collier, a Wigan great from the 1950s and early 1960s, would regularly work a shift overnight down the pit, then nip home for a couple of hours sleep, before turning out for Wigan in the afternoon. Collier was a tunnel-ripper, one of the toughest jobs underground, all hand pick-and-shovel work, and a legendary hard man in the game. The story is told that when transferred to Widnes, he deliberately hung his clothes on the peg used by Widnes' own iron man, the fearsome Vince Karalius, saying 'This thy peg, Vince? There are plenty more in the room for thee to use.'

2

There are now not only no coal mines left in Wigan, there are no longer any miners in the Wigan team. Old-timers mutter about the softness of modern players, compared to those of the old days, when the first twenty minutes of any game would be a brutal war of attrition. In truth, modern rugby league players remain formidably hard men, but they are also highly trained and skilled athletes who would leave their forebears trailing breathlessly in their wake.

Rugby league's roots remain deep in its Northern industrial heartlands, but the patronising view, still occasionally espoused elsewhere, that League is a thuggish pastime, played and watched by working-class illiterates with funny accents, is a country mile wide of the mark. There are stereotypes in flat caps and mufflers to be found on the terraces and some rugby league players are still miners or ex-miners, but the range of characters and occupations among both players and spectators is far wider.

Rugby league prides itself on a family image and crowds mix and fraternise freely. There is no segregation of rival supporters and crowd trouble is rare. Fathers still bring their small sons to watch their heroes, but the game also attracts a substantial audience of women of all ages and supporters are as likely to live in leafy suburbia as the back streets. Racism is also largely absent; most teams have at least one black player, with stars like Martin Offiah, the Widnes winger, and Wigan's own Ellery Hanley, MBE – captain of Great Britain and one of the first black players to captain a British national side at any sport – the biggest names in the game.

Amongst the present first-team squad at Wigan, Joe Lydon has a first-class honours degree, while alongside half-a-dozen full-time professional footballers are an insurance underwriter and an antique dealer, together with the scrap metal dealer and the publican that the cliched view of the sport might have predicted.

Although the highest paid rugby league players now earn incomes well into six figures, the game remains close to its roots; players mix with supporters after the game, use the same pubs, live in the same neighbourhoods. The players may be the aristocracy of Wigan, but they have not yet lost the common touch.

If Wigan rugby league has had a great past, the current side has created an even more glorious present. Under the coaching of a New Zealander, Graham Lowe, and his successor, the Australian John Monie, Wigan have assembled star players from all over the world and moulded them into a side that has won every available trophy, including the World Club Championship. British stars like Ellery Hanley, Joe Lydon, Andy Gregory and Shaun Edwards, rub shoulders in the Wigan side with the finest Australians and New Zealanders. Such is the strength of the squad that two of the best South African rugby union players of recent years, Rob Louw and Ray Mordt, were unable to win regular places in the side after changing codes.

My aim was to follow the fortunes of Wigan over a twelve-month period, beginning at Wembley Stadium on a warm spring afternoon, as Wigan collected the Challenge Cup to bring down the curtain on the 1989–90 season. Though an off-comer from the other side of the Pennines, I spent the next year following Wigan as devotedly as any native of the town christened in cherry and white robes. My intention was not to offer a recitation of matches played, which months after the event would be as exciting as a Runcorn versus Chorley match on a foggy day in February. Instead I hoped to bring out the human stories of Wigan's year, the hopes, fears, disappointments and triumphs of the players and the many other diverse characters associated with the club – management and officials, stewards, hot-dog sellers and turnstile operators, and the thousands of supporters who jam the stands and terraces every week.

My year with Wigan covered the summer close-season, when the players dispersed all over the globe, some sprawled on a beach, some touring Papua New Guinea and New Zealand with the Great Britain side, some earning a fortune in Australian dollars playing in the Sydney competition, while others continued the business of earning a living outside the game, for League remains a part-time sport for many of its practitioners.

I joined them in the pre-season training, the relentless programme of weights, running, sprint and stamina training, skills work and the rest, supervised by the new breed of 'clipboard coaches', monitoring everything up to and including their players' diet.

Throughout the autumn, winter and spring, there was the constant round of training and playing, training and playing, disrupted by injuries, suspensions and all the minor and major human dramas inevitable when some of the greatest players and the greatest egos in the greatest game are concentrated in a single club.

The 1990–91 season began in down-beat fashion, but built to a series of ever higher peaks. The Charity Shield, the Lancashire Cup and the Regal Trophy, were succeeded by the climax of the great competitions of the game: the Challenge Cup and the Championship itself. That was only decided after a frenzied programme of matches in the last weeks of the season which tested to the limit Wigan's right to be regarded as the greatest exponents of the greatest game of all.

Prologue

WEMBLEY Stadium, Saturday 28 April 1990. A packed crowd bellows its triumph as the final whistle signals Wigan's third successive Challenge Cup Final victory; a feat never before achieved in the history of rugby league.

Wigan's captain, Ellery Hanley, MBE, leads his team up the steps to the Royal Box to receive the Cup and their medals. He brandishes the Cup above his head, the crowd's roar reverberating from the roof of the stadium, drowning the players in deafening acclamation. Only a faint echo of the noise reaches the Wigan dressing room, at the end of a subterranean tunnel beneath the terracing. The sparsely-furnished room stands empty, the players and officials still celebrating out on the Wembley turf.

The dressing room, used by some of the greatest names in world sport – Muhammad Ali, Pele, Diego Maradona, Walter Payton, Joe Montana – as well as a myriad of British football and rugby league stars, is scarcely the stuff of legends. It has all the atmosphere of a social security office in Scunthorpe. Harsh neon lighting illuminates the plain white walls. A blue nylon carpet, scuffed, scarred and stained by the boots of players over years of use, covers the floor, the only furniture a treatment table and the blue, plastic benches along the walls. Across one corner of the room a half-partition coyly shields a tea urn on a table also used as a bar, from where two Wembley employees will dispense champagne, beer, coke and sandwiches to the conquering heroes.

The first player into the room is Shaun Edwards. While his colleagues are still circling the stadium, milking the applause of their supporters, the stand-off is being helped down to the dressing room, his face grey with pain. In the tenth minute of the game, he had been flattened off the ball as he chased his own kick ahead. The impact had caused a depressed fracture of the cheekbone and multiple fractures around the eye-socket, but despite the excruciating pain, Edwards had stayed on the field for the rest of the match, playing a major part in the tries that ensured Wigan's victory and doing his full share of defence, not even shirking tackles on the big Warrington forwards.

In another sport, a player completing a game with a similar injury would be an instant national hero, but no such celebrity awaits Edwards. Knocks that would cripple other sportsmen are all in a day's work for rugby league players and the history of the sport is strewn with stories of men who battled their way through games carrying debilitating injuries. So the courage of Edwards will earn him a few newspaper headlines, but will be quickly forgotten – except by the only people whose opinions matter to Shaun, his fellow players.

Edwards had already displayed his courage three weeks before the final. He broke a bone in his hand during Wigan's vital match against their nearest rivals for the Championship, Leeds, but again had defied the pain, staying on the field to steer Wigan to the narrow victory that guaranteed them the title. Although his hand had not properly healed by the time of the Challenge Cup Final, Shaun was determined to play. His reward was another fracture.

The club's 'first-aider', Keith Mills, helps Edwards to inch his jersey over his head and walks with him through to the showers, asking 'Do you feel sick, Shaun? Are you dizzy?' While Edwards is showering, the first of his team-mates arrive back in the dressing room, draped with hats, scarves and banners, thrown to them by Wigan fans in the crowd. The players are whooping as they enter. 'You beauties – we stuffed 'em!' yells one. Full back Steve Hampson comes in wearing a hat, three scarves and carrying a banner, his shirt sodden with sweat. 'Ee, it's a warm 'un, Norman,' he says to no-one in particular, grinning and flopping down on the bench with a can of beer in his hand.

The captain, Ellery Hanley, makes his entrance, the Challenge Cup dangling nonchalantly from one hand, as he promises anyone within earshot 'We're going to have some fun tonight. What happened between you and Des Drummond?' he asks Kevin Iro, the giant Kiwi centre who had a brief flare-up with Drummond after scoring Wigan's final try.

Shaun comes back through from the showers, blood dribbling from his mouth and nose, Keith still at his side. 'Towel for Gizz', Keith calls to Taffy, the kit man. Taffy is lost in inner space, a can of beer in his hand and a seraphic smile on his face and doesn't hear the request.

'Taffy – a towel for Gizz. For God's sake don't get pissed yet.' Taffy comes to attention with a jerk and hands the towel across. 'Two towels,' comes the shout a minute later as Edwards presses the first one to his face, leaving it smeared with blood.

'Right lads, we'll just have a quiet moment before the press come in,' says Ellery. 'Is everybody here?' The players count off by their numbers like soldiers on parade. Number two, Joe Lydon, and number seven, Andy Gregory, are still being interviewed in the tunnel by BBC television. They appear a couple of minutes later and Wigan's undemonstrative Australian coach, John Monie, utters a few laconic words. 'It's been a long time since August. We've done a lot of work and worked very hard to get here. If we do the work we win the prize. Congratulations.' Ellery follows him. 'I normally pay tribute to the younger lads, but today I've got to hand it to the old brigade, particularly Shaun Edwards and Andy Platt. Andy's worked tremendously hard to get here.'

Platt had seemed certain to miss the Cup Final after tearing knee ligaments while playing for Great Britain, but daily hours in the physio room, followed by weeks of punishing work in the gym had brought him back to fitness in time to claim his rightful place at Wembley. The word 'work' appears constantly in the speeches of both Hanley and Monie. They are professionals and sports grounds are their places of employment. For all the magic of its name, even Wembley is still first and foremost a place where they have some business to complete.

The quiet moment is over and the press are admitted, the already crowded dressing room swamped by reporters, photographers and TV camera crews. There is a definite pecking order among the press, with the stills photographers the first in, getting their clichéd shots of players grouped around the cup, arms raised, thumbs up. 'Just one more' is a phrase on every photographer's lips; no-one alive or dead has ever heard a photographer say, 'That's enough.' 'Right that's it, now get lost,' says one player, supplying the phrase for them.

As the photographers retreat, the TV crews home in, their lights making the dressing room even more unbearably hot, sweat dripping from the reporters as well as the players. Kevin Iro, scorer of two tries at Wembley for the third final in a row, and Andy Gregory, Shaun Edwards's partner at half-back, are the principal targets.

Gregory, pocket-sized but bulging with muscle – a Popeye without the pipe – played in the Final despite his own groin injury, which will require an operation in the close season. He performed so well that he took the man of the match award, the Lance Todd Trophy, for the second time, only the second player ever to do so. Gregory's first words were to praise Edwards, however. 'I think what Shaun did shows the incredible spirit at this club. As soon as it happened he told me he thought he'd broken his cheekbone, but just said "I'll be alright." After that, he was still making heavy tackles and knocking blokes down, even though he was in agony. It was incredible.'

The radio reporters hover in the wake of the TV crews, waiting with varying degrees of patience for them to finish, while a scrum of newspaper reporters forms around John Monie and Wigan chairman Maurice Lindsay. Those reporters out of earshot scribble down the quotes second-hand from one of their colleagues after the interviews are over.

'My job finished on Thursday,' says Monie. 'The preparation went great, but I didn't do a lot today. I was just along for the ride. It's the first time I've ever sat on the sidelines, normally I sit up in the stand where I can see the pattern of the play. Today I just got a player's eye view.'

He explains his reasons for bringing on his substitutes for the closing minutes. 'Ian Gildart's been there in winter in Yorkshire when there's been nobody at the ground and he's still knocked out forty tackles. There was no way I wasn't going to put him on today, or Bobby Goulding. If we'd been allowed to put Ged Byrne, Phil Clarke, Ian Lucas, David Marshall and Gerard Stazicker on the field as well, I would have done'.

Maurice Lindsay is still revelling in the club's achievement, an unique one. Wigan are not only the first side to achieve the League and Cup double since two divisions were introduced in 1973, they are also the first side in the 95-year history of the game to win three successive Cup Finals. 'This record will never be broken,' claims Maurice, 'or at least, the only team that will ever beat it will be this lot next year.'

Coach John Monie has equally chilling news for Wigan's competitors. 'We can be better. None of our players are anywhere near retirement. We're going to be back here next year and we'll be even better.'

Amongst the bedlam of television lights and jostling reporters, Taffy battles through with bags of ice for the players, who use it to bring down the swelling on their bruises, muscle strains and 'dead-legs'. There is no sign of sympathy for his traffic problems from the players. 'Get me some ice.' 'Any towels?' 'Ice over here.' 'Where the hell's that ice?' Although surrounded by reporters and photographers, the players strip unconcernedly and push their way through to the showers; even the presence of a woman reporter does not inhibit them, her embarrassment is greater than theirs. The players mostly bear the reporters' endless streams of identical questions with good humour. Only two are not approached for their comments: Shaun Edwards, out of respect for his injuries, and Ellery Hanley. Even the most green cub reporter knows that Ellery never talks to the press, except on the exceedingly rare occasions when he decides he has a story to tell. Even such bland trivia as, 'You must be very pleased with the win?' will remain unanswered, Ellery's usual tactic being to turn his back as the reporter approaches. If the hack persists, a firm brush-off will be administered. Journalists are even forbidden to ascribe the words 'no comment' to him.

As the press leave, the boys who played in the under-11s curtain-raiser, before the Final, are allowed in. They shyly touch the Cup, dumped on the bench by the door, and cluster around Bobby Goulding for his autograph. The odds are that some of them will visit this dressing room again as adults; seven players who appeared in the under-11s match have gone on to appear in the Cup Final as adults, including three of the current Wigan side: Denis Betts, who played for Salford under-11s, Bobby Goulding, with Widnes under-11s and Joe Lydon, who played for Wigan in the first under-11s game in 1975.

Shaun is hurried away to hospital for an X-ray and probable surgery. While his team-mates celebrate the victory, he will spend his weekend in a hospital bed, receiving the best treatment that money can buy. The Wigan players are treated like thoroughbreds – for, like thoroughbeds, they are worth a lot of money to their owners.

The players begin to drift out of the dressing room, heading for the reception in the banqueting hall, where their wives and girlfriends will be waiting for them, all dressed to the eye-teeth for the greatest day in the rugby league year. A few players are still getting changed or just sitting wrapped in towels, savouring their achievement and reflecting on its implications. 'Hey, there should be a bonus for doing the double,' shouts New Zealander Dean Bell. 'It never crossed my mind to think of money until you said that,' says another player with an ironic smile, for money is never too far from the thoughts of these ultra-professionals. 'You money-minded sod, Dean,' calls Andy Gregory, 'well done!'

Two wicker baskets stand ready to receive the soiled kit, boots, shoulder pads and used towels. Taffy irreverently props the lid of one open against the Challenge Cup, shocking disrespect to the game's most sought-after trophy, familiarity perhaps breeding contempt, for it has not been out of Wigan's possession for three years. He and Keith Mills go round picking up the discarded kit and throwing it into the baskets. Every time they pass, they smile or nudge each other in the ribs, as proud of the victory and the record as the players.

John Monie catches Wigan's youngest player, the 18-year-old Bobby Goulding, admiring his winner's medal. 'I got a gold and a silver one from Sydney – won one, lost one. The gold ones are much better, aren't they?'

They walk out together, followed by Maurice Lindsay and the last few players, the Cup retrieved and carried with them. Taffy and Keith lower the lids on the kit baskets, as if bringing down the curtain on the season. They carry them out to the coach, then return for a final look round the empty dressing room, Taffy winking at the Wembley employee, waiting patiently to lock up. 'See you next year, as usual.' They drain their cans of beer and walk up the tunnel into the afternoon sunlight.

Summer Tourists

URING normal summer close-season, the Wigan players would have scattered all over the world, some piling up dollars playing the off-season with Australian clubs, some flat out on holiday beaches improving their tans, some working in their other jobs or businesses, while others worked on their strength and fitness for the next season with punishing sessions in the gym.

This was not a normal summer, however, for the Great Britain rugby league team – the Lions – were to tour Papua New Guinea and New Zealand, entailing ten weeks in the South Pacific for many of the Wigan players. When the Great Britain squad had originally been announced, Wigan had a record representation of ten players. Virtually every British-born player in the Wigan first team had been selected, the major exception being Andy Goodway, omitted not on form but because the British management feared that the individualistic Goodway would disrupt their stringent team discipline during the long overseas tour. He had already had a blow-up with the Great Britain coach Malcolm Reilly in Perpignan after the spring Test match against France; if they could not get through two days in France without a disagreement, the chances of harmony over ten weeks in Papua New Guinea and New Zealand were less than zero.

As the tour drew nearer, however, a dozen top players from Wigan and other clubs joined Goodway on the sidelines. Many had genuine injury problems, other had a variety of personal reasons for not touring. Cynics were quick to say that the number of both injuries and personal problems would have rapidly diminished if the tour had been to Australia rather than the less attractive – in the players' eyes – territories of Papua New Guinea and New Zealand.

Whatever the causes, the Great Britain squad lacked Wigan's Ellery Hanley, Andy Gregory, Shaun Edwards, Andy

Platt and Steve Hampson and half-a-dozen star players from other clubs, leaving the likely Test side unrecognisable from that which had beaten New Zealand in England just six months before. The absence of the superstars opened the door wide for the younger players, however, including some of Wigan's brightest rising stars. It also meant that the squad was free of some of the larger egos that might have caused Goodway-style frictions in the close confines of a touring party.

Despite the withdrawals, Wigan still had six representatives in the final tour squad, five of them under 21. The one veteran, the vastly experienced Joe Lydon, would fly out to join the party before the New Zealand leg of the tour, after having surgery on his injured ankle. Denis Betts, though still only 20, was also already a seasoned Test player, but youngsters like Bobby Goulding, Phil Clarke, Martin Dermott and Ian Lucas had a genuine chance of winning their first Test caps on tour. Goulding, at 18 the youngest ever Great Britain tourist, and Phil Clarke, just a few months older, found themselves in the unlikely positions of being Great Britain Test candidates even though unable to command a regular first-team place with their club.

The tour was to prove a traumatic introduction to international football for all of them, but particularly for Bobby Goulding, whose angelic face seems in bizarre contrast to his powerfully-muscled body. He looks as if he has been snapped by a seaside photographer, with Bobby's face peeping over a cut-out of a Charles Atlas in a cherry and white hooped bathing suit.

His precocious self-confidence on the field could not conceal his immaturity off it and he was also miserably homesick for much of the time. The Lions' management wisely chose the kindly and very experienced Garry Schofield as his roommate and he and the tour captain Mike Gregory kept a paternal eye on Goulding, but they could not be expected to watch over him 24 hours a day, least of all at 2.30 in the morning, as events on a June night in Auckland were to prove.

'I would have cracked up here if it hadn't have been for them,' said Goulding. 'When I've been down, Garry and Mike have picked me back up and when the homesickness has been bad, they've pulled me out of it. I get really homesick when I'm away from home; I went to Australia last year, somewhere I've always really wanted to go and I had to come back three weeks later because I was so homesick.'

Only the watchfulness of Schofield and Gregory, coupled with the soothing effects of Bobby's incessant 'phone calls home to his girlfriend, prevented him heading for home this time as well. His face a picture of misery, he missed his home, his home town and his girl and for two pins would have hopped on the first plane home after just a week on tour.

'I've been on the 'phone back to Widnes twice a day. I'm engaged to get married next year. I 'phone her to get her up in the morning and she 'phones me to get me up twelve hours later. The 'phone bill when I get home will be ridiculous, but it makes you feel better talking to home.'

Goulding's rise through the rugby league ranks had been meteoric. His father, a prop forward, had played for Widnes at 16 and went on to play for St Helens and Huyton during a long career. Bobby, who had been playing for the St Mary's amateur side in his home town of Widnes, turned professional on his sixteenth birthday, like his father before him. 'I was approached by St Helens, Warrington, Salford and Widnes as well. Wigan were the last team in for me. It wasn't just the money that made me go to Wigan, they were the World Champions at the time. I knew Andy Gregory was Wigan's scrum-half, but there has got to be a new era some time, so I thought "Why not start off at the best club in the world?"'

'Andy Gregory has been my hero since I used to watch him at Widnes, he always will be. The things that he can do on the field are just unbelievable. He's been really good to me too. People tell me that I'm the next Andy Gregory, but I've not modelled myself on him completely. I prefer to involve myself in a lot of tackling; I actually like knocking big people down, small people are harder to tackle.'

Bobby made his debut for the Wigan 'A' team when he was 17, and later the same season, in March 1989, he scored a try on his first-team debut. Andy Gregory suffered a run of injuries the following season which gave Goulding the chance of an extended run in the first team and he took his opportunity in style, playing with the panache and confidence of a veteran and without a trace of the nerves one might expect in an 18-year-old.

'I never feel nervous, I've always been told by my parents to look forward, never look back. I have a lucky charm though, rosary beads. I pray to them that the team win, that I contribute and, most of all, that I don't get hurt. I pray like that for five or ten minutes but I have them on all the time except when I'm playing.'

The call to join the Great Britain tour squad came as a surprise. 'I played against Leeds on the Tuesday night and didn't have a bad game. I was round at my girlfriend's later on and my mum rang up and started singing "Congratulations" down the 'phone!'

Although Great Britain also had the very experienced Deryck Fox in the party, it was clear from the opening game of the tour that Goulding was seen as the first-choice scrum-half. He made his Test debut against Papua New Guinea in Goroka, a game disrupted by a crowd riot met with a volley of police tear gas that also swirled around the British players as they awaited the kick-off after scoring the game's first try.

'Crazy wasn't it?' said Bobby. 'People throwing rocks. They seem like nice people, then you see the other side. I've never experienced anything like that, but I wasn't frightened, just wary.' Perhaps partly as a result of the disturbances, the tear gas and the intimidating atmosphere from a crowd held back from the pitch only by the flimsiest of fences, Great Britain lost to Papua New Guinea for the first time ever, an unfortunate start to Goulding's Test career. 'I was very disappointed after the game. Getting beaten by a poor side like that, I didn't know what to think or what to say. I didn't want to talk to anyone. Garry Schofield was sharing a room with me and I don't think we talked for two hours, just stared at the floor.'

Bobby played well and scored in a revenge victory for Great Britain in the Second Test against Papua New Guinea, but soon after arriving in New Zealand, he was brought crashing back down to earth. If his first year in senior rugby league had been a Boys Own story of incredible and uninterrupted success, including a Championship medal, a Cup-winners medal, selection as the youngest ever tourist with the Rugby League Lions and then his first Test cap, his fledgling career now took an abrupt turn for the worse.

Goulding's cherubic face belies his aggression on the pitch, but in the middle of a June night in Auckland, his off-field behaviour was also far from angelic. While most of his team-mates were in bed asleep, Goulding was arrested at 2.30 a.m. in a smart bar and restaurant after assaulting two customers. He was undoubtedly drunk, but that was no excuse for what was allegedly a largely unprovoked assault, least of all in a country where no-one under the age of 21 is permitted to drink alcohol. Released on bail the following morning, he sat alone in the hotel foyer, head in hands, looking like a frightened schoolchild waiting to see the headmaster.

The case made headline news in New Zealand and Britain and there were calls for Goulding to be sent home in disgrace. Instead, Maurice Lindsay, tour director for the Lions as well as Wigan chairman, opted to let his young half-back face the Auckland courts. Goulding subsequently escaped with a $500 fine and a payment of $1,000 in compensation, which satisfied neither the complainants nor the New Zealand press, who hounded him for the rest of the tour.

It was a lapse that his opposite number in the Test series, the Kiwis' equally fiery scrum-half Gary Freeman was to remind him about throughout the series, taunting him in an attempt to put him off his game, a tactic that was only partly successful. Bobby lost his cool in the Third Test, conceding penalties and spending ten minutes in the sin-bin as a result, but by then the series had already been won, with Goulding overshadowing and outplaying his tormentor in both the first two Tests.

The end of the tour put an end to Bobby's homesickness, but it did not signal the end of his troubles. The immaturity that had been his undoing in Auckland was to cause problems, albeit in less dramatic fashion, in the early weeks of the new season back in England, placing a question mark over Goulding's ability to remain the heir-apparent to Andy Gregory as the Wigan and Great Britain scrum-half. Coach John Monie's prediction that, 'We'll have trouble with Bobby this season. After being the Great Britain half-back, he won't like going back to being Andy Gregory's understudy', proved to be absolutely correct.

Central Park

THE GREATEST name in rugby league began its life in very humble circumstances. The original Wigan club was born at Dicconson Street in 1872 and played rugby union, for the great split over 'broken time' – compensation for loss of earnings while playing rugby – was still twenty-three years away.

Even at the modest rent of £2.50 per annum, the club struggled, amalgamating with nearby Upholland and then folding up altogether within the year. Re-formed as Wigan Wasps the following year, the club survived to become one of the pioneers of the Northern Union, as the Rugby League was originally known, in 1895. Like most of the other leading rugby clubs in the North, Wigan had recognised that rules designed for Southern gentlemen amateurs were entirely irrelevant to Northern working men, who quite simply could not afford to take time off work to play rugby unless the wages lost for their 'broken time' were made up. Hence, Wigan was a natural convert, having already been suspended from the Rugby Union the previous year, after making illegal payments to its players.

The wounds left by the split between the two rugby codes have still not entirely healed nearly one hundred years later; while many in rugby league wish to see the game expand to become a truly national sport, there are also some who revel in its Northern isolation. The near-tribalism of the rugby league fraternity is at least in part a reflection of the traditional Northern resentment of the 'soft South'. While there are far more amateurs than professionals playing the game, the word 'amateur' carries no special status, no implication of moral superiority in rugby league. It is widely and correctly assumed that amateur rugby league players would welcome the chance to prove themselves at the highest level – the professional game – while many ex-professionals spend the last years of their careers playing or coaching at amateur clubs.

17

Union players coming into league are usually given a searching, and occasionally brutal, examination; trial by ordeal on the field of play. That reflects the great divide, for union players are often perceived as inferior beings, lacking the hardness and skill of top league players, lazy or flash characters unwilling to undertake the donkey-work, the tackling, that is essential in league. If the old working-class base of the sport has been largely eroded by the changing nature of twentieth-century Britain, the most-admired features of rugby league remain traditional working-class virtues: hardness, skill, taking pain and adversity without flinching and earning a fair financial reward for sweat and hard graft expended.

Central Park, Wigan, is typical of football grounds throughout the country. Built in 1902, it was regularly filled to capacity during the inter-war boom years for professional sport, but the money generated was rarely, if ever spent on improving the ground. Despite recent improvements it still looks what it is – a relic from a distant past. The homely clubhouse, built in 1909, still stands, though it is now held in the rigid steel embrace of the new cantilever stand, built right over the top of it during the 1990–91 season.

The provision of new seats, sponsors' boxes, banqueting facilities and all the other accoutrements of professional sport in the 1990s has slightly marred the folksy charm of the old red-brick clubhouse, but it has also mercifully obscured an ugly concrete extension. That had been built as Wigan succumbed to the 1960s obsession with new buildings in which to house the bars and clubrooms that were to prove cash cows for some and leaking white elephants for others.

The clubhouse end of the ground excepted, Central Park has changed little since the war. Facilities for spectators then varied from basic to non-existent. Seats were hard, stands and terraces cold, draughty places, the toilets for men primitive and open to the elements, those for women scarcely more hygienic and pitifully few. Some things have changed, others remain the same; approach Central Park from any direction but the front and the first impression may still be one of dereliction, coils of rusty barbed wire on top of crumbling walls, mud, pools of standing water and primitive facilities.

The new regime at Wigan took over ten years ago, determined to improve the facilities, but their efforts so far have made little impact on a ground scarcely suitable for the 1960s, let alone the 1990s. Admittedly, like all sports clubs, Wigan has been burdened with safety work in the wake of the Taylor Report into safety at football grounds, but, again like all sports clubs, Wigan had spent scarcely a pound on its facilities in fifty years and arguably had it coming. Though the 'River Caves', as the gents toilets behind the main stand are known, have been roofed, they remain dank and gloomy, with concrete floors, exposed breeze blocks and not a wash-basin, let alone a towel to be seen.

Despite its imperfections, however, a rugby league match at Central Park has an atmosphere matched nowhere else. The Wigan fans are the most numerous, knowledgeable, vociferous and shamelessly one-eyed supporters in the whole of rugby league. They expect success as a birthright. When they get it, they are loud in their praise; when they don't, they are quick to bay for blood. Central Park is the most demanding, but also the most rewarding arena in rugby league.

The Wigan dressing room is painted cherry and white, inevitably, for those are Wigan's colours. The fake wood panelling on the walls is partly obscured by the paint and the floor is covered in red, industrial-grade linoleum. The room has something of the air of a tap room in a down-market pub. The illusion used to be strengthened on match days by the sight of a crate of beers, for post-match consumption, under the battered treatment table in the middle of the room, but the modern professionals prefer fruit, soft drinks and vitamin supplements.

On the dressing-room wall is a control box for the sauna, its temperature setting dial sealed with pink elastoplast. There is also a blackboard and a grubby, smeared and streaked mirror. An advertisement from a dental laboratory in Wigan completes the spartan decor, offering mouthguards in a choice of delectable colours:

Bright ....White

Gruesome...Black

Monster slimy ....Green

Fluorescent...Orange

Grass ....Green

Deep Sea ....Blue

Danger Area ....Red

As the players drifted in to get changed for the first full training session of the season, Andy Gregory was holding court as usual from 'millionaire's row' – the far corner of the dressing-room where he, Ellery Hanley and Andy Goodway have their pegs. While his team-mates sat around or got changed, Andy regaled them with the tale of his summer operation on his persistent and painful groin injury.

'I'd torn the muscles either side of my groin. I was supposed to be in hospital for ten days after the operation, but I came home after three. I'd been there for a couple of days and I'm sitting there thinking: "Here's me, a little lad from the North Country, all on my own in London." So when the doctor came in on his rounds I said to him, "What am I supposed to be doing for the next week?" He said, "Just what you're doing now, resting and going for a gentle walk."

'I said, "Well, I can do that just as easily at home in Widnes." So I 'phoned up Heathrow and booked myself on the next shuttle up to Manchester and I called a taxi to take me out to Heathrow. The doctor stopped on his way back from the ward and said, "Well, see you tomorrow," and I said, "Why, are you coming to the North of England?"'

A few players headed down the corridor to the treatment room so that physiotherapist Denis Wright and first-aider Keith Mills could work on their injuries or ease the soreness from muscles hammered by Bob Lanigan's weights session the day before. Lanigan, a weight-training expert brought over from Australia to build up the players in the off-season, was to remain until the last week in September before returning to Sydney. By then, if his treatment had been successful, the players would be stronger, bigger and more powerful than they had ever been. Already they looked ferociously fit and hungry; it was hard to see any English team standing in their way, but an English team was not uppermost in their minds, as Maurice Lindsay admitted. 'I suppose I shouldn't say this really, but my ultimate objective for this season is to be the first English side to beat the Australians since 1978.'

The 1982 Kangaroos – 'The Invincibles' – and the 1986 'Unbeatables' both swept irresistibly through their tours of

Britain. Lindsay was determined that the 1990 Kangaroos would not achieve the same success and desperately wanted his Wigan side to be the first to beat them. He had one major worry: 'They play St Helens straight off the plane. It would be just our luck if Saints caught them cold and beat them!'

While some players were having treatment and others were comparing notes on the weekend or listening spellbound to the Andy Gregory show in the dressing room, Bob Lanigan was putting Ellery Hanley and Bobby Goulding through a weights session in the gym. Red-painted signs around the walls exhorted them to greater effort: 'Eat, Work, Train, BIG.' 'There is no easy way.' The punchbag carried some contrasting exhortations, graffiti scrawled on the white leather by players in quiet moments: 'No pain, no gain; no pain, no train; no train, no play; no play, no pay.' 'There is no easy way; Oh yes there is – anabolic steroids.'

Lanigan put the two players through a gruelling session, culminating in multiple sets with the boxing gloves, where they punched his padded hands in super-fast rhythm, perhaps 200 punches in 120 seconds. The prodigiously fit Ellery, who had already done a full weights session on his own earlier in the afternoon, finished his sets and then urged on Goulding, while Lanigan eyeballed Bobby from six inches away, shouting at him constantly as the gloves thudded into his padded hands: 'Come on, Bobby, I can't even feel it. Hit harder, harder, harder. Pick up the rhythm. Come on, only thirty seconds to go. Harder, harder. That's better, keep it going. Ten seconds. Hit harder. Finish well. Come on, five, four, three, two, one. That's it. Well done.'

Just before six o'clock the players all hurtled down to the training ground at Robin Park for a gruelling fitness session, Martin Dermott breaking the lap record for the one mile journey across town, laughing insanely as he flung his car through the traffic.

Pre-season

WITH the players all out at training, the kit man, christened Derek Jones, but universally known as 'Taffy', settled down with a cup of coffee in his kingdom, the boot room, a cramped space, lined with wooden cubbyholes full of boots, reached through a door in the corner of the dressing room.

Torn and scarred hardboard ersatz 'tiling' in one corner flanks a white handbasin in which Taffy rinses the mud from the players' boots. The whole room is a dusty, cobwebbed remembrance of times past, but with a move to new dressing rooms under the stand due within the year, there was little point in the club spending time and effort on a re-fit or even a spring-clean.

Taffy is the head groundsman as well as looking after the kit. He came to Wigan twenty years ago from his native North Wales, not to play rugby league, but to join a brass band. Taffy played a mean soprano cornet and in the competitive world of brass bands, that was enough to persuade the Wingates Band to arrange a job for him in Wigan.

'I started at Central Park about 1977. I didn't come here as groundsman, I just came part-time to do kit and that at weekends, just for a bit of beer money, not that you could get much beer for what the money was. My full-time job now is groundsman; I do the kit when I've finished working on the ground.

'I have a good relationship with the players, you've got to, but I don't socialise with them, though after a game a lot of the younger players ask me how they've played. You've got to be honest with them, when they do that. I don't profess to be a great expert on rugby but they just ask, even quite a few of the seasoned players.

'Sometimes you see the players around after they've finished their careers, but not very often. Once they've done that's it, they've done, they don't come to training or anything like that. Very few even come to watch Wigan, a few do, but most of them don't.'

The only man at Wigan who calls Taffy by his real name is Keith Mills, his best mate and sparring partner. 'Me and Keith always keep together, we're a bit like Laurel and Hardy really. We always sit in the front seat of the coach on the away games and we have a few laughs together, especially when we go to Wembley. It's amazing how many friends we all find we have when we get to Wembley. They all 'phone up, they all want tickets, even friends from fifty years ago!

'The way I look at it though, there are people like me work for other clubs and they work for years and years and years, and never get to Wembley. So it never loses the magic for me, it's still special, even though I've been four or five times now. When I started here they weren't a good team really, so I've been very lucky.'

While Taffy was relaxing with his coffee, the Wigan players were sweating it out at Robin Park. They train there during the autumn and spring on the council-owned facilities, which include several rugby pitches, a grass running track, an all-weather soccer pitch and an athletics stadium complete with grandstand.

The only drawback, from Wigan's point of view, is that there are no floodlights. When the nights start to close in, training switches to Wigan's own training pitch, a mudheap just outside the ground, at the end farthest away from the dressing rooms. Trudging past the back of the stand on a wet, cold winter's night to go training on an even wetter, colder pitch is not one of life's greatest pleasures.

That remained a few months away at this stage of the season, however. This evening the weather was still hot and sunny and the players were soon sweating as they warmed up, jogging, stretching and striding out, jogging, stretching and striding out, under the watchful eye of Bill Hartley, once an Olympic medal-winner in the 400 metres hurdles, now Wigan's sprint trainer and conditioner.

The first part of his job done, Hartley handed over to John Monie and his battery of coaching assistants: Graeme West, a former Wigan player and New Zealand Test star who coaches the reserves, the 'A' team; Harry Pinner, a former Great Britain loose forward with St Helens, now Monie's assistant at Saints' most deadly rivals; and Bob Lanigan. About thirty

23

spectators were standing around the touchline, among them an old man in a shabby blue suit, who spoke to no-one but watched the players go through their paces with rapt attention.

Now thoroughly warmed-up, the players were put through an exhausting series of drills, hurling themselves repeatedly at the tackling bags, doing close handling against the tackling pads and running sets of sprints with the 'power sleds', a Lanigan innovation, small sledges, loaded with weights and harnessed to the players.

Monie took the forwards in drills on the tackling bags and Lanigan worked with the backs on the pads, while the juniors went off to do fitness and skills work with West and Pinner. The bags are thick cylinders, perhaps three feet in diameter and as big as a man, which the players repeatedly crash-tackle to the ground; the pads are padded shields about two feet square, held by the players providing opposition to those doing close-passing drills.

Monie spent some time on the technique of tackling, making sure that all his players, from the vastly experienced Hanley and Goodway, to the newest recruit, knew the proper technique. 'Get your foot in close to your target before you make the hit and put your head on the same side as that foot; you've only got one head, you want to make sure you hang on to it.'

They went through the drills at walking pace until Monie was happy with the technique, then built up the pace and intensity over a series of repetitions, carrying out a gruelling series of 'hits' on the bags. Again and again the players sprinted back to the mark, then turned to run up as a line, crashing into the bags, which were put upright again by the forwards waiting their turn. This may have been practice, but there was nothing half-hearted about the way they attacked the tackling bags or did the rest of their training.

After twenty minutes the backs and forwards swopped over, the forwards working on close inter-passing while the backs underwent trial by tackling bag. League is a democratic game: while there are obvious distinctions between back and forward play, everyone runs with the ball and can take and give a pass and no-one can shirk his share of the tackling.

Tackling practice over, Monie drew his players together to point out a defensive flaw in the previous week's game, a friendly, in which an error by one of the players had opened a hole in Wigan's defensive line. The side were operating a modified defensive pattern for the opening weeks of the season and Monie wanted to make sure all his players understood how it worked and what they should be doing in every possible situation.

They had now been training for an hour and the number of spectators, still including the old man, had risen to about sixty. Most were young, a few boys and a lot of girls gazing shyly at their heroes, identifying the new faces since last season and comparing notes on whose autograph they hoped to get. In the final session, both forwards and backs did ball-work, the forwards practising handling and passing, while the backs worked on a series of variations on set moves and practised the defensive pattern against players coming on overlaps, drop-offs – known as 'scissors' in rugby union – and coming into the line between the centres. Whenever the set moves succeeded there was swift praise: 'Good work, good work'.

The star players train as they play, with relentless concentration and intensity, though it is also obvious that they enjoy, and are immensely proud of their skills. During any pause in the training groups of players flicked passes or spiralled kicks to each other, while Bobby Goulding buzzed around burning up enough energy for ten, but enjoying himself hugely, chip-kicking, firing out reverse passes and trying to catch the ball behind his back. Even the famously solemn-faced Shaun Edwards had time for the occasional joke, pretending to 'stiff-arm' Ellery as he came through the middle on a planned move, a smile briefly illuminating Shaun's face before he resumed the mask of total concentration on the job. There was a suspicion of hostility however, between Shaun and Frano Botica, the former New Zealand All Black signed amid much publicity during the summer. Perhaps Shaun was keen to establish his dominance over a man whose preferred position in rugby union had been stand-off. Whatever the reason, there seemed to be just slightly more force than necessary in their confrontations during the practice moves.

That seemed to be the only sign that Botica was not a welcome arrival at Central Park, though John Monie had already complained that signing an ex-rugby union player was 'a risk that a club like Wigan don't have to take. We already had a proven rugby league player, Phil Blake, who was keen to come back from Australia to rejoin us, and now we've filled our import quota with a rugby union player on the wrong side of 25-years-old.'

Union players often face a baptism of fire from opponents resentful of the fat signing fees and media ballyhoo that greets their arrival, but hooker Martin Dermott denied that anyone in the Wigan dressing room would be looking to make life hard for Botica. 'I wouldn't say there's much resentment. When a new signing arrives in the dressing room, we welcome him. The sooner he settles down and gets on with the job, the better. If he's being signed for all that money and plays well, then he's helping the team and he's helping me and the lads win money. At the end of the day, it's your living and if he can come in and add that extra sparkle, or score that try in the last minute, the money is going in everybody's pocket. So he's looking after himself and his family, but he's looking after us as well.'

Botica was a natural target for rugby league scouts, for his path to the All Black Test stand-off berth was blocked for the foreseeable future by the Auckland points machine Grant Fox, but Botica was perhaps as surprised as Monie by Wigan's interest in him. 'My first thought was that with all those stars already in the team, why should they want to sign me? I definitely fancied the idea of becoming a professional league player, but I also felt a little apprehensive about making the switch. If it all goes wrong in league, you've made your decision and there's no going back.'

Maurice Lindsay persuaded Botica that there was room in the squad for him and that his goal-kicking, an under-used asset in union with Grant Fox around, would strengthen one of the few weaknesses in Wigan's formidable armoury. After a hesitant start, Botica worked tirelessly to master the very different requirements of league, though he makes oblique acknowledgement of his early troubles in coming to terms with the new game.

'John Monie is very straight with the players, that's his strength. It's down to the player to be man enough to take the criticism and sort out the problem.' Frano also reinforced Martin Dermott's claim that there was little friction following his signing, paying particular tribute to fellow-Kiwi Dean Bell. 'Dean's been a great help to me. We train together and he's gone out of his way to put me right on the finer points of the game.'

If the transition from union to league is always a giant step, Botica was at least prepared for the pressures involved in playing for Wigan. 'As an All Black, the demand for success was already part and parcel of the job. People just don't except you to lose when you play for New Zealand and at Wigan things are just the same. There's the same fierce competition for places and they're the team that everyone would love to play for and that everyone wants to beat.'

Though aware of his coach's reservations, Maurice Lindsay was confident that Wigan had picked a winner in Botica. Unlike some other clubs, whose policy of recruiting ex-union players amounts almost to an obsession, Wigan had signed very few of them in recent years. The much-publicised capture of two Springbok stars, Rob Louw and Ray Mordt, had ended with the two being quietly – but expensively – released from their contracts. Since then the bulk of the recruitment had been from amateur rugby league.

'I honestly believe that people were under-valuing the quality of young league talent,' said Lindsay. 'Players like Martin Offiah and Alan Tait show that there is talent in rugby union, but from rugby league at a much younger age, you can get stars like Garry Schofield, Andy Gregory and Bobby Goulding. If you looked closely at the players in the English Schools' rugby league team, you'd admit you were impressed. They're ten years ahead of where the same team would have been a few years back, because they're so much more mature and accomplished.

'Of course if you sign a top union player you get the publicity – just look at Widnes and Jonathan Davies. We signed Denis Betts and got a few lines in the local press, whereas Jonathan Davies was on national television, but the judgement of the player is what counts ... and you get the media attention when you win three successive Challenge Cup Finals. We do make signings from union, but we think that English Schools' rugby league is the greatest bed of talent available.'

At Robin Park, the rare exception to the rule, Frano Botica, completed his evening's work. After two hours' intensive training, Monie called a halt for the night and the players jogged from the pitch to their cars, then disappeared from the sun-baked car park in clouds of dust. As usual, the coaches had to dragoon players into taking the training equipment and tackling bags back to the building in which they are kept, and as usual, they finished up carrying most of it themselves. The old man in the shapeless blue suit was the last to leave, gazing around the now-empty field for a last time before walking off slowly towards the town.

The Charity Shield

HAVING already thrashed Warrington in the annual pre-season friendly, the Locker Cup, Wigan now faced another of their trinity of most-hated opponents, Widnes, in the opening fixture for the new season, the Charity Shield. It is usually a contest between the previous season's Champions and Cup-winners, but since Wigan had won both, the Premiership holders had been drafted in as opponents. Widnes had been virtually the only side to dent Wigan's near-monopoly of trophies over the previous four seasons, winning the Championship twice and the Premiership three times. They were also seen by most observers as the only side likely to prevent Wigan from cleaning up the trophies again this time.

The Rugby League was making another of its periodic attempts to foster its long-cherished dream of expansion beyond its traditional northern strongholds, by taking the Charity Shield match into the heartland of Welsh rugby union, South Wales, though the game was to be played on the Vetch Field soccer ground, in Swansea. Previous attempts had ended in failure, most recently with the demise of the Cardiff Blue Dragons a few years before, but the massive television exposure of league, coupled with a flood of Welsh players to league clubs in recent years, had convinced the League that the time was right for another try.

Summer was now emphatically over. The crowd of spectators at Wigan who had watched the pre-season training sessions had now dwindled to a hardy few, huddled under their umbrellas, as the players grunted and groaned their way closer to perfection at the Thursday training session. This finished with half-an-hour working on the set moves, over and over until John Monie pronounced himself satisfied. There were far fewer errors and dropped balls than a week before. The players looked confident and ready for the Charity Shield game, even though Wigan would be lacking seven injured internationals: Steve Hampson, Ellery Hanley, Joe Lydon, Andy Gregory, Andy Goodway, Martin Dermott and Kevin Iro were all ruled out, while an eighth, Shaun Edwards, was on the substitutes' bench, with Frano Botica taking the stand-off role.

The long summer drought had ended in a prolonged torrential downpour; the weekend armada of cars and coaches streaming down the motorway from the North, Wigan or Widnes scarves trailing from the windows, was shrouded in a pall of spray hurled up from the wheels. Despite the rain, the curious locals manned the street corners outside the Swansea pubs, to watch the Northern aliens pass by on their way to the ground. A few thousand Welshmen joined the queues at the turnstiles, celebrating the return of Widnes' Welsh ex-rugby union stars, Jonathan Davies and John Devereux, to their roots.

Wigan began well, the forwards dominating the opening fifteen minutes, with prop Kelvin Skerrett, a big-money capture from Bradford Northern during the close season, in the van, terrorising an inexperienced Widnes opponent, but once Widnes began to spread the ball wide of the ruck, a frail Wigan defence began to fall apart. Several players looked completely at sea with Monie's new defensive pattern. On a couple of occasions half of them were sliding across the field, while the others were sprinting up on their opposite numbers yelling, 'Attack, attack.' Widnes poured through the resultant holes and put the game out of Wigan's reach well before the end.

The Charity Shield went to Widnes 24–8, Jonathan Davies making a triumphant return to Wales with a fine hat-trick, and while Widnes lapped the pitch, showing the trophy to their exultant fans, a dispirited and chastened Wigan side slumped in the dressing room. Dean Bell, one of the senior professionals, was the only man to break the silence, the rest staring at the end of their boots. 'As long as we learn from this. A good whipping doesn't hurt anyone if you learn from it. Sometimes our attitude was outstanding; at other times it was crap. Just so long as we learn from this; and that's got to start from tomorrow at training. We lost this game last year and went on and won everything else, now we've got to do that again.' The Widnes players whooped their way down the corridor to their dressing room. No-one spoke in the Wigan one, the only sounds were the showers and the scraping of studs on the floor.

After a few minutes, the natural ebullience of the players slowly began to return, one or two talking quietly together, one even cracking a couple of jokes. Widnes' woman physiotherapist, Viv Gleave, popped in for a quick word with one of the Wigan players. His team-mates returning from the showers stark naked, didn't give her a second glance. She looked no more interested or embarrassed than them, indifferent to the array of naked flesh or the tattoos, apparently *de rigueur* for Wigan players, that several had emblazoned on their buttocks.

Prop Andy Platt was taken away for routine drug testing, often a lengthy process, for players can be so dehydrated after a game that it can take half-an-hour and several cans of soft drinks to produce enough urine for a sample. 'I hope there was nothing in those pills you've been giving me,' he shouted to Bob Lanigan, as the drug testers led him out. Lanigan laughed, his pills were the perfectly legal amino acids which help to prevent players losing the muscle built up in his gruesome weights sessions.

Unlike Wembley a few months before, there was no flood of journalists into the Wigan dressing room this time, for they and their readers are only interested in winners. Down the corridor Jonathan Davies was besieged by reporters, but only one journalist came into the Wigan room, getting a brief comment for an Australian magazine from John Monie, before disappearing.

The week following the Charity Shield defeat was the last involving the pre-season training routine of six sessions a week: weights Monday, Wednesday and Friday, physical training on Tuesday, more conditioning and ball-work on Thursday and ball-work on Saturday, with the game on Sunday. During the run of the season, Wigan follow the standard winter routine of training Tuesday and Thursday and a light session on Saturday morning, with each player fitting in his fitness and weight training at his own convenience.

Bob Lanigan's main work was already completed. There is little more the players can do to build up their strength once they are on the treadmill of weekly and often twice-weekly games; all that they can hope to do is hold on to most of the gains in weight and power they have made. On his arrival in

31

England, Lanigan had detected a clear difference in strength between the Wigan players and the Australians he normally trains, but after three months at Central Park, he felt the gap had closed. 'I look at football as being in three phases: speed, endurance and power. One of the areas that was a little bit neglected, but has really been addressed in the last five years in Australia is power, which comes through weight training. I brought a weights programme with me that the Australian champions, the Canberra Raiders, have used for the last two seasons and I think that has helped tremendously. Looking at these Wigan players now, I think the Kangaroos are going to get quite a surprise when they play here. The Wigan blokes were probably about 20 per cent short of the players I worked with in Sydney in terms of strength and power, but I'm now very confident that these guys are up to a par with them. Hopefully the extra strength will show on the field in results and less injuries.'

As well as putting the players through a relentless series of weight repetitions, Lanigan also had them working out with boxing gloves, pounding the punch bag and raining blows onto his padded hands. The intention was not to improve their performance in any on-field punch-ups, but to build upper-body strength and stamina and sharpen their reflexes and hand-eye co-ordination. With the season now started, however, Lanigan was winding down the players' workload in the gym. 'The players are down to just two weights sessions a week instead of three and the programme is down to about 45 minutes instead of an hour-and-a-half.'

Though Lanigan's main role was to work with the players in the gym, he usually turned up at evening training too, to give Monie a hand. Joe Lydon had failed to show up for a weights' session earlier in the day, a fact reported by Lanigan as Joe jogged out onto the training field that evening. 'Got a new job Joe?' Monie enquired.

'No, just the same one, graphic design a couple of days a week.'

'Why weren't you in to do weights with "Lano" today, then?'

'I was, but he wasn't there.'

'What time did you come in?'

'Two o'clock.'

'Well, he's at home then. He's in ten till lunchtime and four to six to supervise the weights' sessions. Make sure you're there next time – it only cost about five thousand quid to bring him over to supervise your workout and keep you up to the mark.'

His point made, Monie turned away. Bill Hartley took the players for the running work, putting them through a series of interval runs, running, hopping, high-stepping and even skipping in a way that would provoke derisive wolf-whistles and shouts of 'Mind your handbags' in other circumstances. The Wigan players respect Hartley enough not to question the need for any exercises he orders, however, and they did what he asked without camping it up or fooling about. It was not always so. 'At one time a lot of them didn't realise the value of stretching and they were very immobile, but the game's changed so much now that they can't afford not to,' said Hartley.

Only one or two of the players appeared to be lazy trainers, pulling out a few yards short of the finishing line each time, most pushed themselves hard. It is no coincidence that the best trainers are almost always the best players . . . and Wigan have a near-monopoly on the best players in the game.

While Bob Lanigan was responsible for the players' strength and power training, Hartley's role was to improve their general condition and sprint speed. As in the other areas of specialist coaching, Wigan recruited the best expert help for the players' sprint training and Hartley remains impressed with the club's thorough-going professionalism.

'Compared to this sport, soccer is really in the dark ages. That's not true for all the clubs, but I just can't believe the way they train and the attitudes of a lot of them, whereas rugby league is one of the most open sports there is. If they've had a problem, say with weight training, they say: "Well, we need someone to help us here," and they go out and find the best person they can and bring him in to help.

'My basic job is to condition the players. I work with them individually when we feel they require it or when they do; very often it's the players who will come to me. They either come to training early or come down on a different night.

'I work quite a lot with Shaun Edwards, Steve Hampson, Mark Preston and Denis Betts. I think they realise the value of it, but during the season, when we're playing a lot of midweek games, they don't always get much chance to work on the speed training, so we fit in sessions when we can.

'We work on speed off the mark mostly, over twenty or thirty yards or so, but sometimes they feel their endurance needs topping up as well. You're looking to get a speed gain from most players, but the greater part of that will come from their general condition – weights, power and all that side. So really my main job is with the player who isn't converting that power because he has a poor running style, though to be honest with you, there aren't many of them that aren't good runners.

'It's just making them aware of a shortcoming. Kelvin Skerrett, for example, who's just come here, is 23-years-old and he's been running in the same style all his life, so it's very hard for him to change. It's a very gradual process, you just have to try and build an image in their own mind of what they should be doing and the correct way to do it.

'The hardest part really is varying the training to stop it from getting boring. When I was running, I used to go out and warm up in the same way every time. I mean you've got to stretch and you've got to jog and you've got to stride out, so really it's variations on a theme and you can't stray far from it.'

Like Lanigan, Hartley felt the players were already close to peak condition; the difficult job now was to try and keep them that way, without allowing them to get stale or overtrained. 'What we found last year, particularly when they're playing two games a week, is that you've got to really ease down on them. There are times when it's more important to get them to rest than to get them to train. They're such good pros, you've really got to bang them on the head to tell them to stop rather than to kick them up the backside, because they can tend to do too much. A lot of them are full-time pros and they've got all day, so maybe they go and do an extra session of weights, just to fill in the time as much as anything.

'You pick up from talking to them when they need a little extra training. There'll probably be a time in the season when they're just a little short on the endurance work, so we'll pick that up for a couple of weeks, not just for the physical reasons, the mental ones can be just as important. If they feel they need it, then we do it.

'On the track, you can aim to peak for certain events but it's very, very hard to do that here, plus once you're into the season, you've always got players coming back from injury at varying stages of fitness. So basically you get them in good shape at the start of the season and then the games really keep them fit. I mean Andy Platt played about forty games last year. The biggest problem was that every time we came to weigh him, he'd lost another couple of pounds, and that was just through playing a lot of games.'

The tall, lean Hartley still looks as fit as when he was tearing up the track as one of Britain's top athletes, but while he retains enough speed to give most of the Wigan players a race over the length of the pitch, the power, skill, resilience and endurance that they possess leave him open-mouthed in admiration. 'It was a culture shock when I came to this game. The only way to really condition your body to the knocks you get in a body-contact sport is to play it, there's no way you can really train for that. Parts of the game don't really come across when you're in the stand watching a game, you're divorced from the ferocity of the tackles and the speed of the movements. When I'm out on the pitch working with them, the speed that the ball travels at is amazing and you can really see the ferocity of the hits.'

Monie Talks

FOR defending Champions, Cup-holders and Regal Trophy winners, Wigan's early season form was anything but regal. The defeat in the Charity Shield at the hands of Widnes had been followed by a win, a 70 point thrashing of Second Division Barrow, in the first round of the Lancashire Cup, but on the following Sunday Widnes again proved too good, this time by 24–22, in the second-round tie. The game was a thriller, only won by a last minute touchline conversion, but that was little consolation for another defeat.

John Monie remained philosophical about their exit from the Lancashire Cup, however, believing that the tough pre-season training programme, which had partly contributed to their defeats by Widnes, would pay dividends over the full season. On Monday morning, following his normal routine, he sat down with his assistant, Harry Pinner, to analyse the video of the game and the match statistics.

Apart from his preference for tracksuits and his Australian accent, Monie could easily pass for a city slicker. Well groomed and well turned-out, his whole bearing exudes authority and quiet competence. He rarely if ever raises his voice, in welcome contrast to the old-fashioned breed of coach still operating at some clubs. Monie prefers to achieve his ends by intellect, quiet persuasion and the force of reason, rather than the emotion, bluster and threats which are the stock-in-trade of the old-fashioned coaches. He is a deep thinker about both the strategy and tactics of the game and the equally important areas of physical and mental preparation of players. His shelves are lined with rugby league titles, but also with books on sports psychology and about winners in every sport. A shy and very private man, his social life is strongly concentrated around his home and a small circle of close friends, shunning the pubbing and clubbing in which many sports coaches and their players indulge.

Monie had coached a Premiership winning side, Parramatta, in the tough Sydney competition before coming to Wigan, picking up the reins from the New Zealander Graham Lowe, the most successful coach that Wigan or British rugby league had ever seen. It is a tribute to Monie's abilities that in his very first season he was able to equal, and even better, the best that Lowe had achieved. Monie's blend of Australian defensive organisation and British attacking flair saw Wigan sweep to the treble of Cup, Championship and Regal Trophy. His task now was the even more daunting one of repeating that initial success, but he felt that he had already made the right start. 'When I first came over here, it was obvious that the number one area where we could really improve the players was the off-season training and in particular their weight training. That's why, when I was in Australia this summer, I got Bob Lanigan to come over. The main problem was that we had a lot of players away on the tour with Great Britain and we had other guys on holidays.

'The ones that responded to it and came in – our best three guys were Botica, Bell and Platt – have all benefited from it and have all put on weight. Through past experience I know that whatever they put on, they usually lose half of it once they start running a lot and the season starts, but that's better than starting off at the weight you were and then still losing some. So those three guys in particular are well in front. Next year we want to take it a stage further because there's no tour next summer, so we want to give them a month off at the end of the season and then get the whole squad in and do it properly and then we'll really get some benefits.

'While I was in Australia I used my time to go to games and go to different clubs' training sessions and I spent a couple of weeks with Wayne Bennett at the Brisbane Broncos. I haven't been able to do that in the past because I've been a Sydney club coach, but I was able to get around this time and have a look at different training sessions and pick up some new ideas, so that football-wise, when I came back, I'd hopefully be a little bit smarter.

'By the time I got back, Bill Hartley, who handles all our running training, had started to work with Bob Lanigan and they'd worked out a running programme and a weight-training programme. We let that run as long as we could, but once the season started to get a little bit closer, I had to step in and start to take over the football side of things, the tackling drills and the ball-handling drills and all those sort of things.

'Our programme was aimed at the start of the Championship. Now that the Lancashire Cup has been brought right to the start of the season, we hoped that we could get through the first couple of rounds with the lighter preparation. As it turned out, we drew Widnes in the second round and a side that good is capable of beating you when you've got everything going for you, let alone when you're a little bit short of preparation, so it was unfortunate. There were only two points in it and we could have won that game as well, but that's the way it goes.'

Monie insisted that the new defensive pattern, which some of the players still seemed unsure about, was still on trial. 'It's just the result of having a look at the way the Australian teams have been using their defensive patterns. It's a system we've never used before and we were going to give it a go until we were eliminated from the Lancashire Cup, or until we won it and then we were going to take stock. When we get to those sort of decisions, I don't say to the players, "Well I've got all the answers, here's a new way to do it, we're going to do it that way." I say, "Well, give it a go; at the end of the Lancashire Cup we'll make up our minds whether we're going to use it or go back and do it the way we did it last year."

'The players have got to be happy with it and I've got to be happy to go the way the players want to go, so it's a two-way thing; we've got to work it out among ourselves. We also have team meetings on Tuesday nights when everybody has their say about what happened in the previous Sunday's game. The players can have their say and I can have mine. It's a good discussion night where we sit down and go over the good and bad points from the previous game.

'Usually your gut feelings after the game are correct; if you think a player was poor or he didn't play well or he had a good game, your first thoughts are never far off the mark, but quite often when I watch the video, a player who I thought was at fault, wasn't quite as bad as I thought he was, because something else has turned up on the video. I never talk to the players after the game, not about the game anyway. I'll always give the player something positive or something good after the game, but I never discuss my feelings after the game or on the Sunday night. If you win, everything's fine and you accept some of the mistakes the players make, but if you lose, it's such an emotional game and you put so much hard work into it . . .

'Sometimes I've got to bite my tongue, because I feel like really giving someone a blast. By Monday morning, when you calm down and watch the tape with not that much emotion, because you're not caught up in the excitement of the day, you get a different angle on a few things. So my rule that I don't talk to the players after the game about the game, has probably saved me from some embarrassing situations, because I haven't embarrassed the player in front of the other guys. I mean I've said a few things in dressing rooms at half-time that I wish I hadn't said as well, because they're not always the things that players like to hear, but I think if you eliminate the after-the-game thing, you save everybody a bit of bad feeling.

'Sometimes you've got to criticise a player in front of his team-mates at half-time, but generally I'd never single anybody out and do it with everybody around. On Tuesday nights, everybody sits there and I have my say, but I'm just speaking from facts off the video, so it's pretty unemotional, because I know I'm right. I've probably watched something four or five times, I've watched it in slow-motion, I've re-played it, so I don't really get too emotional, because I know that what I'm telling the players is what happened. Whereas if I'm doing it on Sunday night straight after the game, a lot of it is coming from the heart and the gut and maybe I haven't got my facts straight. I tend not to be a coach that raises his voice and goes off the deep end, anyway, I'm usually pretty calm in those situations.

'The same thing applies to me with motivating the players for a game. The best motivation is preparation. I just think the benefit of getting players excited before a game are zero. It might last them two minutes or five, or they might do something stupid in the first couple of minutes because someone's revved them up. You've got to work hard through the week, get your preparation right so that everyone knows what their job is, do a lot of repetition with your set plays, so it's just sort of locked in there with the player, and then I tend not to do much coaching at all on the game day.

'I don't give the players too much information on the opposition because I think they ought to be focusing on what we're trying to do rather than the other side. I might write a page on the opposition, but by the time I talk to the players, I might only mention four points. That's especially so early in the season, when it's more important that we get our own game together.

'It doesn't matter who the opposition is; Widnes, our opponents last Sunday, were as good as we're ever going to come up against, but we got beaten because we didn't do our own stuff correctly. They were a very good side and they capitalised on all their chances, but we dropped the ball from the kick-off and gave away penalties in front of our goalposts, so the defeat was really of our making, because of things that we failed to do.'

Like the best motivation, the key to Monie's coaching is preparation. He studies his team and its individual components minutely, always looking for imperfections that can be remedied or improvements that can be made. He gives the same scrutiny to the opposition, unerringly fastening on flaws in their game that he can exploit. For Monie, as well as his players, winning on Sunday starts the previous Monday.

'I always do the video on Monday. Harry Pinner is working with me this year, so he comes up to my house on Monday morning and we go through the video, which can take anything from two to four hours, and I make all my notes off that video. On Monday afternoons I usually watch it again. In between the two viewings I'll write up everything that I've noticed and then I might watch it again with the sound up and make a few more notes. I might even watch the tape yet again on a Tuesday morning when I go through and take the good bits and the bad bits off it.

'I get everything written up for Tuesday night, when we have our team meeting, because we want to get everything from the previous weekend out of the way on Tuesday, so that it's finished with. That's how long you live with the win or the loss. After Tuesday night, last Sunday means nothing to me; that's it, it's gone.

'I have Wednesday off, then on Thursday I try to get one or two tapes of the opposition, just to see where they're strong and where they're weak; they might be vulnerable out wide or down the middle. I go over the tap plays and set plays that we're going to use that week and plan the training session and the tactics that we're going to use.

'On Friday I might have a look at the tapes of the opposition again and anything that didn't work as well at Thursday night training as I wanted when I planned it, then I'll change that. Friday night there is usually the Alliance game, I go to that to have a look at all our younger players, then we come in early on Saturday morning, go over things for about an hour and then its back to the game on Sunday.

'When the time comes for the game, I think the players have just got to play. My job is finished, the main part of my job as a coach is to work with the players through the week, work out the problems, what's right, what's wrong, get the tactics right for the game, make sure the training sessions are good and then, come the day of the game, the players have just got to play. Rugby league is a reaction thing, you have to react to situations.

'I don't want to restrict the players and say, "You can't do this and you can't do that." If a player has got natural skills and ability to do things, I want him to express those things on the day. I'll tell a player, "That's a poor percentage play, I don't want you doing that in our own 22", but basically they've got to react to the situations and do what they think is right at the time.'

If his players have a relatively free rein when the side is in possession, however, Monie allows little latitude when the opposition have the ball. Defence is the number one priority, a once-neglected area of the British game, but to which all coaches now pay proper respect. He insists on rigid adherence to the defensive pattern and total commitment, even to the extent of ignoring injuries, when the opposition are in possession. Few things can make the normally imperturbable Monie lose his cool with his players, but one of the surest ways is to miss an important tackle.

By match day, Monie usually has little left to say to his players. The important work has already been done. 'On Sunday we meet here early, I sort out a tape for the bus or if the game is at home, we show a tape here. The players eat early at home, whatever time they usually do, and then they just have a cup of tea and toast here. I send them downstairs about an hour before the game and then I've got other things to do, like meet the sponsors, tell them "Everybody's OK, we're going to win today," and all that, so I do a few official-type things and then I go down and see the players just for ten minutes before the game.

'Apart from all the things I do through the week, we also have specialised sessions: Lano has a couple of weight sessions, Bill Hartley has a couple of sprint sessions, the physio checks the players over, and all that sort of thing. Then there's all the media people, the press and radio reporters that I've got to deal with . . . not forgetting the bloke who's writing a book about us.' He winked and turned back to his study of the video with Harry Pinner, stopping the tape every couple of minutes to freeze-frame an incident or run through it backwards and forwards until he was sure he understood what had happened and who was to blame, if an error had been made.

Derms Gets Dropped

A T THE following night's training session, Monie had a more pressing problem than the analysis of the Lancashire Cup defeat: he had to discipline Bobby Goulding, whose problems had not ended on returning from New Zealand. Within two weeks of the start of the season Goulding was in serious trouble with the Wigan club. He had missed several weight-training sessions, annoying Bob Lanigan and John Monie by failing to turn up even at fixed times. Maurice Lindsay had also received a complaint about an unpaid debt of Goulding's in New Zealand.

Goulding had private problems away from the club, and there were even claims that he had been seen drinking before a training session, the ultimate heresy for a professional sportsman. As a result of all his problems, his form had dropped alarmingly, whereas his hero and chief rival Andy Gregory was playing at the very top of his game.

When John Monie arrived at Central Park that evening, he called his coaching staff together, to ask them to reinforce the message he wanted to drum into his talented, but wayward young half-back. 'Lano, you, Bill and Harry come and sit in with me and Maurice upstairs. I want to get Bobby up there as soon as he comes in.' As soon as Goulding appeared – late – Monie pounced. 'I want to see you upstairs now, Bobby.' Goulding climbed the stairs with all the enthusiasm of a French aristocrat ascending the platform to the guillotine. Confronted by all the Wigan coaching staff, he looked even younger than his eighteen years. Just as in Auckland, he again had the air of an errant schoolboy awaiting his doom outside the headmaster's study.

'You came back here as the Great Britain number seven,' said Monie, as soon as all the protagonists were seated, 'but since you've been back, you haven't done any work. You played half-back at Swansea and we both agreed that you had played pretty poorly, but the main thing I want to talk to you about is that, apart from team training, you haven't done any work. Lano's been in the gym waiting for you to come in and do some weights and you haven't turned up. Bill's wanted you to do some running and you haven't done that.

'Somebody said you'd had a drink one night before training. Now I said I didn't think you would, so I'll just ask you.' Bobby shook his head, eyes downcast. 'No? Fair enough, but you have had trouble with your father, you've had a bit of a problem with your girlfriend too, and you've also still got some problems from your legal troubles in New Zealand – you know about those?' Still not speaking, Bobby nodded his head.

'What I suggested to Bobby the other day is that the best thing for him is if we bring him over here to live,' Monie continued, talking for the benefit of the room at large, but directing his comments at the top of Bobby's bowed head. 'Do you have a job, Bobby?'

'No, I'm unemployed. I could do with a day job, not so much for the money, but just to keep my mind occupied. I'd like a job just to fill in the time, though I wouldn't work for nothing.'

'Well it's not possible for the club to fix you up with a job. You don't know, but football clubs fix players up with jobs and then the players don't turn up for work and it causes all sorts of problems. So we won't be able to do that, but we might be able to get you some accommodation, to help you out, and there will be a lot more you can do over here to keep you occupied. For example, on Monday you can come and watch the tape of the game at my place. Tuesday you can come in the gym and do some weights. Bill has some sprint sessions on Wednesday. I mean if you're not working, there are going to be plenty of things to do over here.'

Bobby was unemployed only in the sense that he had no job other than rugby league. While that was a situation that many of the players actively preferred, describing themselves as professional footballers, Bobby was in the last year of the contract he had signed when first coming to Central Park and was well short of the sort of income that would have given him financial security without other employment. He still lived at home, and was one of his large family's chief bread-winners.

While Wigan's total wage bill for the season would total around one and a quarter million pounds, with several of the biggest stars collecting six-figure incomes, Goulding's earnings would be miles short of that. Though he earned the same bonuses as the others, his contract money might only be one tenth of that of the club's top earner.

'If you did come over here how would your girlfriend feel?' asked Maurice.

'She'd come over here, no problem.'

'If you're happy off the field, then you're going to be happy on the field, aren't you?' said Monie. 'If you're having a good week your preparation is good, but if you're in trouble with your parents, or you haven't got any transport, or you're fighting with your girlfriend . . .'

'What do you feel yourself, Bobby,' asked Bob Lanigan, 'John's pointed out all the plusses of you being over here.'

'Yeah, it would be better for me,' said Goulding with the air of someone who would have agreed to move to Reykjavik if it would have earned him a few moments respite.

'How will your parents feel about you moving out?' added Lindsay.

'They'll be a bit upset I suppose, but in the end they'll just want what's best for me.'

'In that Third Test in New Zealand you were the fittest and fastest I've ever seen you,' said Maurice, 'but since then you've lost that sparkle. Players like Andy Platt and Dean Bell maintain their form pretty consistently over years, so that's the example you've got to follow.'

'What we'll do is give you a week to see if you can sort things out at home, make some enquiries about places, that sort of thing,' said Monie. 'If you haven't been able to find anything after a week, then we'll see some agents over here, but if you can sort it out for yourself and find somewhere where you want to be, so much the better. Try and sort it out for yourself. OK?'

'Yeah, OK.'

'Now the other thing is,' Monie said, 'with Greg playing well at number seven . . . we all think you're going to be the next number seven at Wigan, but at the moment, you've got to admit it, Greg's on top of his game. Now Martin Dermott's form hasn't been that good recently, so the best opportunity for you to force your way into the side would be at number nine. I know you'd prefer not to be playing at hooker, but if I stick you in as hooker this week, would you try and make that position yours? I don't want you sitting on the bench every week; I mean I'll always use you as a sub but that's not helping you either.

'What I'm saying is that I'm ready to give you an opportunity to play number nine and just tell Martin "You're going to have to play Friday night football, Bobby's got your position, make the best of it." Now after saying that, you don't really deserve for me to do that for you, because you haven't trained. You deserve to be sitting on the bench, just getting a bit of football, but if you're prepared to work hard at it and you show some form, I'll put you in the starting side. If Greg gets hurt, then of course I'll put you in at half-back – but otherwise you'll be at hooker.

'If you're playing in the first thirteen you're a mile better off than just sitting on that bench, getting half a game here and a few minutes there, but you've got to say, "I'm going to go all out and make the number nine jumper mine." It's no good me making you hooker and then next week you saying to some of the boys in the changing room, "I want to be number seven." If we're going to give you the job, you've got to go all out.

'If Greg gets injured, you'll play half-back,' said Monie, 'but when the seven comes back and he's all right, you'll go back to number nine. Right, that's it, go and get ready for training.'

Martin Dermott, known around the dressing-room as 'Derms', the player about to be shunted aside to make way for Goulding, was as aggrieved at being demoted as Bobby had been at not getting a run as first-team scrum-half, for he too had been Great Britain's first choice in his position on the summer tour.

Dermott was an old enough head, even at his young age, to know that there was nothing to be gained and much to be lost by making an issue of his demotion. John Monie's word on team selection is final. To argue, sulk, or stay away from training in protest would merely lengthen the period that he would have to spend in the 'A'-team wilderness.

Like any other player dropped from the team, Dermott's

task was now to knuckle down, train hard and prove to Monie by his form with the 'A' team that he deserved the number nine shirt ahead of any other player, including Bobby Goulding. Within a few weeks he had achieved that aim, the Goulding experiment being aborted. Though still occasionally exasperating his coach by following a 'blinder' one week with an indifferent game the next, once back in the first team, Dermott held his place for the rest of the season, except when injured or suspended.

Wigan born, Dermott had been playing rugby league since the age of six, and had represented Wigan at every available age group, under-11, -13, -15 and -16, before joining the top amateur side, Wigan St Patricks. He signed for Wigan in 1984 at the age of 17, played in the 'A' team the same season and made his first team debut in 1985. He still remembers his first nervous entry into the dressing room.

'The first time you go in there as part of the first team, you don't really know where to go. If you pick the wrong place, you either get a kick up the arse or a clip round the ear. When you're a young lad it can be a bit frightening when a big forward comes up to you and throws you away.

'I played against Hull on my debut and had a few first-team games but it was when I was about 19 that I started to make the first team more regularly. Last season was my best one so far, because I was chosen as the number one hooker and I kept my position. I've always watched Wigan and it's always been my dream and my ambition to play for them. To walk about in the same dressing room as players like Brett Kenny, Henderson Gill, John Ferguson and Nicky Kiss was my dream come true.'

Nicky Kiss was Martin's predecessor as Wigan hooker, a flamboyant character who wore two gold earrings off the field. Martin limits himself to one earring, to the amusement of Maurice Lindsay. 'I think all Wigan hookers must have been fathered by Nicky Kiss! The first sensible hooker we got, we'd be very disappointed.'

'They always used to say I was Nicky's apprentice,' said Dermott, 'because Nicky's got two earrings and I've just got the one. Some people still call me Nicky. With Nicky being part-gypsy he's got it in him, but with me it's just a bit of a trend really.'

The scrums in rugby league are increasingly treated as a

way of restarting the game as quickly as possible, with the side putting the ball in almost invariably taking possession. Many people, perhaps including Dermott's coach, see the specialist ball-winning role of the hooker as largely obsolete, but unsurprisingly Martin disagrees.

'I think it's still a specialist position. Sometimes the ball actually does go in the scrum, it's very rare, but when it does, its a fifty-fifty ball and when you put a non-hooker in that position, the specialised hooker has got a lot more chance of getting the ball. Nowadays though I think the hooker has to have a lot more vision than the old-fashioned one, who used to be head down and in. Now the hooker has a more varied role. He has to distribute the ball, do plenty of tackling and kicking, like a scrum-half, and as well as all that he's got to do a lot of organising, plus the scrummaging of course. You've got to sort the forwards out, take the lead.'

Derms is one of the 'party animals' of the team, enjoying the wisecracking in the dressing room as much as any of them. He's single. 'I never married, never bothered. I spend my time training and just enjoying myself. I take the odd girl out, like. If I want a quiet night I'll go for a meal or something like that. People don't really mob us around the town, though. We don't go out nightclubbing because of fitness. It's very rare that we go to a nightclub. If we do it's usually after a final or a victory or something, but we don't make it a regular thing. You've got to look after yourself and rugby and night-clubs don't mix. Usually we go out for a drink every Thursday after training. We have a few drinks and a few sandwiches. Any problems or anything we need to discuss out of rugby hours, we do it there. It's good to get the lads together, it's a great atmosphere, gets the team spirit going.

'So we socialise on Thursdays but I have my own friends back home in Higher Ince, and it's good to have that part as well. I have a local pub, I go there every Sunday night after the game, have a game of darts with the lads and have a few drinks around my local town. I know everybody there and nobody treats me differently. We have a good laugh and just generally do what I've always liked doing.' Though Martin clearly regards Higher Ince as quite distinct from Wigan, to the untrained eye the distinction is not that easy to make, Higher Ince being some houses, a few shops, a pub or two and a set of traffic lights about a mile from the town centre.

Dermott is one of the full-time professionals of the team, in the sense that rugby league provides his only income, though much of his daytime work involves the paid coaching of children in the sport. 'I passed my Grade 1 coaching certificate a couple of years ago. I'm in rugby league development, coaching kids from 9 to 13. It's brilliant, I love kids and I like helping them. I've always wanted to coach kids and I got my opportunity with the Wigan council. I go to about seven different schools and do about three hours with one of them every day.

'I'd like to coach a team at an amateur level but I don't think I'd get into coaching a professional side, not because I don't think I'm good enough, but when I've finished playing, I want something stable that I can fall back on. Coaching is like playing really. When you're playing, if you get a bad knock you're out; in coaching, if you keep losing it's a very insecure future, but I'd like to keep in touch with rugby league in some way.

'It can be a good living, we've been doing well. If you look after yourself and look after your money, at the age of 30 or so I think you'd be able to retire on what you've earned. We have a weekly wage as well as winning money and so on, but if you don't play you don't get paid. If you're injured, you don't get winning money, you don't get a basic, you just get SSP – sick pay of £60 a week. So you've got to be there to make the money. Only you know if you can go out there and give 100 per cent for 80 minutes. Obviously if it's a really bad injury, you just don't play, but a bit of an injury you can soon run off. You're fit, you're taking the right food and the right vitamins and the adrenalin takes over, your body just clocks on and you get on with it.'

In The Boardroom

A T THE team meeting that week, Monie discussed the new defensive pattern with the players. They weren't happy with it and after a few minutes discussion of its merits and drawbacks, he agreed to lay it quietly to rest and revert to the system which had served them well enough on their way to the Cup and League double the previous season.

The change back to the familiar pattern had no immediately discernible effect on the quality of the defence, however. The early-season record already made less than cheerful reading at a club accustomed to uninterrupted success: two defeats against Widnes, with the only victory the thrashing of Second Division Barrow. The one piece of good news was the return of Ellery Hanley after a long absence with a groin injury that had at one stage looked likely to end his career. He made his comeback in the first Championship match of the season, a home game against Sheffield Eagles, and came through the eighty minutes without ill-effects.

Despite the boost of Hanley's return, Wigan were surprisingly held to a high-scoring draw in a game which they were expected to win convincingly and, as a result, John Monie lost patience with his side. His humour was not improved by Bobby Goulding's failure to turn up for a weight session with Bob Lanigan on the Monday, despite the previous week's bollocking. As a result, when Goulding finally did turn up on Tuesday, 'Lano' put him through it without mercy. 'Get in the gym, Bobby. I'm going to work the guts off you until six o'clock and as soon as I've finished with you, you're going training.' Lanigan was as good as his word, not sparing Bobby at all, forcing him through an intimidating series of weight repetitions. Much of the work focused on his shoulders, upper back and arms. Hookers need stronger shoulders than scrum-halves and the conditioning work to turn Bobby from a half-back into a number nine was already being pushed.

Monie came into the gym towards the end of the session, watching as Lanigan drove on the near-exhausted Goulding, who was now wearing the boxing gloves and punching Lano's padded hands. Every few seconds Lano was screaming at him: 'Harder Bobby, I can't even feel it. Pick up the intensity. Come on, punch it. Get your arms up. Thirty seconds, come on work. Get angry, punch it. Keep going, faster, faster.' As Lanigan finally called halt, to give Goulding a moment's breather, Monie called out, 'When Bobby gets his breath back Lano, ask him where he was yesterday,' and then walked out, without waiting for a reply.

The Tuesday night team discussion became a lecture. 'Normally when we have the meeting on Tuesday, we'll talk about the game,' said Monie, 'but I don't want to hear you talk about Sunday's game. We're not doing things right, we're spilling the ball, we're forcing the pass, we're missing tackles – we missed eight in the first half and eight in the second on Sunday – so I'm not going to listen to you this week; this time I'm telling you what we're going to do.

'We're going to keep it tight for six tackles and then kick to the corners. I don't want any fancy football and I don't care if we get booed off the pitch, we're going to keep it simple. Once we get back on the rails, once we get the basics right, then we can start to build on that, but we need to get that right first. We won't even beat Second Division teams playing the way we have been.

'I've also been a bit concerned about the running in the last couple of games. We've done a lot of weights, but we've dropped that to twice a week now, so I've got some news for you, the first thing you're going to be doing tonight is half-an-hour's running – shuttle runs. You'll start off sprinting the length of the pitch, turning round and sprinting back. You're going to do that for five minutes. Then you're going to rest for five minutes, then you'll sprint for four minutes and rest for four, then three, then two, then one. That'll take you half-an-hour. That's it. Get to it.' The players filed out in silence.

As the players began their shuttle runs, Wigan's four directors were settling down to their weekly board meeting. The Wigan boardroom has the air of a recently-revamped lounge bar, unsurprisingly, since a brewery had funded the improvements as part of a sponsorship deal. Leather Chester-fields flank the walls, surrounding a fine boardroom table. The floor is plushy carpeted and a bar stands ready in the corner. Steps lead up to a lounge area overlooking the pitch.

Maurice Lindsay chaired the meeting, flanked by his three co-directors. Lindsay is a small, sandy-haired man, with a soft voice and a disarmingly – and sometimes misleadingly – gentle smile. As well as his chairmanship of Wigan, he is also a powerful voice on the board of directors of the Rugby Football League and manager of the Great Britain side. He had led the drive that had seen Wigan rise from near-insolvency in the depths of the Second Division to a position of prosperity and undisputed pre-eminence in the British game, in less than a decade. He can be charming or ruthless as the occasion demands, and though he is always willing to see both sides of a question, the suspicion is that the two sides that Lindsay has in mind are always his own and the enemy's. He has unquestionably been one of the most important influences in transforming Wigan from mediocrity to excellence, bringing strict financial disciplines and a shrewd business brain to bear on the running of the club, as well as a gambler's instinct developed in his other occupation as a rails bookmaker. There is probably no better or harder school in which to learn the art of making instant calculations and decisions.

Jack Hilton, a former Wigan chairman, sat on Lindsay's left at the boardroom table. A former Wigan player, Hilton is the oldest member of the board, a white-haired, old-fashioned figure with the look and the ideals of a Victorian businessman, summed up in his first contribution to the discussions. 'I'm a profits man myself, if it's costing us £200 a week to video the games, let's get rid of it.'

Tom Rathbone, the local bread magnate, a round, florid, avuncular man, sat facing Lindsay at the far end of the table. He ignited a huge cigar at the start of the meeting and dis-appeared into a fog of expensive smoke, emerging from the wraiths from time to time when asked his opinion. He sat closest to the telephone on the bar and rose to answer it frequently during the meeting.

The fourth director and vice-chairman, Jack Robinson, whose business interests include antiques shipping, sat on the chairman's right. He is closest to Lindsay in both age and outlook and has a dry sense of humour which is frequently employed during the meetings. While the other three wore business suits, he had arrived late for the meeting, straight from work, and was still wearing a pair of muddy, oily jeans.

Lindsay had joined the Wigan board in 1980, during a financial crisis that almost sent the club into liquidation. In a series of negotiations conducted while the club teetered on the edge of bankruptcy, Lindsay and his allies, Jack Hilton and Jack Robinson, held off the creditors and managed to persuade the old ten-man regime to yield up their voting rights, their powers and their shares to the streamlined new board.

The club is now run as a business, though the directors still have one eye on glory, and today's multiple Cup and Championship winning side is light years from the ramshackle outfit that suffered the ignominy of relegation in 1980. Lindsay pointed to the reduction of the board to four members as the crucial factor in setting the club on its upward path. I reminded him of the definition of the ideal board of directors: 'Three, with two away sick.' Maurice had an improvement on that joke, his version being: 'Two with one dead!' However, he will not be going to those extremes at Wigan, believing that the present four-man board is the ideal size, but the days when a seat on the board was the entrée to membership of an unwieldy debating society and social club have gone for ever.

Lindsay was born six miles from Wigan, but went to school in Bolton, a soccer-playing town with no rugby league team. His introduction to league came through the 160 boys who came to the school from Wigan every day. 'I was soon going to watch Billy Boston and all the other Wigan stars and I got hooked. Once you're hooked, you stay hooked, even when you've grown up and gone into business.

'Joining the board at Wigan was never a particular ambition, but I had friendships within the game because my company had sponsored various games. In the late 1970s I sponsored Wigan, Salford and Warrington, but my heart was always at Wigan. Harry Costello was chairman of Wigan in 1980 and out of the blue one morning he was waiting for me when I got to my office. He said that things were pretty critical and asked me to join the board. Jack Robinson joined at the same time. I had only dealt with him in a professional capacity before, but we discovered we were both pretty tough negotiators and struck up a good relationship. The same week they asked me to take over financial matters; no one else was willing or able to do it.

'They were very angry times, the state the club was in has not been exaggerated. There were three letters from the bank sitting on the desk when I started, none of which had been answered. In fact I honestly believe that if events had carried on the way they were, when the approach from the local soccer club, Wigan Athletic, finally came, they would have swopped grounds and that would have been the end of Wigan as a major club.

'I was vice-chairman inside two months with Jack Hilton becoming chairman. I wanted it to be run from the heart, because it is a rugby league club and I didn't want us to lose sight of the affection that everybody holds for it, but also run it like a business. There had been no vision, no courage, no management for years; it needed a complete strip down and some aggressive management.

'We approached Tom Rathbone after about six months and we put in £100,000 between us, the immediate injection of cash it needed, introduced financial disciplines and got the support through the turnstiles. We reduced the board to four directors because trying to run it with ten was just impossible. We had luck, the four of us, but if we hadn't come along at the right time, it would have been curtains. I always felt the supporters were disillusioned because there was no obvious effort coming from the boardroom. The club had slipped into Division Two with no-one taking responsibility. Supporters lost patience and the gates dwindled, but we knew that if we took the supporters into our confidence and told them our ambitions, we felt that they would support us.

'They did, even if they were a little impatient sometimes! Every year our receipts increased until we were self-supporting. We changed the administration, and brought in overseas players like Brett Kenny and John Ferguson from Australia, who revitalised the image of the club to British players – they realised we were going places and wanted to be part of it.

'You can't ignore the illustrious history of the club though, just the colour of the jerseys excites a lot of people, so we didn't want to do things in a dour manner. We wanted trophies, but with verve and panache. We knew we were in the entertainment business and wanted to play in front of packed houses because we were bloody good at what we did. We're famous for style and class and they became our watchwords.

'We've had several coaches here in that time and I have always felt that we never appointed one who gave less than 100 per cent or who didn't give us something different. George Fairbairn gave us dedication, Maurice Bamford commitment, hard work and Yorkshire grit, Alex Murphy an atmosphere of excitement and tension.' Lindsay said this with a smile, knowing the legendary status of their final parting when the volatile Murphy emphasised a point by throwing a telephone at his chairman.

As well as a short fuse, Murphy had a host of idiosyncrasies that made him in equal parts the most loved and the most hated man in rugby league. His ideas on coaching were occasionally as unorthodox as his method of terminating discussions with his chairman. Maurice Lindsay recalls one of the many occasions when Murphy left the training session to his assistant.

'We had a big match coming up at the weekend, a cup-tie, so I went down to training to make sure Alex was there. He got on the bus to go to the training field with the team, but I was still a bit uneasy, so twenty minutes later I drove down myself. The team were there but there was no sign of Alex. He'd arranged to go to the greyhound racing with a friend and as soon as the coach left Central Park, he changed out of his training gear into a suit. When they got to the training ground, his mate was waiting for him in his car and Alex hopped in and disappeared for the night. We lost the cup-tie.

'We were stabilised and brought into the modern era by Alan McInnes and Colin Clarke and won the classic Wembley final against Hull in 1985 under them. By then we knew we were on the verge of something pretty great, but to achieve it we needed the final ingredient, someone with Australian experience at a high level, provided they were willing to give us some style and verve. Graham Lowe was ideal. It was heartbreaking to explain to McInnes and Clarke but we needed new methods from Down Under to raise Wigan into a class of its own.

'We were the first club to employ an overseas coach long-term and our judgement was right, we got what we hoped for. After Lowe we had to maintain it. We thought seriously about home-grown talent but felt Lowe had left a little prematurely and that the Australian education he had brought had to be furthered and advanced. We didn't want to de-stabilise the club, we wanted someone with the right temperament, but the Down Under knowledge too.

'We have the backbone of the Great Britain side at Wigan, people like Ellery Hanley, Andy Gregory and Shaun Edwards, and they wouldn't settle for anything less than the best. We had to have someone they would respect and admire as Graham Lowe's equal. In John Monie we found even a new dimension, different from Graham, quieter, more reserved, but bright. We call him a rugby league educationalist, whereas Graham was an evangelist. Graham would coach from the passion of the side, whereas John coaches from the intellect.'

The recruitment of Monie provides a perfect example of Lindsay's relentless determination to have his own way. He had made up his mind that Monie was the coach for Central Park and the fact that John did not even want the job when first approached was a trifling impediment. Lindsay merely ignored Monie's refusal and continued to ring him at least once a day, cajoling, persuading, pleading and steadily increasing the terms being offered, until it reached a point where Monie could no longer keep saying 'No'. He gave in and accepted a three-year contract.

One reflection of the increasing professionalism of modern rugby league, exemplified by coaches like Lowe and Monie and players like Hanley and Edwards, is that more and more of its protagonists have no other occupation than the sport. Some observers worry that this will eventually lead to a break in the bond between players and supporters which is one of the most cherished features of the game. Supporters have always known that their sporting heroes drink in the same pubs and work in the same factories as they do, but that, like much else, has changed. Several of Wigan's present first-team squad already list their occupation as 'pro footballer' and others spend their time in paid rugby league development work in schools, but Lindsay remains unperturbed by this change in the game.

'I'm delighted that our players are becoming full-time professionals now,' he said. 'The demands of modern sport, particularly rugby league, require full-time commitment from the players and they can't give that if they're working at something else. The way to create the opportunity to become full-time footballers was to pay them the correct remuneration. At Wigan they are getting it, but the game had to grow nationally first, so that we had the sponsorship and gate income to pay it.

'I don't think that full-time professionalism necessarily threatens the bond between players and supporters that has always been such a feature of rugby league, though. The only people who can destroy it are the players. If some don't have the intellect or generosity of nature, they will destroy it. I don't accept the theory that where a player acts abnormally towards his fellow men, people say, "That's what makes him a great player." I abhor arrogance, I admire style – the quality that separates them from their fellow athletes, not their fellow men.

'We're also very aware of the links between the club and the town. We know that when Wigan win, more beans go in more Heinz cans at their factory here. I'm also proud of the atmosphere at Central Park. When we have 20,000 people there, no-one runs on to the pitch, obscenities are few and the opposition get applause for good football. We appealed to the fans not to run on to the pitch against Manly, when we had 36,000 in the ground, and they stayed off. Against Featherstone, when we won the Championship for the first time in twenty years, six kids ran on to the field and were booed off again. The discipline established in the boardroom runs right through the club; we're responsible to our community.

'Society generally is growing more dangerous, sport too, but rugby league seems to be the last bastion where you maintain a charged atmosphere but without feeling threatened. It's safe to go into Central Park with your 6-year-old daughter, you know she won't be trampled. Opposing supporters stand next to each other, there's a bit of banter, but nothing more.'

In parallel with Wigan's rise to the summit of the game, has been Lindsay's own meteoric ascent. Having joined the Wigan board as a complete unknown within the game, he has become one of the most influential figures in the Rugby League within a decade.

In the course of his rise, Lindsay has won plenty of supporters and admirers, but he has also inevitably ruffled feathers and made enemies. A fierce row with a journalist accused by

Lindsay of denigrating the British team, undid a little of the good work that he had achieved in fostering relations with the media, while many question whether the rulers of the game itself should be quite so closely identitifed with individual clubs. Lindsay is not unique in this, since all the seven members of the Board of Directors are identified with particular clubs, but as chairman of the game's most successful club and the most high-profile member of the board, Lindsay attracts most of the flak.

Maurice shrugs aside the criticism and his record of success speaks for itself, but his impatience and his brusque treatment of those who do not see the world his way have fostered deep-rooted resentments. Just as there are many journalists praying for the day when Ellery Hanley is on the slide, there are people within the game eager for Maurice Lindsay's feet of clay to be exposed; not that the prospects cause either man to lose much sleep at night.

Like many of his players, Maurice Lindsay is now also a virtual full-timer at Wigan, though unlike them, he draws no salary from the club. 'When things started to move pretty quickly, about 1983, I had an offer for my business from a national company and I took the money and ran. It gave me some financial independence and the opportunity to have a go at running Wigan full-time. I don't go to Central Park from nine to five though, I still have other interests and a private life. I am also a part-time racecourse bookmaker, which takes me all over the country. You've got to be pretty alert when you're taking on the big boys like Hills and Ladbrokes.

'Wigan was exciting me so much though that I wanted to finish it off and I couldn't do that from a remote office. Brett Kenny, Graham Lowe, John Monie are all full-timers, I wanted to be full-time too. Now we have a secretary, an assistant secretary, a pools manager, a commercial manager and an accountant who are all full-time, but when we started there was nobody.'

Though Wigan had been to Wembley three years running, earning a healthy slice of the gate receipts as well as the prize money, Lindsay rejects the widely held view that getting to Wembley can be the difference between profit and loss for a club. 'Wigan is profitable now, we made a profit of £280,000 in the last balance sheet, but it's not because of our share of the Cup Final receipts. We only made £34,000 out of

Wembley, that's because we paid all the lads £5,500 for a win, there were bonuses for the coaches and everyone at the club, and we threw a banquet for everyone, that cost £20,000. We take all our sponsors and their guests to Wembley, that's 192 people.

'Our money is made during the season; when you get 27,000 watching a league game against St Helens, you're into money. Our gate receipts for the season are around £1,250,000. There's no magic formula to it, you don't even have to be a dyed-in-the-wool rugby league town like Wigan. Our commercial activity has leapt up because we have become a fashionable club. There is no reason why Leeds, Sheffield, Nottingham or anyone else can't do it.

'Nor is it true that we can outspend anyone; Leeds would lick us. They have the backing of the income from the cricket ground and some wealthy board members, it's a bottomless pit, but so far we've never lost anyone we really wanted. We beat off Manly and Leeds for the services of Kevin Iro, even though Manly offered jumbo-sized prawns. All we've got in Wigan is fish and chips, but we matched them financially.'

One rather more expensive commitment made by the board during the previous season was causing them plenty of sleepless nights. The replacement of the old terracing at the clubhouse end of the ground by a new, cantilevered stand was months behind schedule and soaking up money at a frightening rate.

The stand was originally scheduled to be completed in time for Wigan's game against the touring Australians in October, but by the start of August, Lindsay was admitting, 'We've lost a couple of months through delays and our ambition of having it finished in time for the Australian game is definitely doomed. Nevertheless, we shall be pressing on as quickly as possible and the stand will certainly be finished by Christmas.'

By November Lindsay was forced to admit that Christmas was no longer a feasible completion date and as the contractors ran into more and more problems, particularly those caused by the maze of old coal mine workings below Central Park, further revisions became necessary. The 'Wigan four foot seam' on which the town's prosperity had been built, passed directly under Central Park. The contractors were forced to spend unscheduled weeks of their time and unbudgeted tens of thousands of pounds of Wigan's money, pumping concrete grouting into the old mine workings to secure the foundations of the new stand.

In early February Lindsay was able to announce that the stand would definitely be finished by the end of April, by which time, unless they made progress in the end of season Premiership competition, Wigan's season would already be over. In fact even that proved optimistic, the new stand did not see service until the start of the 1991–92 season.

Many soccer clubs have come close to bankruptcy after investing heavily in new stands, but Lindsay remained convinced that the Wigan board had made the right decision, whatever the temporary problems. 'I always felt that one fault of Widnes was that in the 1970s and early 1980s when they were a great side, as dominant as Wigan have been more recently, nothing seemed to happen inside Naughton Park. We vowed if ever we were lucky enough to achieve that success rate, we would do something permanent at Central Park, something to be proud of. First we put in undersoil heating, then we refurbished the clubhouse, the players' lounge and the boardroom and now we have a £1.5 million development of the clubhouse end of the ground. There will be another 2,000 seats, private boxes and eventually new offices, dressing rooms and a gym.

'Of course in some ways it would be easier to move from Central Park, demolish it, sell the land for development and build a new stadium on the outskirts of Wigan, and if anyone offers me £30 million, I'll snap their hands off, but Central Park is ideal for many reasons. We have thought of alternative locations, but there is something lovable about the ground, like Anfield. The car parking is inadequate but many of our supporters live near the ground and they love it.'

The prime business of that night's board meeting was a report from Elaine Mitchinson, the commercial manager, new in the job since her predecessor transferred himself to the Wigan Athletic soccer club during the off-season. Maurice interrogated her, doing most of the talking, but ensuring that she committed herself to a recommendation for action on each point.

Elaine was clearly still feeling her way in the new job and in her relationship with the board, and offered her opinions hesitantly, diffidently.

'I think that you might want to consider dropping the videos we produce from each game,' said Elaine. These videos were made by the club and sold to supporters and other outlets; however, as Jack Hilton had already pointed out, they cost £200 per week to make.

'So is that your recommendation?' Maurice asked Elaine.

'Well they are costing us money . . .'

'So what do you recommend?'

'I'll be sorry to lose it but . . .'

'So what are you saying?'

'I'll be sad to lose it . . .'

'You've said that, what are you saying?'

'I think we should drop it.'

No vote was necessary on that or any of the other agenda items, but Lindsay was careful to sound the opinion of each board member and reach a consensus, before moving on. (The decision was taken to drop the videos, but after a deluge of irate 'phone calls from Wigan supporters, it was swiftly rescinded.)

Perhaps prompted by the arrival of sandwiches and coffee, the discussion turned to the celebration lunch before the Australian game. Lindsay was anxious to preserve a certain tone for the occasion. 'We don't want the brewery turning it into a boozy do for their customers who buy the most beer, we're not after that for this game.'

The final item for discussion was the discovery that the house next to the Wigan shop was coming up for sale in the near future. 'It could come in very handy,' said Tom Rathbone, 'particularly for Bobby Goulding – very topical.'

Ged Gets Transferred

WIGAN bounced back from the lapse against Sheffield with a 38–18 thrashing of Castleford away from home the following week, but while John Monie was pleased with the win, he was still unhappy with the error rate and the defensive frailties of his side.

His theme for the week, hammered home at every training session, was 'pride in defence' and the result of the next game, a 24–2 beating of newly-promoted Rochdale Hornets, left him more content with that aspect of his side's performance. Bobby Goulding once more came in for some private criticism on the following Tuesday, however, both about his form and his weight.

'You're getting the ball away from dummy-half all right, Bobby, but you haven't been doing any runs. Their guy has only taken the ball up six times, but you haven't had a shot at all from your own half. So to be truthful with you, if Derms had played for the "A" team on Friday night, I probably would have dropped you. I've given you the chance to claim the spot but you've got to do the work. Now what did the scales say tonight?'

'I had all this on,' said Goulding, pulling out two tee shirts from under his tracksuit top.

'But what did the scales say?'

'Thirteen stone ten.'

'Well get your weight down to thirteen-seven and when it's down there we'll have another look at it, but I want you down to thirteen-seven by next week, so you've got to lose some weight. You know what I'm after, I just need some more action out of you.'

As they walked downstairs towards the dressing rooms, they passed half-a-dozen girls sitting on the staircase by the office. Though the numbers vary a little, at least four are there every Tuesday and every Thursday evening. Each one shyly admitted to having a bit of a crush on one of the Wigan players. 'Well I've not, but the rest of them have,' said the group spokesperson, going on to reveal that Andy Gregory, Joe Lydon, Shaun Edwards, Dave Myers, Ged Byrne, Denis Betts, Martin Dermott and Bobby Goulding each had their own admirer.

The girls' judgement seems to be based not so much on good looks as on how nice they think the players are, though one greedy girl, an exception to the general rule, claimed both Joe and Denis as her special favourites and clearly did not have their niceness uppermost in her mind. All the girls were agog at Joe, a player most of them thought a bit flash, who had spent a long time out on the car park, chatting to two fans in wheelchairs who had been brought to meet the players, long after his team-mates had trooped back inside.

'I never thought Joe was like that,' said one. Her friend, who had said she liked Joe the best, preened herself at this unexpected compliment to her hero. 'We could tell you a few things about the players, things nobody else knows,' said the spokeswoman. 'Though nobody knows it all ... I'll let you see my diary, if you like, that'll show you something.' While she talked, one of the other girls laboriously did her school homework, sitting on the stairs.

Like her mates, the spokesperson seemed to be ascribing an importance to her knowledge of the players and their activities that bore little relation to reality. None of the girls appeared to have anything more than the most passing acquaintance with the players, as was demonstrated when Shaun Edwards came down the stairs on his way to training, saying, 'Evening girls,' as he passed them. Only one was brave enough to reply, the rest sat in embarrassed silence and then burst into giggles and recriminations when he had gone. I asked if many of the players acknowledged the existence of the group. 'Some of the players just walk past us and ignore us, others say hello. There's a couple, not many, that'll stop and chat with us.

'You should go out with them on a Thursday night, you'd learn a lot,' said a girl who didn't look old enough to be allowed out with them on a Thursday afternoon, never mind a night, and was undoubtedly speaking from hearsay.

I asked them if the players were like pop stars to the girls of Wigan. 'It doesn't seem to affect the ones who were born in

Wigan as much. Ellery is like a pop star, he likes being God, but others are more down to earth, like Ged Byrne. Some make a habit of being seen, going to functions, that sort of thing. I was actually going to say like Joe, but, I couldn't believe what happened just now, Joe still talking to those two lads when everybody else had come in. Ellery is . . . well a lot of times little kids go up to him to ask for his autograph and he'll just write his name, he won't say anything. A lot of the time he'll just say no, actually.'

'Yeah, he'll just get in his car and shut the door,' chimed in her friend, looking up briefly from her homework.

I asked why they sat there night after night, when most of the players hardly acknowledged their existence. 'You see, something will happen every few weeks, and it makes you stay.'

'So it's like a soap opera is it?'

'Yeah, "Neighbours" with a Wigan accent.'

They all go to Wembley when Wigan are in the Cup Final, despite the problems in getting a ticket. 'It's like the January sales here, you have to queue all night. We got here at 7.30 the night before the tickets went on sale last year and they were already queueing right around the back. Some lads had been camping outside the office since Monday morning and the tickets didn't go on sale till Friday. It was like a party, we were all playing rounders on the car park in the middle of the night. I think the players should come down and keep you entertained quite honestly though, when you're queueing up.' It was hard to tell if she was joking or quite serious. 'We stayed all night. The office opened at 9 in the morning and my friend who was in the queue right down by the stand, didn't get her ticket until about 12.'

The spokesperson had already revealed herself as Ged Byrne's number one fan and that meant she was in for an anxious evening, for Wakefield Trinity had made a £60,000 offer for her hero. 'I just hope he doesn't go that's all.' John Monie shared her hopes, but was less than sanguine about the likely outcome. 'I've already told the board that I want him to stay, because I think he's a valuable part of our squad, but I think they want to sell him, so they're trying to sort it out now. It'll leave us short if he does go – he played thirty-some games last year.'

While his team-mates were at training, Ged was closeted in the boardroom with the directors. After half-an-hour, he emerged shaking his head. He had wanted to know if they wished him to stay or go, but while there was little doubt they would prefer to sell him, they had not made that clear to Ged. 'I've not been looking for a move at all. You get a bit frustrated when you're in and out of the team all the time, but it makes you more determined as well. I don't know whether I'd be better off or not over at Wakefield. It all comes down to how many games you're winning. You get bugger all for losing in this game ... and there's not many teams win as many games as Wigan. I don't know what the travelling would be like either, but I suppose you adapt soon enough, don't you?'

While he was musing, the boardroom door opened and Tom Rathbone stuck his head out, calling, 'Right Ged, can we have you back in now?' Ged followed him back into the boardroom to discover his fate. Five minutes later he came out again, still shaking his head, but this time in disbelief rather than bafflement. He mimed putting a gun to his head and pulling the trigger, shook his head again and walked out. His own particular girl fan chased him out across the car park to find out what had happened, while her mates clustered at the window halfway up the stairs, giggling. 'She's hopeless, I just can't believe that girl.'

As Ged drove out of the car park, John Monie returned from training at Robin Park and went up to make his weekly report to the board. It was a brief one. 'Well the side is just the same as it was last week, that's about it really. Now how did you go with Ged, what's the story?'

'Well I know you'll be disappointed and I know you don't agree with us, but we've decided to sell him,' said Maurice. There was a pregnant pause as the directors waited to see how Monie would greet the sale of the third player in less than a fortnight, following the sale of young back John Gilfillan to Salford and prop Shaun Wane to Leeds.

'It just makes it tough on the squad, that's all.'

'We appreciate that, but £60,000 is an inflated bid. I know you would argue differently, John, but we feel it would be bad management to reject sixty thousand quid. Our own valuation would have been a bit less than that. Also, don't get me wrong, but you said you had Joe to back up Kevin and Dean and you also said you were quite impressed with Denis, and even Ellery can play centre, so if we hit a patch of injuries there are players who can step in.'

'Well when it's all said and done, I've just got to coach whatever you give me.'

'But don't be thinking that we don't give a toss.'

'The position we're in now is . . . say Joe's playing on the wing, then the backline players we've got left that I feel comfortable playing in the first team are Botica, Marshall and Preston. Now Botica's OK on the wing and at this stage we could move him in to six if anything went wrong there and possibly he could play full back. Marshall is just a winger and a full back, nothing else and that leaves Preston, who's just a wingman.'

'Could Botica cover centre, John?'

'Well I don't think so, he couldn't handle a big centre. He's still pretty green, in fact his wing play isn't that great, to be quite honest with you, I'm going to have to do quite a coaching job on him.'

'But if something happened to Kevin, or Dean got suspended or something, you have got Joe.'

'But the problem with Joe is that he's not fit enough to play in the centre regularly. You saw what happens to him when he plays in the centre for two or three weeks, he breaks down, doesn't he? He can't take the knocks. I mean I hope he can, because we can use him, but really . . . If you've got to sell a player, then I'd rather you sold Mark Preston, if we're getting down to the nitty-gritty, because I've got David Marshall who can cover his wing, and we've also got Botica. Preston is a player who looks very poor in the "A" team, I tell you he doesn't look any good at all.

'I said to Preston the other night, "Look, I'm the first-grade coach here. It's my job to get you back into the first team. How do you think I'm going to do that, because David Marshall has only come back for one game so far, and straight away he's put himself ahead of you. So now it's not just that you aren't in the first team, but if one of the wingers got hurt, I'd put David Marshall in ahead of you." Well he's saying to me that he's not doing the weights like he used to and he's not doing the sprint training, but I can't use him at this stage. So he's a bit of dead wood.'

Preston was one of the fastest players on the club's books

and had been the club's leading try-scorer the previous season. Monie remained unimpressed with his overall play and particularly his defence, however, consistently preferring Joe Lydon and the new signings Frano Botica and David Myers.

'The "A" team last Friday, Preston didn't go, said he had an ankle injury, Martin Dermott pulled out, saying he had a groin injury. I also told Martin and Bobby Goulding tonight that Bobby wouldn't be in the team this week if Martin had played on Friday night, because Bobby doesn't deserve to be in the side the way he's playing. I've told him he has to lose three pounds by next week. I also told Martin that if he hadn't pulled the pin on Friday night, he would have been in the first team, but he's cost himself the spot. So he knows exactly where he is.

'Kelvin Skerrett is going a bit slowly too, according to the doctors. I told them I didn't want him pulled out of Sunday's match, I wanted him on the bench so that we could give him half a game, which would get him ready to play next week. I mean those big guys – he's nearly seventeen stone – we wouldn't even get twenty minutes out of him at the moment.'

Skerrett had been the biggest disappointment of all for the Wigan fans. He had taken on and destroyed the Wigan pack practically single-handed when playing for Bradford against Wigan at the end of the previous season, and had been signed on massive personal terms to do the same to other teams for Wigan. However, a combination of niggling injuries and a breathing problem caused by asthma had reduced him from a leading player to a series of walk-on parts, rarely completing a game. The granite-hard prop, who had reputedly scared one of his former team-mates so much that he had asked for a transfer just to get away from him, had yet to look the best prop at Wigan, let alone the best in the League.

The most important consequence of Skerrett's arrival at Central Park seemed to have been to make everyone who was already there discontented with their financial terms. In theory, all players' contracts are confidential, but in practice, within a couple of weeks of Skerrett signing his contract, the other big earners at Wigan had a fair idea of his terms. If the rumours were true, Kelvin would be picking up £75,000 a year, before he even laced a boot. With appearance money, winning pay and bonuses, Skerrett's income would be comfortably into six figures.

Shaun Edwards, who was out of contract, was only re-signed after tortuous negotiations which netted him a very substantial increase for an unusually short one-year contract. Andy Gregory's contract still had a year to run, but he was quick to demand a meeting to press his own case for an increase, which was also granted. No-one at Wigan was saying anything to outsiders, least of all to the chronicler of Wigan's year, but the common currency of gossip around the League was that Wigan's board were in almost permanent negotiation with their star players for weeks, trying to keep the lid on the inflationary spiral that had started with Skerrett's massive contract.

The player's earnings were of little concern to Monie, but the expiry date of some of his top players' contracts was very much on his mind. 'Now the last thing I did want to talk to you about, which is your business again, but we've got Shaun Edwards coming to the end of a contract next year, we've got Ellery coming to the end of a contract, so's Kevin Iro and so's Andy Gregory. You renegotiated with him and gave him some extra whatever, but you didn't extend his contract. So you've got those four coming to the end of their contracts and it would be advisable for you to get them on your agenda.'

'It's a very, very skilful and delicate business negotiating with them John, and it will take some time,' Lindsay said.

'Sure that's your business, all I mean is that with the Australians coming . . . they'll be sniffing around them.'

'We've already discussed all of them, in fact. We've already agreed that we've got to get Kevin Iro fixed up, because we've worked out it won't be very long before he comes off the overseas quota. Now that is better left with me because I know what makes Kevin tick and I can assure you that he's not the sort of guy you can go to on a Tuesday and say, "Here's a good deal, take it home with you overnight and sign it tomorrow." He will make you sweat for months before he signs. He's different, he won't be rushed into anything, but that also means he won't be rushed into signing for anyone else.'

'Well once he is off the quota, his brother might be an added attraction for Kevin and the club . . .'

'That's right and Tony has told me that he'd love to come back,' Lindsay interrupted.

'. . . and you could do the deal with Kevin saying, "As soon

as you come off the overseas quota, we'll sign your brother.''
That might help you keep one and get the blockbuster as
well.'

'Of the others, it will be very much up to Ellery and how
his form goes, won't it? If he recovers from the mechanical
problem, and it seems to be OK doesn't it?'

'Just sign him anyway, couldn't you, providing he's medi-
cally sound. I mean, I'd sign him up for ever and say, "Whenever you want to play rugby league this is your club and when
the doctors rule you out or you rule yourself out, well that's
the finish." Because they just don't come along every day,
players like Ellery, he's one in a lifetime.'

'OK. So same side as last week?' Lindsay asked.

'Yeah, just a problem with the two hookers. One doesn't
deserve to be there and the other one blew his chance by not
playing for the "A" team. I'm going to have to have a word with
Ian Lucas too. You watch the tape and you watch him play
and he does everything right. He takes the ball up plenty, he
hits the line hard, his tackle count is high, he can pass, but he
doesn't worry anybody, he doesn't bruise anybody. I mean
Ellery had a go at me because I dropped Ian from the Wednesday side, but I dropped him on ability because I know Andy
Platt is playing better.

'When I drop him – and if he keeps going the way he is, I
will be dropping him – it's very hard to say, "I'm dropping
you for . . ." because he says, "Is my work-rate all right?"
and I say, "Yes," and he says, "Well have I got a lot of
mistakes?" and I say "No". He does everything right, that's
why it's hard to tell him why I'm dropping him. I'm going to
have a go at him soon, though, because otherwise he'll just be
waiting to lose his jumper like he did last year. Sooner or later
it is going to happen and like I say, I haven't got a lot of
ammunition to drop him on.'

'There are a couple of other things we'd like to discuss with
you John,' said Maurice, 'but . . .' There was a pause. 'Er . . .
Neil, you wouldn't mind waiting outside for a minute, would
you?'

'Not at all,' I said, gathering up my notebook and pinching
a couple of sandwiches and one last cup of coffee, before
exiting stage left. Some things are too sensitive for even the
most trusted of outsiders.

Within fifteen minutes, Monie also came out of the

boardroom. Andy Platt, who had been waiting to talk to the board about a problem, went in. When he came out a few minutes later, Monie, who was watching a video of an Australian game in the next room called out, 'Goodbye, Ged. Oh sorry, goodbye Andy.' It was a joke, but only just.

Pride in Defence

IAN Lucas, known to his team-mates by the nickname 'Mal', the prop forward in danger of being dropped simply for not being nasty enough, had already packed up his training gear and headed for home. Born in Wigan, he had lived in the town all his life, playing his way up through the Wigan School-boys, the under-13s, -14s, -15s and -16s before signing pro-fessional forms at 17. Unlike the signing of Shaun Edwards or Bobby Goulding, Lucas's capture made no headlines, even in the Wigan paper, and there were certainly no record fees being offered or demanded. 'It was just a matter of what I and my parents thought was acceptable, we didn't have any agents or anything like that and I still don't.'

Ian played for the Colts for a further two years, before breaking into the 'A' team. He began to appear regularly for the first team, but the arrival of New Zealand Test prop Adrian Shelford pushed him back into the 'A' team, though that seems only to have increased Ian's resolve. 'Adrian was here for three seasons. When he first started, I was just coming into the first-team reckoning anyway. It was healthy com-petition and by his third year he actually played less first-team games than I did. I kept him out for most of the season. It was just unfortunate that I ended up with an eight match suspension at the back end of the season. I couldn't get back into my position for the last couple of games and he finished up playing at Wembley.'

Lucas must have heaved a sigh of relief when Wigan announced that they would not be renewing Shelford's con-tract, but the immediate signing of Great Britain prop Kelvin Skerrett from Bradford Northern showed him that he would still face the same fight for a first-team place. 'I'm here to play rugby, but I want it to be first-team rugby and if Wigan don't think I'm good enough to play first-team rugby for them, then if they just tell me, I'll play somewhere else, because I

71

play for the love of the game. I don't play for Wigan because it's Wigan, my home town, I don't play for glory, I play for love of the game.'

Ian Lucas is unusual in several respects. Unlike many of the other members of the first-team squad, he is not a full-time professional player and has no intention of becoming one. He does not enjoy nights out with the lads, preferring his home and the company of his wife. Nor does he seem to have the short fuse or the 'devil' in him that characterises many of the game's number eight forwards. He is big, powerful, but, as Monie complained, 'he doesn't frighten anyone'. Most surprising of all perhaps, is his occupation, for he is an antiques dealer, as improbable to those brought up on the Eddie Waring 'Ee, by gum, flat 'ats, whippets and pigeons' view of rugby league as it would be to find a coalminer captaining the English rugby union side.

'I have my own business, antiques. It's a small shop but it's a big interest for me outside of rugby. I've never really been a collector, I've never had the money to be one, so when I did get a bit of money, I just decided to buy and sell anything that I came across that I thought I could sell.

'I have a stall at an antiques market which is open seven days a week. About twelve months after I started the stall, I got myself a shop as well. The other players don't take the mickey out of me about it, I think they find it fascinating really, they keep bringing things to me and asking me about things.

'People go on a lot about players being full-time professionals, but there's a lot of people in the game today who earn enough money to become full-time pros, but they don't wish to put all their eggs in one basket. They want to keep something going for when they finish their career, because obviously it's a very short one and if you don't manage to get into coaching or something related to rugby league at the end of it, it can be very hard work.'

Like most of the players, Lucas keeps his financial affairs to himself. 'Money is a very private matter. It's very personal. It's nobody else's business, you get what you're worth. I suppose sometimes it could help to know what somebody else is on, it could give you an idea of what you could get, but nobody wants to tell anybody else their financial situation.'

His wish for privacy extends to treating Central Park as his place of work, and the other players as workmates rather than friends. 'Basically I train at the club and go on match days but otherwise I don't hang around. I have a full social life away from the club. I don't train every day. I run three times a week and train once or twice a week on the weights plus the game. Weights and any other fitness work you want to do, you do in your own spare time. They don't test us individually for things like sprint speed but if they did see any deficiencies they'd let you know.

'It was different training twice a day with Great Britain on tour but after the first week I got into the swing of things and I really enjoyed it because when you're away on tour there's nothing else to do apart from train and play.' Lucas was also far removed from the stereotypical rugby player on tour; he missed his wife terribly, sent her flowers regularly and never once joined the single players in the bars and discos of Cairns or Auckland. Back in Britain, his priorities remain his wife and his home. 'My wife comes and watches me play. She wasn't interested in rugby when I first met her, but I've slowly converted her. Most of the players' wives and girl-friends attend the games.

'After the game they usually go up into the bar, but mine doesn't, she goes straight home with her parents, because she goes to the match with them. I go up into the players' bar, where there's a bit of a buffet on, have ten minutes there and then shoot off home.'

Although he doesn't socialise much with his team-mates, Lucas is as careful as they all are to avoid outright hostility or long-running arguments with his colleagues. The occasional row is inevitable but no-one is allowed to nurse a grievance, for the admirably professional reason that it may cost them all money.

'I don't think there are any upsets between players really, it's all about playing performance. If you're not in the right frame of mind, you won't perform well. Everybody is aware of that, so no-one wants to put anyone else in the wrong mood. When you're out there it's just thirteen men and if one player is in the wrong frame of mind because you've put him there, then you're down to twelve men and that's no good.'

Like all the players, Lucas is resigned to the well-meaning, but often irritating attentions of fans. 'It doesn't bother me if they're talking common sense. Everybody's got something to say, got an opinion, and as long as it's a sensible opinion, I'll listen. I have a very private social life, though. I and my wife are very close, we do a lot of things together and if I don't want a lot of people bending my ear, I don't go into their company.'

No doubt to the distress of the fans, their attempts to bend his and the other players' ears by shouting from the terraces are equally unsuccessful, according to Lucas. 'You don't notice the crowd when you're out there, all you're intent on is getting on with the game, playing to to the best of your ability. You don't hear any individuals, you hear the roar but that's part of the atmosphere; if you went out and didn't hear the roar, that's when you'd think there was something up. So they're wasting their breath when they keep shouting at you from the terraces.'

His preparation for a game usually starts on Tuesday. 'You play on Sunday, on Monday you're just thinking about the game you've played and then on Tuesday you stop thinking about the last game and start thinking about the next one.

'We do the fitness training on Tuesday. Wednesday I might go for a weight session. Thursday there's another fitness session, probably a shorter one with a bit of ball-work at the end of it. Friday I do a light weight session and we do ball-work on Saturday morning. All through the training you're thinking about who you're playing against. When the weekend comes they might have changed their team – and you might not even be playing against them – but at least you're actually thinking about your game and how you're going to play; knocking your opponents on their backs basically.

'Whether you spend a lot of time thinking about the opposition depends on the team you're facing. If they've got a lot of strengths or particularly strong players, you concentrate on them, but overall if you know that you've got a far better team, if you're stronger than them from one to thirteen, then you don't concentrate on any individual on the other side.

'Big matches always do get a lot more attention. If you did it week in week out, it wouldn't have the same impact when you got to a big game. So they take it a bit easier on the psychological approach for the smaller matches; you've still got to have a good approach but it is a little bit easier than for a big match.

'We arrive at the ground about ninety minutes before

kick-off and go up into the vice-presidents' lounge. First of all there's usually a video of a game in which we've done particularly well or it could be the last game against the team we're playing. Then John Monie has a talk and after that he puts a motivational video on, American Football or something like that. Then we have a small team talk and then go straight down and get changed.

'There are people who get themselves up by talking, doing a lot of shouting, or banging their heads against a wall, but I'm not like that at all. I just sit down and go through the routine of getting changed. We go out about a quarter of an hour before the kick-off to have a run around and do some stretching and I find that's a big help in the build-up to the game. Then we come back in and have a team talk and then we're off. John does talk to us, but then he leaves us on our own for the last couple of minutes. Basically anybody who has anything to say will say it.'

Despite Monie's reservations about the lack of 'mongrel' in Ian Lucas's play, there was no mistaking the young prop's quiet determination and will to succeed. 'I always want to win, I never want to lose, but if you take it away from being a game and you lose the enjoyment, it takes so much physical effort it would become a bind. The game is the utmost, I enjoy the game and the money is like a bonus. You get your injuries but you just have to live with them, it's part of the game. Then on Thursday, when you get your pay-check, you think, "Well it was worth it." You might be very sore on Monday and still a bit sore on Tuesday but you have the training session on Tuesday night and by Wednesday you're OK and ready to go again.'

True to his word, Monie took Lucas on one side after training the following week and warned him that he was contemplating dropping him. Lucas was first baffled, then annoyed, which failed to impress his coach. 'Don't get angry with me, save your aggression for out there on the pitch – that's where you need it' said Monie. Ian obviously took the warning to heart, however, for to Monie's delight, he began to turn in a string of dominant performances at prop, 'monstering' several highly-rated opponents. Mrs Lucas's boy remained a thoroughly nice bloke off the pitch, but on it, his play had an added dimension. 'No more Mr Nice Guy' appeared to be his motto as he even outdid the formidable Kelvin Skerrett in subjugating opposition prop forwards.

The two had a beneficial influence on each other, with Lucas's example helping to restrain the wilder side of Skerrett, while he in turn stoked the fires of Lucas's once-dormant aggression. As Joe Lydon put it, using a word not normally associated with rugby league players, 'It's symbiosis. Ian looks up to Kelvin and has borrowed some of his aggression, while Kelvin has taken on board some of Ian's tolerance. Kelvin has definitely calmed down since his Bradford days, while Ian has beefed his game up. The result? The two best props in the English game.'

The transformation of Lucas still lay some way in the future at this stage of the season, however, and meanwhile pride in defence appeared to be a fairly short-term phenomenon. In Wigan's next game they were beaten 31-30 by Bradford at the cavernous Odsal Stadium after being down 19-6 at half-time. It was 'the most exciting game I have ever seen, in 30 years of covering rugby league' according to one journalist, but that was small consolation for Wigan who lost and also had Ellery Hanley sent off for arguing and abusing the referee, charges which Ellery strongly denied. It was the first time in his career that he had been sent off but he faced the near-certainty of suspension by the disciplinary committee on the following Thursday.

On Tuesday night, the players sat watching the television while waiting for the team meeting to start. Two enormously fat Sumo wrestlers were grappling on the screen, the players yelling out, 'Come on Bobby' and 'Get him Derms', in sarcastic reference to their struggle for the right to wear the number nine shirt.

At the meeting Monie again laid into his team. 'The way we played on Sunday could be a result of our week's preparation. We did a lot of running on Tuesday night, which was OK. Thursday night we had a very poor training session, a very poor session indeed. Then Saturday morning, we had a couple of players who couldn't train, so we couldn't really get into it then either. I think the way we played was a reflection of the way we prepared for the game.

'You can't just be great on Sunday; it's a week's work, you've got to do the hard work, and then be ready for it when the weekend comes. If we have a poor week at training, we're not going to get into the groove and we're going to have a poor start to any game.

'There's just one more thing that I want to enforce. It doesn't matter what's wrong with you when you're injured, I want you on your feet and in the defensive line. Now the incident on Sunday when Frano stayed down hurt and they ran the ball up and they were inside our 22 . . . I don't care if the physio's out there and he wants to examine you and all that stuff. That's not important. What's important is – this is for everybody – you've got twelve team-mates tackling their guts out, defending like anything inside the 22 and we've got the physio telling a guy to see if he can straighten his knee out.

'I don't care what's wrong with you; it doesn't matter what's wrong with you; if the opposition's got the ball, I want you on your feet and in the defensive line. As soon as we get a break in play, if you've got a broken leg, you get off the field and we'll replace you, but whenever you can get on your feet, whenever you're conscious, I want you on your feet and faking it in the defensive line. As soon as there's a break, if you're injured, get off the field and we'll replace you.

'There are no exceptions to that rule. So from now on, the only reason you stay down hurt and get attention from the sideline is because there's a break in play or you're unconscious – no other reasons will be accepted. I want everybody on their feet in the defence all the time. Bill or the physio will come out with water and if you're hurt, tell him you need to be replaced and we'll use our replacements.

'Right. Now you did it very tough with the referee on Sunday, but our problem is we let them score 31 points. Like I've said before, we've got to base the team on pride in defence, everybody tackling their guts out. You shouldn't have to score 32 points to win, regardless of the referee, regardless of anything, you shouldn't have to score 32 points to win any game. You should be able to win a game by scoring 15 points or 12 points. I know you can score points, you'll score 25 points pretty well every time you run out onto the field, I know that you can do that, so what we've got to do is restrict the opposition to 10 or 12. I don't care what they get, but they can't get 30, I know that's too many. We've got to say we don't want them to get any. If they get 5 that's too many, but they can't get up around 20.

'I don't want to talk too much about last Sunday's game. We let too many points in to win the game, so that's the end of it. Now we've got to beat Hull on Sunday. People will say it's early in the competition, there's nine months to go, everything's alright. Well I'm telling you everything is not all right. Hull are 3 points in front of us now. If they beat us, they're 5 points in front. I don't care who you're trying to pick up, 5 competition points is a lot to make up. We've got to be spot on this Sunday, so I want us to have a good week, starting with tonight's training.

'I don't particularly want to go down to Hull the night before, because then you're out of your own bed and out of your routine. So we'll go down there early on Sunday, have something to eat on the way, have a light training session where we can move the ball around a bit, have a good video, get to the ground an hour before we play, get changed, get stuck into them, beat the shit out of them, get on the bus and get home. Alright, let's get training.'

Next door, the board meeting had just begun. A hand-delivered letter from the Council had arrived that afternoon, threatening Maurice with prosecution because their inspector had found that the electronic counters on the turnstiles, used to prevent the risk of overcrowding, were not working. In the wake of the Hillsborough disaster, all local authorities were understandably strict about enforcement of ground safety work, but the threat baffled the Wigan board, because new electronic equipment had only just been installed and thoroughly tested. Jack Robinson made a series of calls and discovered that the contractors working on the new stand had severed the wires to the turnstiles while demolishing a wall. The directors heaved a sigh of relief that there was at least a good reason for the failure and passed on to the rest of the business.

The telephone rang. Tom Rathbone, in his customary role of telephonist, as the one sitting nearest to it, got up from the table, picked up the 'phone, listened for a moment, then said, 'I don't know love, I'm only the night watchman here, ring the office during the day tomorrow,' then hung up and sat down again, winking at his colleagues.

They had completed their business by the time John Monie arrived back from training to make his weekly report. After accepting the directors' criticisms of the way his side had played at Bradford, particularly in the first half, Monie offered them some words of hope: 'Watching the game and having seen them on video, I was confident even at half-time that they were a side we could beat, but when I got in the sheds at half-time and found Ellery had been sent off, well, with twelve men you just hope you can win, but I think the way we played last Sunday in the second half, that'll be the spring-board and we'll go on now from that.'

He also told them that Andy Gregory has been breathalysed at ten o'clock on the previous Thursday night and the test had been positive. 'How he can be done for drunk driving at 10 p.m. on a training night, I just don't know,' said Tom.

'He was in a filthy mood when he got to training that night,' said Monie. 'He just ruined the Thursday training session because he wasn't talking to anyone. I had him in on Friday and he complained about having to do all the work, make it all happen, call all the moves and so on. So on Saturday I got the guys I haven't been happy with to come in and talked to them individually and I told Gizz I wanted him to get more involved.'

Business completed, they went next door to the vice-president's lounge for the monthly awards to the players. They are donated by their sponsors, Norweb, every month throughout the season and given for 'hit' (tackle) of the month, defensive player of the month and player of the month, for both 'A' team and first team. The first team awards went to Andy Goodway, Ian Lucas and Dean Bell.

Lucas and Bell both said a brief word of thanks, Bell well enough versed in the etiquette of such occasions to mention the sponsors, Norweb, by name. Goodway – 'B. A.' in the dressing room, standing for 'Bad Attitude' – marched up to the podium, collected his award, flashed a V-sign at his team-mates and was on his way back to his seat when Lindsay recalled him to make his speech of thanks. 'Thanks very much,' said Goodway, immediately returning to his seat, having zealously guarded his reputation as the most surly and truculent member of the squad. Perhaps he wanted to assert his independence and indifference, but the effect was more like a rather gauche schoolboy, embarrassing himself and everybody else at an end of term prize-giving.

Wigan were forced to go into the vital game at Hull without Ellery, who was suspended for two matches, reduced to one on appeal, for his sending-off at Bradford. A combination of indiscipline, bad luck and sheer brilliance by Hull saw Wigan crushed 24–4. The indiscipline surfaced as early as the fourteenth minute, when Joe Lydon was sent off after flattening a Hull player, though both he and his coach were convinced that it had been a perfectly fair tackle. Dean Bell also spent ten minutes in the sin-bin for an off-the-ball hit on another player and a succession of penalties for arguing with the referee compounded Wigan's problem.

The bad luck manifested itself in injuries to Andy Gregory and Dean Bell, who was badly concussed after a collision with his own team-mate Denis Betts, receiving a hideous gash to his mouth which required thirty stitches. Phil Clarke also suffered a serious injury, being carried off near the final whistle. Despite all that, there was no disputing Hull's right to the points. Wigan left Humberside in black mood, leaving the jubilant Hull players celebrating a 100 per cent record and a 5 point lead over the champions.

The Hull defeat and an ever-lengthening injury list was hardly the ideal beginning to a week culminating in Wigan's match of the year against the Australians, who had cruised through their opening tour matches with ominous confidence. At Tuesday night's board meeting, the first item on the agenda was the size of the bonus to be offered to the players to beat Australia. Maurice Lindsay set the ball rolling. 'We paid £1,500 per man for the defeat of Manly (the Sydney champions) in the World Club Challenge three years ago, what are your opinions about the bonus for the Australian game?'

Jack Hilton carefully maintained his reputation for financial prudence. 'I don't think they could play any harder than they already do, whatever size of bonus you offer.'

'Alright, we'll just offer them a fiver then,' said Maurice with a smile.

For once, his natural ally, Jack Robinson, was as bearish as Jack Hilton. 'I think you've got to get control of these bonuses. I think £1,500 is enough, bearing in mind the contract payments that we've been giving lately.'

Maurice was unmoved, bullishly arguing for £2,000. 'It's only once every four years and it is the Australians.'

'Let's go for it,' said Tom Rathbone through his cloud of cigar smoke. The two opponents subsided into silent assent, and Lindsay, not for the first time, had his way.

There were problems with three players to discuss, almost inevitably including Bobby Goulding, who still had not paid his New Zealand legal bill. His father had now been on the 'phone to Maurice, asking for a loan to enable Bobby to pay it. Since he already had an outstanding loan of several thousand pounds from the club, this latest request did not meet with universal approval. The directors turned from the tangled state of their players' off-the-field activities to John Monie's report on the night's training and the team news with relief.

'We've all been saying, "Let's stuff the Aussie swine," but we can't really say that when you're here, can we John?' asked Maurice.

'You can say it; doing it is the hard part . . . Dean was up there trying to train when I got there. He's got those thirty stitches in his mouth. I told him that as soon as he got warmed up and the blood was pumping round, the gash would probably split wide open again so I sent him home, but he's confident he'll be alright for Sunday and so's Kevin Iro. I think Dean will be OK; he isn't going to want to miss playing against the Australians, you know what he's like about them.

'I want to play Kevin too, but he's got to be alright mentally for it. I'm going to leave it until Saturday morning and then have him stretching out; if his hamstring is OK, then he'll play. He was trying to test it out by playing last Sunday but that's not the way to do it. By the way, if Joe Lydon doesn't get suspended, I'm going to give him the hit of the month award for the tackle that got him sent off. I thought it was a great tackle.

'The forwards are all OK, so the pack is going to be about as strong as we can put out, apart from Andy Platt of course. Our top thirteen is about as strong as we can get in fact, providing Dean, Kevin and Joe all come through. They all trained really well tonight, apart from Shaun Edwards, but everybody else was fine. It's the best they've trained for a while.'

'Is that because of the pressure you've put Shaun under?' asked Maurice.

'Could be.'

'Er . . . Neil . . .' began Maurice. By this time I was beginning to get the hang of the routine. 'I'll just wait outside for a minute Maurice,' I said, setting off in my perennial pursuit of a cup of coffee.

A Tale of Two Fathers

SOMEONE at the club had told me at the start of my year with Wigan that 'a few of the problems at Wigan are caused by two fathers'. The paternal duo he had in mind were the fathers of Bobby Goulding and Shaun Edwards. Both were ex-professional players themselves and they were seen, by at least some people at the club, as having too strong an influence on their offspring for their own good. That view was by no means wholly fair, but perhaps just as important, it was widely believed.

While the influence of Bobby's father was alleged to be mainly concerned with the remuneration being offered to his lad, Jackie Edwards was seen as a dominant influence on Shaun in every area, credited with an almost Svengali-like hold on his son. That view of Mr Edwards senior is repudiated by Shaun's present coach, John Monie, however. 'Jackie has never once intervened in my coaching of Shaun. The only thing I've got from him has been a bit of help with information on some of our opposition.'

Whatever his present role, Jackie Edwards is happy to confirm that his son's rugby league career was literally kick-started by him. 'I did not push Shaun, I kicked him,' he said with a smile. 'It was obvious that he had a natural talent as a youngster. That alone is not enough, however. He has worked very hard and he has always had a ruthless winning streak.'

If the influence of Edwards senior seems too strong to outsiders, however, Shaun himself has no doubts about the importance of his family to him. In his personal profile in the Wigan programme, under the heading 'My Greatest Moment', where players usually mention appearing at Wembley or playing for Great Britain, Shaun had written 'The birth of my baby brother' and under 'Heroes' were the words 'My family'.

Shaun knew from early childhood what his destiny was to be. 'I was pretty good at schoolwork, but I knew from a very early age that I was going to be a professional rugby league player; it's the only way to make money around here.'

An incident from Shaun's schooldays, related by Maurice Lindsay, perfectly illustrates this self-belief and obsessive dedication to rugby league. Until the age of 14, Shaun had been a model student, bright, hard-working and regularly in the top half-dozen in his class. After his fourteenth birthday, however, all that stopped. His academic performance deteriorated, he seemed disinterested, sullen and withdrawn. One of his concerned teachers raised the matter with him, asking him what was wrong.

'I've finished with schooling now,' was the reply.

'What do you mean you've finished? You don't leave school for another two years, you could get qualifications, go on to college.'

'No, I've finished.'

'But what are you going to do, when you leave school with no qualifications?'

'I'm going to be a professional rugby league player.'

Shaun was not only unshakeable in his conviction that school had nothing further to offer him, continuing to while away the time until he could leave, he was equally correct in his belief that a professional rugby league career awaited him.

Shaun had played for England schools at both rugby union and league, but there was never much doubt that he would be joining the 13-a-side code as an adult. He was a record signing as a schoolboy, a precocious talent, schooled from an early age towards the lucrative career with Wigan and Great Britain that he now enjoys.

All the clichés of the young sports prodigy can be found in Shaun's story. His father's own career was cut short by serious injury, causing him to channel all his own ambitions into his child. While other kids smoked furtive cigarettes and opened negotiations with the opposite sex behind the bike sheds, Shaun honed his rugby league skills under the watchful eye of his father, sacrificing everything, including some emotional development, on the altar of his own and his father's driving ambition.

Edwards signed for Wigan at midnight on his sixteenth birthday, a throwback to his father's era, when club directors would camp in a player's living room on the evening before his sixteenth birthday, keeping other clubs at bay until the moment when the lad could legitimately be signed on professional forms. Such cloak and dagger stuff had become obsolete by the time of Shaun's signing, but the midnight ceremony was retained at the insistence of his father, though it may also have appealed to Maurice Lindsay's sense of theatre, guaranteeing a few extra lines of press coverage.

Jackie played his professional rugby league for Warrington, but Shaun never had any doubt that he would play for Wigan. 'I never saw my father play, I wasn't born when he was playing, and I never really considered playing for Warrington or anyone else. Wigan was the team I wanted to play for, but at first they wouldn't offer me anywhere near the money that other clubs were willing to pay. Even when I signed, I still didn't get as much as I could have got at other places, but I wanted to play for Wigan. My father helped me with the negotiations, but no matter who's helping you, I think the club know how much they're prepared to offer you and they're not going to up it beyond that.'

Neither awe of his peers at Wigan nor a lack of self-confidence were a problem for Shaun. 'To be honest I couldn't even remember who was at stand-off when I came to Wigan, they were a pretty poor team then. The first game I played, I showed the opposition a bit too much respect, but after that I just got on with my own game. I was always confident, I always thought that I was better than the players in the team, even as a kid.

'I can play either scrum-half or stand-off, I don't really mind which, but the last few years I've been playing mostly at stand-off because we've had Andy here. The biggest disappointment of my career was getting injured in the first match of the 1988 Great Britain tour to Australia because, with all due respect to the people who took over, I think that if Andy and I had been the half-backs against Australia, we would have done a lot better and caused them a lot of problems.'

Shaun's father remains the sharpest critic and keenest student of his son's play. 'My dad doesn't come to the games any more but he watches the videos and tells me where he thinks I'm going wrong and so on. John Monie certainly helps you too, but you just use your own brain as well. When you watch the video, you can see yourself where you're going wrong, though sometimes you can be just a bit blind about something you're doing and then you need other people to help you and point it out.'

Jackie's helpfulness extends to correcting the press when they either criticise his son or wrongly accuse him of error. When Wigan lost to Warrington on New Year's Day, Mark Forster's ninety-yard interception try appeared to many of the press to have come from a Shaun Edwards pass, though the real culprit was actually Dean Bell. Those who blamed Edwards in their reports received a long letter from Mr Edwards senior, defending his son's honour and pointing out the error of their ways. Suggestions earlier in the season that Shaun was playing below his best may have had the endorsement of the Wigan boardroom, but journalists who mentioned this loss of form received another lengthy missive from Mr Edwards.

Before the start of the season, there had been speculation that Shaun would leave his home-town club to play in Australia. Although he did eventually sign a new contract at Wigan, it was only for one year, an unusually short duration, further fuelling transfer speculation. Shaun still denied that he was planning a move, however. 'I only signed a one-year contract last time just to keep my options open, make sure Wigan are still happy with me and I'm still happy with them. Sometimes you can get a bit stale if you stay in the same place too long.'

Shaun has an astonishing, perhaps rather daunting, maturity for a 22-year-old. He doesn't drink or do the rounds of the Wigan pubs or clubs, unlike those of his colleagues who revel in their near-pop star status in the town. Edwards gives few clues to his private self to outsiders and still lives at home with his family, dedicating himself single-mindedly to the game at which he excels. He seems always a loner in the Wigan dressing room, aloof from the wisecracking and horseplay, serious-faced while his team-mates are cutting loose. Ellery is also a teetotaller, but he is accepted as one of the lads. Shaun, the outsider, prefers the company of his family and a few friends from his schooldays. Ian Lucas is no different in this respect, but while he is well-liked, a few Wigan players seem to reserve the sort of dislike for Shaun that schoolboys have for the form swot.

Wigan fans are also aware that Shaun is somehow different from the rest. At a meet-the-fans evening, during which the players answer questions from the floor, usually about favourite movies, or their best try, one supporter swayed unsteadily to his feet. 'I've got a question about Shaun Edwards,' he said to the chairman. 'Is he still a virgin?' Shaun's team-mates collapsed in fits of laughter, while Shaun sat red-faced and silent, battling to control his anger.

If there are those who find him wanting as a mate, however, none question his value on the field. In the end it is perhaps his obsessive pursuit of excellence that sets him apart from his team-mates. There is a tempting and not altogether fanciful analogy between Shaun and Geoffrey Boycott, another supremely gifted sportsman, whose self-absorption and obsession with perfecting his skills left him short on friends, if long on admirers. There may come a day when Shaun will regret that his youth and early adulthood did not include more experiences than those on the training ground and the rugby league field. He will be a very wealthy man when he retires from the game, but not necessarily a completely rounded personality.

Shaun feels that the reasons why the players do not socialise more with each other are to do with their advancing years as much as any personal antipathies. 'I suppose in each team, you all get on all right, but there'll be certain players you'll get on with really well and others less so. The players don't go out together as much as they used to a couple of years back. A lot of the players have got families now and obviously they come first.

'All my mates are from around Wigan; basically I still knock around with the same blokes as when I was at school. I don't tend to go out much around Wigan though, being recognised can be a problem. It does get on your nerves a little bit sometimes, especially when you've lost and everybody is getting on to you. You know, I don't get on to them about their jobs, I don't know why they should get on to me. It's all part of the job I suppose but . . .

'If we lose a couple of games people say, "Oh, they can't play anymore." When Mike Tyson lost a fight they all said he couldn't fight. When the San Francisco 49ers lost the Super Bowl they all said they were finished, but all it really means is that you've had an off-day and we all have them. We haven't played to our potential this year, on a week-to-week basis, but some of our spectators think that there is only Wigan can play, you know. They don't give credit to the other teams and to all the good players they have.

'When we do lose a game, you're a bit despondent for a couple of days but then you just can't wait for the next game. I love playing, but I suppose a lot of people do treat it as a business. If you weren't getting paid I suppose you wouldn't put in the hours that you do, especially the training and preparation, or when you're having physio for an injury, but it's different when you get out there playing. I particularly like it when you're losing and the crowd get behind you – which doesn't happen all that much at Wigan to tell you the truth – and then you come back and you win and it's a tight game, I enjoy all that kind of thing.

'Other people have to get up early and go to work, I just love playing. I like the big games and the build-up to them best, though, and it's not always easy to prepare yourself the same for all the games. You've just got to have a bit of pride in yourself to keep your motivation high and also I do like scoring tries. I get a bit sick if I don't score one for a while. Sometimes obviously you're more motivated than others and I must admit now having played for so many years and played so many big games, that I look forward to the big games more than the others, whereas when you're 17 they're all big games.

'I try to get my mind on the job a couple of days before, mentally prepare myself, think about who I'm playing against, especially when you're playing against a really good player, like Garry Schofield. In the not-so important games, perhaps your aggression and your concentration might slip a little, but for a big game, playing against a top player, if you let your concentration slip for a moment against him, then he'll be past you.'

Before a match Shaun is grim-faced, features drawn into his near-permanent frown, concentrating, distilling his aggression, tuning himself to the peak of his game. He plays a vital role for Wigan, occupying the pivotal stand-off position and acting as the team's midfield organiser, shouting, cajoling and supervising the defensive line, as well as unleashing the full range of his own formidable talents.

His error rate is probably as low as anyone's, he rarely misses tackles, reads the game like a veteran, has a superb kicking game, blistering pace off the mark, a combination with Andy Gregory that sometimes borders on the telepathic and does not shirk the toughest exchanges, taking the tackle rather than throwing out a speculative or 'hospital' pass. 'He never gives a bad ball,' one of the Wigan centres remarked approvingly. As a drinking companion Shaun might be regarded as a bit of a disaster, but out on the rugby field, he is one of the best players around and a tough one as well, despite his slight build, taking hits that would hospitalise the chronicler of Wigan's year.

'You don't get the same feeling if you watch a game from high up in the stands', says Edwards, 'but if you watch it from the touchline level, the likes of Wigan against Widnes, I've sometimes thought to myself, "How do I play that game?", but when you're on the field you just don't feel it.'

Edwards also makes his tackles, frequently on big forwards breaking through around the ruck. He did so repeatedly at Wembley in May 1990, despite his fractures of the cheekbone and eye-socket. 'I knew I'd broken it as soon as it happened. I couldn't see properly for a few minutes, but I knew that if I didn't get stuck into somebody straight away, I'd go off the field. So I made myself go in for a couple of tackles as soon as I could, just to get straight back into the game and try to forget about it as much as I could.'

Even from the press box, it was obvious that Shaun was seriously injured and the pain must have been agonising, so what had possessed him to stay on the field? 'It was agony, but I didn't come off because I didn't want them to know that they could hurt me. I knew that if I'd pulled a muscle or something like that then I couldn't have gone on, because I'd have been a hindrance to the team, but I knew that the injury was only pain and I could put up with it. Well I thought it was only pain anyway, I got a bit of a shock at the end when they told me I could have blinded myself.' That injury had healed during the close-season though the psychological damage took longer to cure.

Shaun would have had no problems with motivation for Wigan's next match, for games do not come any bigger than the one against the touring Australians, but after weeks of build-up, the 'Fourth Test' – as the match had been unofficially billed – proved to be a cruel anti-climax. Despite John Monie's optimism earlier in the week, Dean Bell's mouth had

(TOP LEFT) Andy Gregory takes a sideways look at Steve Hampson's chances of evading St Helens defender George Mann.

(TOP RIGHT) John Monie accepts Bill Hartley's congratulations as the final whistle blows at Wembley. Andrew Pinkerton seems remarkably laid-back about the whole affair, while an apprehensive Alex Murphy awaits his turn.

(ABOVE) Wigan take their annual afternoon constitutional around Wembley. From left: Phil Clarke, Ian Lucas, Andy Goodway, Shaun Edwards, Dean Bell, Frano Botica, Ellery Hanley, Martin Dermott, Dave Myers and Bobby Goulding.

OPPOSITE PAGE

(FAR LEFT) Tea-break. Dave Myers, Andy Gregory, Frano Botica (back to camera), Ged Stazicker and Steve Hampson take a little tea and toast after training.

(LEFT) A defender's eye view of 'Mean Dean'. Dean Bell about to side-step St Helens' Shane Cooper.

(BELOW) Andy Platt looks for an escape route as two members of the Wigan fan club close in for the kill.

THIS PAGE

(RIGHT) 'Put the lid on his head, Maurice.' Every photographer's favourite cliché as Wigan chairman Maurice Lindsay and coach John Monie celebrate with the Championship trophy in the dressing-room at Headingley.

(ABOVE) Train hard and one day you too could have one of these. Dean Bell arrives for training in his sponsored motor.

(LEFT) Kelvin Skerrett proves he can be friendly as the next man . . . off the field. Bobby Goulding stages a cover-up.

(BELOW) Almost there. Wigan's players celebrate victory in the Challenge Cup se final. *From left on the top row:* Dave Mye Ian Lucas, Denis Betts, Dean Bell, Fran Botica, Steve Hampson. *Lower tier:* And Goodway, Ellery Hanley, Shaun Edward Martin Dermott, Andy Platt, Joe Lydon.

OPPOSITE PAGE

(NEAR RIGHT) The Beast. Kevin Iro looks to unload the ball during the Challenge Cup Final, his last game for Wigan before joining Australian club Manly.

(FAR RIGHT, TOP) Alas, no more. The Wigan clubhouse and offices before the new stand was built right over the top. (MIDDLE) Do you have it in cherry and white? Phil Clarke trie on his Wembley suit. Dave Marshall, a sales assistant at the shop as well as a Wigan wingman, offers expert advice. Mike Forshaw and Ian Gildart await their turn.

(BOTTOM) Match day at Central Park. Wigan fans do a little Sunday shopping on their way to the game. In the background, the skeleton of the new stand rises over the Riverside club alongside the club offices.

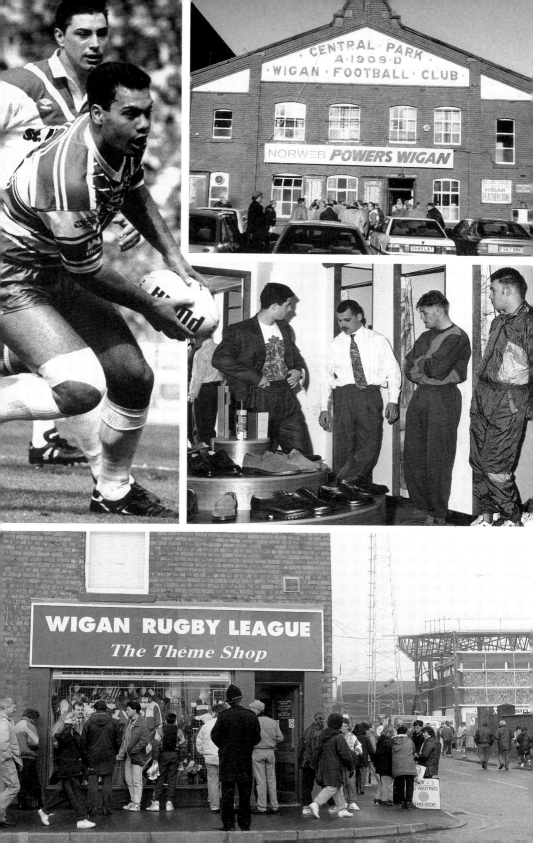

THIS PAGE

(TOP LEFT) A Wigan fan appa[...]
offers £10 for the Championsh[...]
Trophy. The shop assistant h[...]
out for £20.

(TOP RIGHT) John Monie,
auditioning for the role of Phi[...]
Marlowe, as he checks his ma[...]
the Wigan offices.

(LEFT) Gizz. The fierce
concentration of Shaun Edwa[...]
he picks out a supporting run[...]
Andy Goodway backs up on t[...]
inside.

OPPOSITE PAGE

(TOP) 'You get bugger all for [...]
in this game.' Ellery Hanley,
aider Keith Mills and Dean [...]
contemplate losing money aft[...]
Regal Trophy defeat by Brad[...]

(BOTTOM LEFT) Featherstone[...]
Derek Fox makes the tackle, [...]
Shaun Edwards is still on his [...]
and looking to off-load.

(BOTTOM RIGHT) Future lead[...]
Phil Clarke, the young loose
forward tipped to succeed El[...]
Hanley as both Wigan and G[...]
Britain captain.

(ABOVE) Bobby Goulding apprehended by two avid foll of 'Neighbours with Wigan accents'.

(LEFT) Your number's up. T Wigan backline's jerseys awai occupants in the dressing-roo before the game.

not healed and he joined Andy Platt and Frano Botica on the sidelines. Although both Andy Gregory and Kevin Iro took the field, neither looked completely fit.

Nonetheless, with a 25,000 crowd baying for Australian blood, Wigan began like the champions they were and for twenty minutes they looked the equal of the formidable Kangaroos. They ripped into the Aussies from the kick-off and had twice been within inches of scoring before the referee awarded them a penalty try, after Shaun was felled as he chased his own kick towards the Australian line. Joe Lydon's conversion put Wigan 6 points up and they continued to pound the Australians, with Iro and Hampson both going close.

They couldn't add to their lead, however, and having survived the early onslaught, the Australians killed off the Wigan challenge with almost contemptuous ease. Big second-rower John Cartwright had a try disallowed, but it scarcely mattered as the Australians ran in four in the fifteen minutes before half-time. At the break, 20 points to 6 down, Wigan already knew the game was lost.

The Australians scored three further tries in the second half, without ever seeming to get out of second gear, as Wigan slumped to their biggest-ever defeat against Australia. They scarcely penetrated the Australian half and the huge crowd was reduced to near-silence, many of the supporters slipping away long before the final whistle, leaving their shame-faced heroes to slink back to the dressing-room, eclipsed by a far better side.

Knowing they had a three-week break before their next game, John Monie had already arranged for his players to have the following week off. He now had those three weeks to restore the injured players to health and forge some will to win and team spirit in his increasingly fractious and out-of-sorts squad. Although the season was only eight weeks old, the break represented what was already looking like the last chance to get the once-unstoppable Wigan juggernaut moving again. The summer optimism about emulating or even exceeding the previous season's achievements was looking as illusory as the hopes of becoming the first side in twelve years to beat Australia on British soil.

While most of the Wigan players could rest and train for those three weeks, free from the pressure of big matches, some of the most important members of the side, Hanley, Gregory, Platt and Edwards, were on international duty for Great Britain against Australia. Britain took the first Test at Wembley, with Hanley in particular in magnificent form, but narrow defeats in the next two Tests gave Australia the series and the Rugby League Ashes.

As a patriotic Australian, John Monie was delighted with his compatriots' victory, but a more direct concern was the impact the gruelling series would have on the club form of his key players. The jury remained out on that. Andy Platt continued to be the most solid, consistent and hard-grafting forward in the game and Hanley went from strength to strength. On the other hand, Andy Gregory, after playing some of the best football of his career earlier in the season went into temporary decline and Shaun Edwards, perhaps smarting from the indignity of being dropped by Great Britain during the series, played to his potential only fitfully.

The three key positions in a rugby league team are scrum-half, stand-off and loose forward. Wigan's dominance of domestic rugby league in the late 1980s had been built on the foundations of having the top player in Britain in each of those positions – Andy Gregory, Shaun Edwards and Ellery Hanley. The three have skills that can turn any game and they often combine in play of such breathtaking audacity and ruthless efficiency, that lesser mortals can only flounder admiringly in their wake.

There was a price to be paid for having such prodigious talent in the Wigan ranks, however, and it wasn't entirely a financial one. The three of them had egos to match the size of their talents and friction was a constant danger. They had already proved a handful for Monie's predecessor, Graham Lowe, and Monie himself occasionally found that life with Wigan offered rewards and headaches in about equal proportions. The three of them, plus the equally intractable Andy Goodway, had reduced less imperturbable coaches to helpless rage in their time, but to his own surprise, Monie found the problems of coaching Wigan's star-spangled squad far less daunting than he had expected.

Andy Goodway was simply Andy Goodway, magnificently talented, the most explosive running forward in the British game, but with enough chips on his broad shoulders to fill a fair size butty. Goodway seemed to wander through life with two fingers permanently raised against every authority, apparently interested in his club or his team-mates only in so far as they could be of benefit to him. Great Britain's team management had decided that they could live without his talent rather than put up with his disruptive influence on the team. Wigan had apparently reached the opposite conclusion.

Ellery Hanley was ruler of the Central Park roost, captain of both Wigan and Great Britain, acknowledged by his peers as the foremost player in Britain and one of the best, if not the best, player in world rugby league. He had had his moments with Monie's predecessor, during which he had been stripped of the captaincy and left out of the team for several weeks, but under Monie he had re-emerged as leader in every way, revealing still more of the skill, strength, power and unbreakable will that made him close to the complete player.

Secure in his position and supremely confident of his own ability, Ellery could remain largely aloof from the constant jockeying for position between Gregory and Edwards. Both had remarkable talents, which when fused together were more than a match for virtually any other half-back pairing, but their struggles for supremacy could sometimes be at best an amusing distraction and at worst a dangerous irritant to team harmony.

Both saw themselves as the dominant influence on the team and would bicker about the other one monopolising the ball and not allowing them a fair share. Their personalities were as different as could be imagined, Gregory the showman, always talking, joking, holding his team-mates spellbound and helpless with laughter, while Edwards was taciturn, monosyllabic, often appearing grouchy and self-obsessed. For all his humour, however, Gregory could be as wilful and intractable as a bad-tempered child at times. He had gone into dispute with both his previous clubs, Widnes and Warrington, walking out on them in mid-contract. He had forced an increase in his money at Central Park by threatening the same thing. On one occasion Gregory had even turned his back on John Monie and walked out of the room, while his coach was still trying to talk to him.

Like Hanley, Edwards had been installed as team captain and had then had the captaincy stripped from him by Monie's predecessor, Graham Lowe. Hanley was now in charge once more, but perhaps having been demoted continued to rankle

Edwards; who could tell, for Shaun's thoughts on the subject, as on so much else, remained a closed book to all but a handful of people.

When not arguing about their on-field roles, the greatest potential for conflict between Gregory and Edwards – inevitably in a professional sport – came over money. When Shaun's contract expired at the end of the previous season, his negotiations for a further contract with Maurice Lindsay had been protracted and difficult, partly as a result of the inflationary effects of the 'Skerrett factor'. Shaun had eventually agreed a one-year extension at vastly increased money, 'world record money' in the words of one disgruntled board member. In theory players' earnings are totally secret, but in practice Andy Gregory soon got to know that his rival was now earning substantially more than he was.

Though technically in breach of his contract, which still had a year to run, Gregory marched straight into the boardroom, demanding a substantial increase in his own contract payments. Faced with an ultimatum from one of their key players, the Wigan board did what many other boards have done in similar circumstances – they gave way. If Gregory was mollified, Edwards perhaps felt shorn of some of the fruits of his victory. The wheel of petty jealousy and mutual suspicion was set for another turn.

The physical damage caused by Shaun's hideous injuries at Wembley had healed, but the psychological scars might have run deeper, affecting his form and confidence. Whatever the reasons, there was no doubting that his performances in the first half of the season had fallen a long way short of his best. As Andy Gregory turned in a string of match-winning displays, Edwards drifted fitfully in and out of the games. Then, just like the nursery rhyme about good bear and bad bear, as one got better, the other got worse. Perhaps troubled by his recurring groin injury, perhaps just losing the edge of his form after a brilliant spell, Gregory began to make mistakes and ceased to dominate games as he had been doing.

Perhaps coincidentally, perhaps not, Edwards, whose form had been so poor that the Wigan board and coaching staff were already searching around for a replacement for him, began to improve. As Gregory lost form and missed a number of games through injury, Edwards was able to dominate the midfield, call the plays and become the mainspring of the team.

For all the potential and actual personality clashes at Wigan and all the dire warnings he had received before taking up the Wigan job, John Monie claimed to have found his man-management problems to be surprisingly small-scale. 'To be honest, I've only really had a problem with Andy Gregory, and then only once. Sometimes he can be great, he can be everybody's best friend in the world, but if he's the wrong way out, because something or other has happened, he can completely wreck a training session. In fact he has, simply because he didn't want to know.

'I was warned about the others before I came here but . . . Well Ellery is the most coachable player I've come across. He won't accept what you say blindly, he'll ask questions and talk about it, but then he'll do it. His attitude to training and playing is just remarkable, in fact both he and Andy Platt could play first grade in Sydney, right now, without any trouble at all.

'I don't have a problem with Shaun, while the one I was warned about before I came, Andy Goodway, has not been the slightest problem to me either. Nor have I had any inter-ference from the board. They have their areas of re-sponsibility, I have mine, and they don't interfere in how I run the team. We might not always agree about what's the best thing to do, but when it comes down to it, it's my job to coach whatever squad of players they buy for me.'

Monie's calm, methodical approach to coaching may well have made life with the Wigan superstars easier for him than it had been for more emotional coaches, such as Graham Lowe, but Monie admits that he was not always so impassive. 'When I was a young player, I used to get so pumped-up before a game that I'd bring on a severe migraine. More than once I've missed a game through being stuck in bed. Years of mental training have taught me to cope with both the migraine problem and the pressure of being a rugby league coach. I have learned to push the pressure aside in the interests of self-preservation.'

Monie's ability to push aside pressure looked likely to be an increasingly valuable asset, for Wigan's fans have never been slow to turn on their team and the coach, when they are not sweeping all before them. At this stage of the season, with the honourable exceptions of the two players Monie had singled out for particular praise, Ellery Hanley and Andy Platt, few of the Wigan players could have looked themselves in the eye in the murky dressing-room mirror and pronounced themselves completely happy with their form. Results and the manner of the team's play remained wildly variable and, apart from injuries, the most plausible cause seemed to be dressing-room disharmony, disrupting the selfless team spirit that all winners need to pull them through.

False Dawn

WIGAN'S players returned from their three-week break knowing that they had reached the point of no return. They had to rediscover their form, start winning and winning well or they could wave a fond farewell to their Championship title. They began the process with a comfortable home win against struggling Oldham at Central Park. Then on a cold, grey November night, they set off for a potentially difficult away match at Hull Kingston Rovers.

The coach pounded along the M62 motorway to Hull, pausing briefly at a service station to pick up the Yorkshire-based players, Ellery Hanley and Kelvin Skerrett, both signed from Bradford Northern and still living east of the Pennines despite their change of club. Just short of the ground, Monie took his players on a five-minute walk, to pump some air into their lungs and begin the loosening-up process. Then they piled back onto the bus and it swept through the gates into Rovers' Craven Park ground.

The dressing room looked like a section of an underground car-park, with its lagged pipes, metal ducting and harsh neon lighting. John Monie normally regarded his coaching duties as ending the day before a match, believing that if he hadn't got his message across in training, it was too late to start issuing instructions in the changing room, but as if emphasising the importance of this match, he broke with his previous practice and called his players together an hour before the kick-off.

'I know most of you think the Challenge Cup is the most important trophy, but it isn't to me. The one that counts for me is the Championship. That's the one that proves we're better than any of the other teams, because we have to win more games than any of them to do it.

'Now a successful team needs two things: a captain and a half-back. Well you've got the most inspirational captain in the world and you've got the best half-back in the world. So you know what the rest of you have got to do, don't you? You've got to graft and tackle. Don't worry about scoring points, we've got plenty of people who will score some points for us. I just want to see you tackle all night, and any player who doesn't tackle tonight – I don't care who he is – will find himself dropped.'

After Monie's speech, there was near-total silence. The players collected their kit from Taffy, who presided over the two baskets, one filled with boots, shoulder pads and shin pads, the other with each player's kit, neatly rolled inside his shirt with the number showing. Bill Hartley and Andrew Pinkerton, a new addition to the back-up team, were at work with the 'hot stuff' on the treatment table, massaging liniment into the calves and thighs of each player in turn, while Keith went round strapping-up the players with whatever strapping they required. Some have the third and fourth fingers of each hand taped together to minimise the risk of dislocation, others have wrists, ankles or knees bandaged to protect old injuries or prevent new ones.

Martin Dermott, back in favour after the shelving of the experimental switch of Bobby Goulding, wrapped electricians' tape around his forehead, pinning down his ears, while Ian Lucas donned an Australian-style helmet, a more substantial version of the old-fashioned scrum cap.

Someone brought in a pile of programmes for the night's game and the players seized them eagerly, studying them intently, grateful for the distraction. Monie paced around the room, exchanging a quiet word with individual players, emphasising one key part of their job for the game. The first players to be changed, Shaun Edwards and Dean Bell, went through their warm-up routines, stretching and running on the spot. Edwards sprinted to and fro diagonally across the dressing-room, ignoring the other players, a loner as always. There was the sound of a player throwing up from the shower cubicles, as the mounting tension began to grip everyone.

Some are so nervous before a game that they are physically sick, others sit in silence, a few burst into nervous chatter. Andy Gregory talked even more than usual this night, but all the others were silent, except for an occasional few muttered words. There was palpable tension in the atmosphere, the silence broken only by players' irritable shouts to Taffy for tie-ups and tape and Monie muttering to his players, one by one. I was careful not to distract the players or get in the way. I took up a perch on the kit basket in the corner and stayed there.

Monie broke off to address all his players once more, talking as much to vent his own tension as to get any information across. 'The first twenty minutes, it's kicking into the corners and tackling practice. If we get down there, bang! get the thing over the line. You know they're going to give it their best shot for twenty minutes, so let's have good control in the first twenty and field position and tackling, field position and tackling.'

Even though there were still twenty minutes to kick-off, someone was now asking the time every two minutes. Monie spoke yet again. 'Let's make the middle tight in defence. Make it tight, don't let them come down the middle.' A few of the players were now joining in, exhorting each other as the adrenalin began to flow. 'Move up quick, let's have lots of talk out there'. 'Let's meet them in the middle, you know what this lot are like when they get a start.' 'It's a long way to come for nothing.' 'Get these props sorted out Kelvin and Mal.'

The two touch judges came in to check the players' fingers for rings and inspect their studs, feeling for dangerous sharp edges, while passing on the referee's instructions. 'If the stand-off is creeping up offside at the scrum, we'll tell the winger and he can shout to him to get back. It'll save a load of whistle.' Monie nodded curtly and they filed out.

There were now just ten minutes to go to the kick-off and Ellery rose to address the team, stressing his familiar themes. 'Basics are what's going to win this, good defence. If you make a mistake, don't be looking for excuses, grabbing your muscle or your leg.' Monie chimed in once more. 'Just do your job, that's all you've got to do, play the way we train. In the line all the time. If you're injured, you come off, if you're not, stay on your feet.'

Shaun Edwards spoke for the first time in an hour, directing a remark to the forwards. 'From a tap they're just going to take a settler, so you can gang up on one of them and waste him.' Not to be outdone, his half-back partner and rival Andy Gregory added his five penn'orth. 'You know what they'll be saying next door? They'll be saying, "This lot don't want to be here on a Tuesday night, let's hit them hard." Well let's hit them harder and do it first.'

John Monie grabbed the last word. 'The only talk I want out there is positive talk. It's a fifteen man team and you've got to help each other. If someone makes a mistake, pick him up, help him over it. Now the last thing I'm going to tell you is this. This is the best football team we've had on the field since Wembley last year. I don't mind sticking with this team for the rest of the season. So if everybody does their job, you can stay together for the season. It's up to you.'

The players all stood and began to move towards the dressing-room door. Normally they would have warmed up out on the pitch and then returned to the dressing room for the team talk, but tonight they were going to warm up and then stay out there for the kick-off. As they got ready to leave they were all talking and shouting at each other. They stormed out in a thunder of metal studs on concrete.

Wigan ripped Hull KR apart from the first tackle, three forwards piling in and driving the Rovers ball-carrier back ten yards. They scored five fine tries in the first 40 minutes and conceded only one, to a piece of individual brilliance from Rovers' New Zealand centre Dave Watson.

At half-time, the Wigan players roared back into the dressing room, high on adrenalin and the buzz of taking the opposition apart. In contrast to the pre-match cathedral calm, the dressing room was now a hubbub of noise, all the players talking and shouting at once. 'Does it make any difference if we score again? Nooooo, just as long as they don't.' 'They're going to be looking for us out wide now, so let's bust them up the middle.'

'Let's have a rest now and save a bit of air,' said Monie, trying to calm them down. His first attempt was totally unsuccessful. After a five second pause, Gregory, Edwards, Goodway and Bell were all talking at once again.

'Listen,' said Monie, 'when we're at Wembley and we're 20 points down, I'll get lost and you can do it. We're up 30 points and suddenly everybody's a coach. Let's just have a drink and save some air. Just shut up for a bit.'

Half a minute later Edwards was off again, discussing some complex move with Ellery. 'Let's not turn into scientists,' Monie interrupted, 'let's keep it simple. Shut them out, shut them out, that's our priority, nil them in defence this half. Kelvin and Mal are doing good hitting them high but let's have the next man coming in low and really ripping the legs out of them. Then we can really do some back-slamming.' In the pause while he was considering his final thought before the second half, retching sounds could again be heard from the showers. 'OK. We don't want any stars in this team. Team work, doing your own job and helping your mates, that's what we want.'

The second half was slightly anti-climactic for Wigan's travelling supporters, with only one further try, scored by Ellery, to celebrate, but Monie's aim of nilling the opposition in the half was achieved, the final score being 36–6.

In the dressing room everybody was smiling and laughing. It appeared that the early season derailment was over; Wigan were back on track. On the coach back home, the players swigged beer, cracked jokes and played cards, the buzz continuing throughout the journey. Keith Mills looked over his shoulder as we neared Wigan, turned back and winked. 'There's no happier place than a winning bus, is there?'

With Wigan now back on the treadmill of once- and often twice-weekly games, the injuries began to mount again and Keith's workload increased with them. He had joined Wigan as a player in 1965, but his playing career was ended prematurely in 1971 by a bad shoulder injury. Perhaps stimulated by his own lengthy sessions on the treatment table, he took over the role of 'first-aider' to the team. 'It's a bit of a hobby you know, I still work at Leyland-Daf, though not in anything like this.

'I've been first-aider since 1972 and I've never missed an "A" team or first-team game in all that time. I've been trying to reckon it up, it must be something like 1,500 games. Even the day my dad died. He died during the night and we were due to go to Barrow or Whitehaven, I can't remember which. The rest of my family told me there was nothing I could do staying there. They were saying, "Your dad would want you to do it anyway," so I went with the team.

'My wife's always said that there's no-one who's been to more parties on her own; a lot of people thought she was a widow! She's involved as well now though. A few years back the lady who washed the Wigan kit was going into hospital for a couple of weeks and they asked me if I knew anyone who could wash it, while she was away. So we tried a few but couldn't get anyone and in desperation my missus said she'd come down and do it for a couple of weeks while this woman got herself right. That was over ten years ago and she's still doing it. So it's now got in her blood as well, she can't leave the place alone either.

'I work under Denis Wright, who's the official club physiotherapist. He does most of the diagnostic stuff, but I do the basic stuff on the field. Mostly we try to keep the player on the field till they've discussed it on the touchline, but the player knows himself if he can carry on. Sometimes you don't hear a crack from the touchline, but the player will tell you he heard one, when you get out there and then you know it's more than just the normal sort of injury. If it's an injury that could be made worse we usually try and get them off the field, but we've had players stay on with cuts that have required up to ten stitches. You get to know your players too, some go down dead and as soon as they've seen the opposing player penalised or sent off, they're suddenly not so bad again. Some used to go over the top a bit with that and I don't think that's a good part of the game.

'Denis may often miss half-an-hour of a game, because he's in the dressing room, working on an injured player straight away. We've found that a good system, because if you can start treating an injury straight away, get it packed in ice and get pressure bandages on and that sort of thing, you can save a week or sometimes a fortnight on a player's injury.

'You get to recognise the standard injuries; I would think you could go to every club and on every treatment table you would find a sprained ankle or an ankle ligament injury. There will be 'dead legs' – what the Aussies call 'corked thighs' – there will be sprung shoulders, where they spring the AC joint in the shoulder and there'll be broken hearts and a bit of the old sham when things have not gone right. You also get the head and face cuts which are inevitable when somebody just mistimes a tackle, or often enough they happen in a collision with one of your own players, like that mouth gash Dean Bell got when he collided with Denis Betts.

'On a match day, Denis and I do the strapping between us; he has his regular customers and I have mine. You get to know what players need. There is some friendly banter and you get a lot of flak as well, but you put up with it, knowing the lads. You've got to sit there and take a bit of stick sometimes, knowing it's just a player venting it before a game. It affects different players in different ways, some lads are physically sick, others like a joke to ease the tension.

'You strap what might have been an injury to give it some support and then what often happens, if they have a good game, the next thing they're saying is, "I'll leave on that strapping." It becomes like a superstition, they won't leave it off in case they have a bad game.

'There used to be a hell of a lot of superstition in the game. Colin Whitfield, who used to be club captain, always wanted to go out last, even at Wembley. I've watched a player run out at Central Park, literally with a bare backside, pulling on his shorts as he ran down the tunnel. That was Brian Juliff, the Welsh lad, that was his little foible, he used to pull his shorts on, running down the tunnel bare-bummed.

'We've been through fourteen different coaches while I've been here, but Alex Murphy was one on his own. When he was here, his own little thing was to send a message on to somebody every minute. He'd have you going on with ridiculous messages, it was his way of geeing players up. He'd say, "Go and tell so-and-so that if he drops the ball one more time he's coming off." But I hope we've seen the last of that, because there's nobody knows more than the player himself when he's just dropped a crucial ball. He'll not want someone coming on with a cold sponge and saying, "If you drop it again you're off."

'So there have been times when I've used a bit of discretion. When I thought it wasn't right going on with a message like that, by the time I've got out there, I've conveniently forgotten to pass on the message. There are crucial messages sometimes, though, like, "There are four minutes to go, let's just play for field position", because players can get so carried away sometimes they lose all sense of time and not all the grounds have a countdown clock.

'Sometimes I'd get back from taking a message out for Alex and he'd say, "Have you told him?" and when I said "Yes" he'd say, "Well get back on and tell him again." He was so nervous that he actually didn't spend a lot of time looking at the pitch. He had his head down, buried in a programme or something and he listened to the comments around him and then looked up and acted on impulse.

'Murphy was what you might call the old-fashioned style of coach, a motivator, completely different from John Monie and Graham Lowe. Lowe used to do a bit of a Billy Graham sort of thing in the dressing-room. It would be really still and quiet, with Graham giving each player their individual instructions and they weren't allowed to speak. I had to laugh one day though. Graham was talking to Joe Lydon before a game against Widnes: "I warn you, if you hesitate going for the corner, Kurt Sorensen will knock you into the Sullivan Bar." Andy Gregory whispered, "If he does, bring us back a pint of lager."

'I've had my moments with some of the coaches here, but the club do look after us well, especially when we go to Wembley. I went to America with them last year as well, I'd never have had the chance to do that otherwise. I was also lucky enough to be asked to go to Australia with the Wigan Colleges team. I put all that down to getting a little bit back for the hours I've put in.'

Denis Gets Married

THE FINE victory at Hull Kingston Rovers was followed by another equally comfortable, if less impressive win against Featherstone, but a midweek visit to Wakefield ended in a shock defeat. Wigan old boys Adrian Shelford, Nick du Toit and Ged Byrne all turned it on against their former colleagues, with Byrne scoring the decisive try in a 14–12 scoreline.

John Monie refused to rise to the promptings of the journalists after the game, who were baiting him about being beaten by a try scored by a player Wigan had only just sold. Whatever his private feelings, in public he was noncommittal, playing down the significance of Byrne's involvement and praising the overall performance of the Wakefield team, while bemoaning Wigan's luck. 'Last season we seemed to get the breaks and won the close games. This time the luck is going dead against us. Byrne's winner was very controversial. Joe Lydon was taken out after kicking the ball. He was flattened and lying on the deck. Ellery appeared to get to the ball first and kick it dead, but Byrne was given the try.'

Whatever the cause, another defeat had increased the pressure on Monie and his side. By their own abnormally high standards, the season so far had been a bit of a disaster: beaten in the Charity Shield, beaten in the Lancashire Cup, 5 points adrift of the leaders in the Championship and with an injury list as long as the faces of their spectators, Wigan needed to find some consistency and quickly, for every time they appeared to have got the engine running smoothly again, the next match would produce a breakdown.

The last hope of ensuring a really happy New Year at Central Park was to make progress in the Regal Trophy, a competition that Wigan had won for the last three years. An away draw at Second Division Whitehaven promised a fairly easy passage into the second round, but before that game, second-rower Denis Betts had an equally important fixture to fulfil.

Betts had been a precociously talented schoolboy, with both soccer and rugby league clubs monitoring and chasing him from an early age. He played for the Salford under-11 side at Wembley, but then turned his back on rugby league for a couple of years to concentrate on soccer. By the age of 13 though, he was playing both sports, soccer on Saturdays, rugby league on Sundays.

'I was more athletic than a lot of the lads at the time I think. I wasn't that big, but I was quite quick and I was quite strong as well.' Manchester United were sufficiently impressed with the look of the young centre forward to offer to sign him on schoolboy forms and for Betts it was 'a dream come true. I never really thought about playing professional rugby league, I used to think about football, rugby league was just something that I did, that was there. If a teacher came up and said, "Play rugby" I'd play rugby for him.

'So when United came along to me at 14 and said, "We'll pay your expenses to come down to training and we'll give you boots and training kit if you sign schoolboy forms," they didn't have to ask me twice. I signed a piece of paper right away. I used to go training twice a week with them and played in the "B" Team, the "A" team and the youth team a couple of times.' Though Betts was a promising footballer, it was a rugby league club that first offered him a professional contract and in the absence of any sign that Manchester United would do the same, Betts jumped at the chance to join Wigan.

'Derek Standish took me along to Wigan when Phil Clarke's dad, Colin, was coach. I went to see them, came away for a week, went back and told them I'd sign. I went downstairs to sign the contract and Phil's dad and Alan McInnes were there. They were saying, "You'll have to work hard" and all that sort of rubbish and I was saying, "I will. I will work hard and train hard" – all that kind of stuff you do say when people ask you these kinds of questions!

'I think they got me really cheap because I didn't know anything about rugby league contracts then and a lot of things were missed out that I think I should have got. Just talking with the lads afterwards, they'd say, "I get paid for that" or, "I get contract money for that" and I was thinking, "I don't get paid for that" and "They never told me about contract money for that." I never really knew about rugby league. A lot of lads were advised by their coaches, who had played professional rugby league. All I had were my mam who knew nothing and my dad who knew nothing, but thought he knew everything, and I just sat there not knowing anything myself. It's all changed since then of course!

'I played in the Wigan first team when I was 17, played a full year at both 18 and 19 and then went on tour with Great Britain last summer as the third youngest player. It seems like I've been playing a long time and I've played with a hell of a lot of good players. I think that's seen me in good stead. I've played in a lot of pressure games and a lot of finals too. I'm only missing one medal, that's the Premiership. I'd won every medal in the game before I was 20, apart from that one.

'I still go to college, so my only income is rugby league. After I finish, I'll maybe open up a small business, a shop or something and just enjoy life. You've just got to invest your money now so that when you finish you don't have to worry about where your next wage packet is coming from. Mind, I've got no money put by at the moment, I'm getting married. That's why I've got no money saved, because I've had to spend it.' Betts was not just precociously advanced on the sports field. At the age of 14 he was already the father of a daughter. It was both touching and remarkable that Denis and his girlfriend, Val, survived all the traumas of having a child so young and had stuck together through their teens, when their friends were falling in and out of love every couple of weeks, to the point where they were now getting married, seven years after the birth of their daughter.

The wedding was set for a Friday, depriving the non-teetotal Wigan players of a major celebration, the Regal Trophy game being at Whitehaven that weekend. Denis's own priorities remained firmly business first, pleasure second. 'Where are you going for your honeymoon?' I asked.

'Whitehaven on Sunday,' he replied, smiling. 'We'll have to wait until the end of the season for a proper honeymoon.'

Although rugby league is his business, like most of the players Denis finds the training far from a chore. 'I enjoy training and you can't call it work when it's something you enjoy doing. Rugby league helps you meet a load of people; every sport must bring you up to people that you admire and you hate – brilliant characters. You can laugh, joke and listen to some stories about when they were your age, the kind of people they've met, funny stuff.'

Like Ian Lucas, Betts does not spend much time out on the town with his team-mates, preferring to socialise around his home-town of Salford. 'I only go out now and again round Wigan with the lads, sometimes on Thursday night and occasionally after the game. No-one really seems to mither (bother) you then, but I don't go out in Wigan every weekend, I don't go out to nightclubs in Wigan, in fact I've never been to a nightclub there. It helps me a lot because I can get out of it. I don't have people mithering me, either getting on my back or patting me on the back all night. People in Salford don't really know who I am, it happens occasionally, that's all.

'Sometimes it's nice to be recognised; you're standing in a place in Wigan and everybody's coming over and recognising you, patting you on the back and that. It's all right for five or ten minutes but when they're at you all night when you're trying to chat to someone else about something other than rugby league, then it gets on your nerves.'

The Wigan players clearly hadn't extended Betts' wedding celebrations too far into the night, for they disposed of Whitehaven 24–6. Though far from a vintage performance, Monie pronounced himself happy with his favourite area, defence, for Whitehaven did not cross the Wigan line until the final minute.

The draw for the second round gave them another tie against Second Division opposition, Keighley, and this time it was at Central Park. The result of that game was another comfortable win for Wigan, but Monie was far less happy after the match. The winning margin was similar, but the 36–16 scoreline revealed a very different game. 'We opted to throw the ball around, which is the sort of rugby league that excites our supporters, but it doesn't excite me. A more methodical approach would suit me far better,' said Monie, reflecting on a game that saw several breathtaking Wigan tries but also a hatful of dropped passes and unforced errors.

The match brought the inevitable injury problems as well, forcing Monie to delve even deeper into his depleted squad. For young winger David Marshall, the game was a catastrophe. He was carried off with a hideous knee injury that seemed certain to bring a very premature end to his playing career. Andy Platt's broken finger was nothing but a minor inconvenience by comparison. In addition to the injuries, Wigan finished the game with only twelve men, because

Martin Dermott was already in the showers after being sent off for a high tackle. It was to earn him a two match suspension and bring a brief recall to first-team action for Bobby Goulding.

Wigan were again drawn at home in the third round of the Regal Trophy, but this time the opposition was far more testing, for they faced their bogey team, Bradford Northern, who were on a three-match winning streak against them, including that bizarre 31–30 scoreline in the Championship.

Wigan took the lead after an inspired substitution by John Monie, who sent Andy Goodway on to replace Kelvin Skerrett and saw the big second-rower romp in for a try from Andy Gregory's pass within thirty seconds. With Gregory troubled both by a recurrence of his groin injury and by the harrying of Bradford's scrum-half, Brett Iti, and with several of his colleagues out of touch, Wigan lacked pattern and conviction. Bradford stuck to their tried and trusted no-frills style and scored either side of the interval to take control, though both tries owed much to Wigan errors.

Bradford's loose forward John Pendlebury, a former Wigan player, strolled through some feeble tackles for their opening try, while Paul Medley added the second, hacking the ball past a stationary Steve Hampson, who waited in vain for the whistle as the referee played advantage to Bradford. Ellery Hanley was in magnificent form and he was in the van as Wigan laid siege to Bradford's line for the last twenty minutes, but their defence held and Wigan had crashed out of a competition they had dominated for three years. To rub salt in the wounds, their own fans booed, jeered and whistled at their increasingly frenzied attempts to find a way through the defence in the closing minutes, while to make a grim day worse for Wigan, there were more injuries. Andy Gregory's groin trouble looked bad enough to require a lay-off and perhaps another operation, while Denis Betts had suffered a broken nose.

A pitiful crowd of barely 5,000, one of Wigan's lowest in years, were streaming away well before the final whistle. Many fans had stayed away in protest at Wigan's poor form and some of those who had turned up for the Bradford game left vowing not to return. The Wigan dressing room was like a funeral parlour, dispirited players, coaching staff and directors united in deafening silence, broken only by the sounds of

Bradford's celebrations from the other side of the wall. In the corridor outside, the normally loquacious Monie struggled for words to explain the defeat. 'I'm naturally very disappointed, but I just cannot understand what is wrong.'

By the Tuesday team meeting, Monie had studied the video tape of the game and was less down-hearted about his side's performance. 'We made six times as many clean breaks as they did; they had four, we had about twenty-four, but they scored from two of theirs and we just couldn't get over their line. I thought our defence was good, apart from the errors that led to their tries, but we didn't score the tries we should have. I don't understand what's going wrong, but I want you to have a private meeting now, so that if there are any problems amongst yourselves, you can sort them out.'

One possible source of discontent, Andy Gregory, sat stone-faced at the back of the room while Monie was talking, only opening his mouth to yawn ostentatiously three times. Monie walked out, leaving the players alone to thrash things out.

The Bradford game should have been Wigan's last before Christmas, but spurred both by the need to get the team back on the winning track and the even more pressing need for a pre-Christmas boost to the cash flow, Wigan had approached the League's other 'Bank of England' club, Leeds, to bring forward their Championship fixture.

With Wigan's top players on much-improved contract money, which had to be paid whether or not Wigan had a game, and the new stand soaking up cash faster than the foundations were swallowing concrete, the Wigan board had pressing reasons to give a boost to the club finances. The Bradford game had drawn only 5,000 spectators, but a clash with the main Yorkshire pretenders to Wigan's crown was guaranteed to attract around three times that number. For their part, the Leeds board perhaps felt they would never have a better chance to put one over Wigan on their own turf, and they readily agreed to the change.

Whatever had been said behind closed doors in the players' private session seemed to have had the desired effect. There was only one change in personnel from the previous week, Bobby Goulding switching to scrum-half in place of the injured and disgruntled Andy Gregory and Andy Goodway filling in as emergency hooker in the continued absence through suspension of Martin Dermott, but Wigan looked a very different side on the field. Shaun Edwards revelled in the absence of his chief rival as creator and prime mover and with Ellery Hanley again in peerless form, contemptuously striding past the Leeds defence for a try and playing a hand in two others, Wigan had the game won well before the end.

Monie was less than delighted with a loss of concentration that allowed Leeds to score two tries in the last three minutes, but the 22–16 scoreline saw Wigan back within hailing distance of the Championship leaders Hull and left both players and spectators in rather more festive Yuletide mood. The return of Phil Clarke after a three-month injury absence was another boost for Wigan, though that was more than countered by another injury blow, Andy Goodway having fractured his arm.

If the Wigan fans tucked into their Christmas turkey, brandy and cigars with rather more relish than had seemed likely a week before, Wigan's players had to make do with a more frugal repast, for they faced the traditional Boxing Day derby against their oldest and most bitter rivals, St Helens. Saints had been having an even more troubled season than the champions, but a season of defeats interrupted only by success against Wigan would still count as a successful year at Knowsley Road.

Wigan fans had the same feeling, as Monie's forerunner, Graham Lowe, had discovered. On his first day at Central Park, Lowe was approached by an old man. 'You're the new coach, are you?' Lowe admitted he was and waited for the words of welcome. 'It doesn't matter about anything else,' said the fan, 'you can lose the lot, but just make bloody sure you beat St Helens.'

Unlike the majority of their supporters, Christmas Day was an alcohol-free day for the Wigan players, though this was nothing unusual for the teetotallers like Hanley and Edwards. The players met at Central Park at 10.30 a.m. on Christmas Day and spent an hour going through their drills and set moves before Monie sent them home to their families with a laconic, 'Do the job at St Helens tomorrow and we'll celebrate tomorrow night.'

The Boxing Day weather was atrocious, driving wind and incessant rain, and though 14,000 brave supporters of both sides defied the elements, that total was well down on the normal crowd for the holiday fixture. Both sides were under-strength, with Wigan missing four internationals, Andy Gregory, Joe Lydon, Kelvin Skerrett and Andy Goodway.

St Helens twice nosed in front, at 7–2 early in the first half and 15–14 early in the second, but the Santa Claus impersonator who had wandered round the crowd before the game handing out sweets to the children, had obviously also infected the Saints players with Yuletide spirit, for they presented the game to Wigan with a burst of seasonal generosity. A ridiculous Saints pass gave Wigan the first of three tries in ten minutes, some woeful tackling allowed Betts to create the next and the referee then got in on the Santa act, overlooking a sackful of knock-ons and forward passes as Hanley added the third to clinch the game 28–15.

The try of the game was undoubtedly Wigan's first, however, scored by Frano Botica. Having had some defensive frailties exposed by a couple of missed tackles, Frano showed the other side of his game with a scoring run that must have covered at least 125 yards. He scooped up a St Helens kick on his own line in the left-hand corner and set off on a curving run past five defenders. Passing to Kevin Iro, Botica looped round to take the return pass on the outside and then held off a despairing challenge by the St Helens full back to cross in the opposite corner for a try that had the Wigan fans shouting themselves hoarse.

A bonus for Wigan was the return to top form of Bobby Goulding, who had an outstanding game in his preferred scrum-half position. Shaun Edwards also looked a different player, the continued absence of Andy Gregory giving him undisputed dominance of the midfield. The Wigan faithful streamed out of the ground at the final whistle with a renewed appetite for Christmas cheer and the players, too, could look to the New Year with more confidence than had seemed likely even two weeks before. Though Wigan still trailed the leaders Hull by 5 points, they had a match in hand and were at last beginning to play with something of the blend of defensive solidity and attacking flair that had characterised their play in the previous three all-conquering seasons.

New Year's Day held another formidable challenge, however, another derby match, this time against Warrington. If clashes between Wigan and St Helens were usually characterised by fine tries and good football, Wigan's games against

Warrington were normally wars of attrition, with no quarter asked or given. Like Christmas Day, New Year's Eve would be a low-key, alcohol-free occasion for the players as they faced up to the next game in the marathon run towards the League title.

If there is no happier place than a winner's coach, as Keith Mills had remarked a few weeks before, there is certainly no sadder place than a loser's dressing room. The Wigan players sat or stood around the dressing room in total silence, having lost the New Year's Day game against Warrington, a defeat that made hopes of retaining their Championship look very fragile.

Three hours earlier, the players had watched video highlights of the wins against Leeds and St Helens which had put them back in the Championship race, before going downstairs to change. John Monie had a warning for them. 'The worst thing you can do in this game is to think about last week – we were great last week, we were great in the Cup Final – what's important is being great today.

'There's one more thing I want to say. It's my job to worry about the team and the team work, all you've got to do is concentrate on your own form. Make sure that your own form is good and leave me to worry about the team and the team work. Alright, let's go.'

After eighty minutes of rain-swept, mud-soaked football, it was hard to know which was more worrying, the individual form of several players or the team work. Both were well short of what was needed to beat a cohesive and determined Warrington side. Perhaps things would have turned out differently if Wigan had accepted any of the early chances they created, but they were lost in a flurry of wild passes and knock-ons, a fault that was to recur on the rare occasions when they threw off the shackles of Warrington's well-organised swarming defence later in the game. The normally masterful Dean Bell had probably his worst ever game in Wigan colours, his co-centre, Kevin 'The Beast' Iro played as if auditioning for the role of the dormouse in Alice in Wonderland, and so many others were well below par that even titanic efforts from Ellery and Andy Platt couldn't galvanise Wigan into action.

The 'Wigan Walk' was in evidence long before the end as many of the 16,000 crowd streamed away, too wet and dispirited to stay, but not before the sound of boos, jeers and cat-calls had greeted some of their heroes' ineffectual attempts to breach the Warrington defence. Wigan's only score, a Dean Bell try in the final minute, was an irrelevance; they had been well-beaten by a side lacking no less than ten injured players.

In the dressing room there was none of the buzz and chatter that greets a win. For several minutes the loudest noise was the steady drip of water from a pile of sodden shirts on the table into a muddy pool on the floor. At least half the players needed treatment for minor injuries, which they might have ignored in the excitement of a win. Maurice Lindsay paced around the room, trying, without much success, to conceal his bitter disappointment and anger. One of the players made the mistake of calling out, 'Are the baths hot?' to Andy Gregory, back as a substitute after injury, as he came back into the room. 'That's the least of our worries at the moment,' spat Lindsay, turning on his heel and storming out.

Thirty minutes' later, Shaun Edwards and Dean Bell still sat wrapped in towels, brooding on the defeat. The 'A' team coach, Graham West, brought in the news that the leaders Hull had been beaten as well, which merely deepened the gloom. Wigan could have been breathing down their necks had they won, but now they were still 5 points adrift of both Hull and Widnes, who had won against St Helens to go top on points difference.

In the whole of the previous season, Wigan had dropped only 12 Championship points. Less than halfway through this season, they had already given up 9. With Widnes and Hull setting a hot pace at the top and Castleford moving into contention as well, Wigan could scarcely afford another defeat if they were to be sure of retaining their Championship. A man walking past the open dressing room door called out 'Happy New Year'. No-one smiled or responded.

Great When They Have to Be . . .

AFTER Wigan's erratic form over the season so far, it was all but inevitable that the home defeat by Warrington would be followed by the annihilation of their next opponents. So it proved, for Wigan went to Sheffield Eagles' Don Valley Stadium the following Sunday and came away with a 46–4 win, a score which included the 300th and 301st tries of Ellery Hanley's remarkable career.

The victory was achieved without Bobby Goulding, however. With Andy Gregory back to full fitness, John Monie restored him to the starting line-up, despite Goulding's impressive form in his hero's absence. 'I suppose the harsh term is that Bobby has been dropped,' said Monie, 'but I have to pick the side that I think will win. Bobby has grumbled about it and I've left him to think it over.'

Goulding's thoughts were predictably rueful. 'I feel terribly disappointed. I really don't know what I have to do to keep my place at Wigan. I will not be creating a fuss, but something like this really makes me think about whether I have a future here.'

Bobby's roller-coaster year was on another down-slope. After staying away from training in protest at Monie's selection of Shaun Edwards at scrum-half for the game at Whitehaven in early December, Goulding had met with the directors to discuss his future. 'I was Great Britain scrum-half on the summer tour,' said Bobby. 'I have always been prepared to be second fiddle to Andy Gregory – he's the greatest – but there is no way I am going to play second fiddle to Shaun or anybody else.'

Goulding and the directors emerged all smiles from their discussions, with Bobby saying, 'It all seems sorted out now and I'm satisfied with what they've told me.' Maurice Lindsay added: 'We've indicated to Bobby and his father that we are quite happy to sit down and talk about a new four-year

113

contract to replace the present one that runs out in 1991. The details haven't been discussed, but the directors agree that the player's future lies here at Wigan.'

Within a month, Bobby was evidently no longer willing to play second fiddle, even to Andy Gregory, and his future as a Wigan player was once more in doubt. Talks on a new contract did not take place.

John Monie had been under mounting pressure from the Wigan public during the team's lean run before Christmas. A stream of letters to the local paper berated him both for his team's failure to win every game and to play the flowing football associated with the Lindsay watchwords, style, verve and panache.

The ever-fickle Wigan fans forgot the achievements of the previous season and rounded on him. Like most complaints from the terraces, the criticisms of Monie and his team were overblown and exaggerated, but there was a mounting feeling of unease, only partly dissipated by the victories around the Christmas period.

I drove out to his house in a quiet suburb a few miles from the centre of Wigan in the week following the Sheffield victory, to see how Monie was reacting to his first real taste of public hostility after a year-long honeymoon in which his side had swept all before them. Maurice Lindsay was there when I arrived. Even in a tracksuit, Monie still looks like a business-man, and the only clues to his occupation are the shelves bulging with video tapes and books, virtually all of them sports books, on American football, boxing, basketball and some rugby league, but all about getting an edge and winning.

Monie did not seem unduly worried by his side's in-consistency. 'Injuries to key players mean a lot. We've been missing Andy Gregory, Joe Lydon, Kevin Iro, Andy Good-way, Phil Clarke and Andy Platt for long spells at various times and that certainly doesn't help. Despite the fact that we've sold some players this season, I don't see the size of the squad as a problem; you can only play thirteen at a time.'

He remained philosophical about the complaints and the invective from the Wigan public. 'The fans do get to me a bit, to say you don't hear what they say to and about you wouldn't be true – and what they say can be quite cutting – but as long as I know that I've done my best, at the end of the week I'm the one I have to satisfy, though obviously it makes it easier if you're winning.

'I really don't think the general public realise how critical the bounce of a ball or a goalkick can be in this game though. If Jonathan Davies hadn't kicked six out of six, including four from the sideline, I have no doubt at all that we'd have won the Lancashire Cup this season. Against Bradford Northern in the Regal Trophy, they put quite an innocuous kick through, our players all stopped, waiting for the whistle, and they scored the crucial try.

'Every now and again you lose a game you should have won, but basically I think our main problem has been that we haven't been able to put our best team out consistently. Last year we would keep virtually the same team for six weeks at a stretch, this year we've scarcely had the same team out two weeks running.

'I'm worried about Hull and Widnes having the break on us, but if we're good enough to beat Widnes twice and Hull once between now and the end of the season, we'll be good enough to win the Championship, and that's my main goal. The players' main goal is still Wembley, but mine isn't, it's the Championship, because that's the one that rewards the team that is consistently the strongest. Don't get me wrong, I want to win at Wembley as badly as they do when the time comes, but at the moment, my priority is to win the Championship.'

His chairman, Maurice Lindsay, chipped in with another explanation for the side's pre-Christmas blues. 'I think the hangover after the Australian Tour affected everybody, particularly our players who were involved in the Tests.' Lindsay's main worries were not about playing matters, however, except as they affected attendances. 'There is an economic downturn and one of the first things that go in a recession are the luxuries and watching Wigan is a luxury for most of our potential supporters. That new stand though – I've just been on the 'phone about it – it's crippling us. It was supposed to be completed by January first, then they said the end of February and now they're talking about April, so realistically it's gone for this season.

'So, with falling gates and the new stand bleeding us white . . .' He did not complete the sentence, and did not need to. Wigan had to have success to keep the cash flowing in to cover the torrents going out. Getting to Wembley may not have been essential to Wigan's financial well-being in the past; this year it looked as if it might be.

Wigan's financial equilibrium, not to mention Maurice Lindsay's mental equilibrium, were further destabilised the following week, by the sort of cock-up that only Sod's Law could adequately explain. One great advantage Wigan have over most other rugby league clubs is that they have an under-soil heating system, which keeps Central Park playable, whatever the winter weather. The announcement that Wigan's home game against Bradford had been postponed because the pitch was frozen, was therefore the cause of some considerable surprise.

Unfortunately the under-soil heating has a design flaw; it only operates when switched on. The groundstaff neglected to turn on the heating and by the time anyone noticed the error, it was too late to defrost the pitch. A last-minute attempt to switch the game to the following day was torpedoed by the police, who refused to supply officers to police the match at such short notice, leaving Wigan with no alternative but to postpone it until later in the season.

The deeply embarrassed groundstaff had to endure the players' merciless ribbing, while the Wigan directors had to grin and bear it too, facing the temporary loss of much-needed income and praying that a decent crowd would still turn up for the match in an increasingly congested programme towards the end of the season. If the board had to pay the financial price, one of the groundstaff responsible for the error paid a higher one; there are now two groundstaff at Wigan, where there used to be three.

As the season moved beyond the half-way mark, virtually every game became a vital one, for any defeat would yield possibly irretrievable ground to Wigan's rivals in the Championship race, Hull and Widnes. For all that, however, the away game against Widnes on Saturday 19 January was arguably Wigan's most important game of the season so far. If defeat against anybody would have been a major blow, the loss of the 'four-pointer' against Widnes would be irreversible.

Wigan's players needed no reminding of the importance of the match and little motivation facing the side that had already beaten them twice that season. The training sessions leading up to the game were formidably intense and single-minded. The injury situation had continued to improve and only Andy Goodway, still nursing a broken arm, was unavailable. The team was the strongest Wigan had fielded since the game at Hull Kingston Rovers, two months before: Hampson; Lydon, Bell, Iro, Botica; Edwards, Gregory; Lucas, Dermott, Skerrett, Betts, Platt, Hanley. There could be no excuses for defeat.

John Monie preferred Frano Botica to David Myers on the wing, citing Botica's better scoring rate, though his goal-kicking ability was perhaps equally relevant. Myers was relegated to the substitutes bench, alongside Phil Clarke, leaving no room for Bobby Goulding. Widnes were also close to full strength, missing only Jonathan Davies from their first-choice line-up and they, too, were well aware of the game's significance.

When the Wigan players entered the dressing room, they were greeted by a sign that John Monie had ordered to be put up there. Lettered in red, it announced:

To win the Championship we must:
1. Have the *proper attitude.*
2. Be in *great physical condition.*
3. Help each other *work together.*
4. Place *team goals* above *personal goals.*
5. Always remember that no-one can beat Wigan *unless we beat ourselves.*

If further proof was needed of the importance of the game, John Monie's pre-match demeanour supplied it. The normally cool and unflappable Wigan coach appeared hot-wired, pacing up and down the dressing room, snapping out instructions and endlessly repeating the message he had been drumming into the players all week.

On their day, Widnes are good enough to beat any team in the world. They can score tries from any part of the pitch, the ball whipping through a dozen pairs of hands, with the freakishly fast Martin Offiah usually completing the move with his customary flamboyance. The flaw in the Widnes approach was that they rarely played a percentage game and would continue to throw the ball about, even when pinned deep in their own territory. Sometimes it paid off, creating unexpected openings and overlaps, on other occasions it failed, yielding the ball to the opposition in dangerous attacking positions.

John Monie's strategy for Wigan was to eliminate all risk of error when in possession in their own territory, using the forwards to grind out the 'hard yardage' down the middle, before employing the varied kicking game of Gregory, Edwards and Lydon to establish field position. The kicks would all be directed away from Offiah's left wing, reducing his opportunities to run the ball back at them. Once in Widnes territory, Wigan would employ savage and unyielding defence to pin their opponents there. 'Don't let them hit the advantage line,' said Monie. 'If they can't dominate us up front, if they can't stand over us and be bullies, they can't get the freedom they need.'

The Widnes playmakers, Tony Myler, Les Holliday and Phil McKenzie were singled out for especially close attention, for each of them had the handling skills to unlock the most secure defence, if allowed any latitude at all. Wigan's main attacking threat would come by exploiting the fringes of the ruck, where Widnes often appeared vulnerable, and by targeting the Widnes centres, whose tackling technique was not always according to the coaching manual.

It is of course one thing to formulate a strategy, and quite another to employ it successfully against a team as individually and collectively talented as Widnes, but Monie's urgency and tension was mirrored by that of his players. They knew they could not afford to lose, not that the thought of defeat ever entered their heads. They were coldly, implacably determined to prevail.

Live television coverage kept the attendance below capacity, but there was still a substantial crowd as Widnes kicked off on a perfect winter's afternoon. The early exchanges of a game are always bruising, as both sides come onto the ball at top speed or pile into the tackle. In this vital game, the battle for early midfield dominance was ferociously intense, but Wigan gained an early and potentially crucial edge. The Widnes ball-carriers were repeatedly engulfed in three and four man gang-tackles, the impacts of the hits echoing like pistol shots, breath forced from battered lungs in involuntary grunts, as a tackler's shoulder drove upwards into the ribs.

The much-maligned Kelvin Skerrett was back to his fearsome best, putting his injury and breathing problems behind him. Ian Lucas also made his tackles and his drives with a force that made a nonsense of the early season suggestions that he lacked 'devil' and hooker Martin Dermott harried and broke up the Widnes defence with darting runs from dummy half. With their front row gaining the advantage, Wigan's running forwards, Platt, Betts and Hanley, prompted by the irrepressible Gregory, began to punch holes in the defence. Out wide, Dean Bell and Kevin Iro were a formidable centre combination, Bell showing sheer class on attack and ferocity in defence, while Iro had shed his apparent torpor of previous weeks to batter Widnes' defensively uncertain centres.

Frano Botica put Wigan on the scoreboard with a beautifully struck forty metre penalty goal after ten minutes and within two minutes of the restart, Wigan had crossed for the first try. Andy Gregory used the plunging decoy run of Denis Betts as a foil before unloading to Andy Platt, and the second-rower, having a towering game even by his own phenomenal standards, burst through the first-line defence.

As Ellery Hanley ghosted up on his shoulder, Platt delivered a pass that left Hanley with only the young Widnes full back, Stuart Spruce, to beat. Ellery strode past him with a contemptuous ease that would have sapped the confidence of a veteran, let alone a newcomer, feinting to the inside and then sweeping past Spruce on the outside on a curving run. Hanley touched down without a finger laid upon him. Botica missed the conversion, but added a second forty metre penalty a few minutes later, to put Wigan 8 points clear.

A penalty to Widnes, kicked by Les Holliday, scarcely threatened Wigan's apparently unshakeable grip on the game. Their forwards were so dominant that Widnes were forced to send on both their substitutes, the granite New Zealander Kurt Sorensen and the giant Tongan Emosi Koloto, in a desperate attempt to stem the tide. They were little more successful than their team-mates in stopping Wigan's forward onslaught, Koloto being met by a juddering hit from Skerrett that must have come close to putting out the Tongan's lights, but each played a part in two controversial incidents that changed the complexion of the game.

Four minutes before half-time, Andy Gregory went down to a tackle from Kurt Sorensen. It seemed a little high, with Sorensen's forearm finishing across Gregory's face and when the referee blew his whistle, virtually everybody in the ground was expecting a lecture for Sorensen and a penalty to Wigan. Instead the referee called Gregory to him and then pointed to the dressing-room, signalling that he was sending him off for biting. An incredulous Gregory left the field and Wigan faced a daunting task, playing the remainder of the game a man short, with their attacking mainspring already in the showers.

The Widnes fans, cowed into silence by Wigan's superiority, came to life and roared their team on, sensing the chance to reverse the flow of the game. They were to be disappointed, for Wigan shrugged off the loss of Gregory to stretch their lead with another try, right on the stroke of half-time. Shaun Edwards, switched to scrum-half in Gregory's enforced absence, made the initial break, scorching through the defence. His pass to Ellery Hanley left only the luckless Spruce and the powerful winger Devereux between Hanley and the line. Spruce bravely made the front-on tackle and Devereux also hit Hanley from the side, but such was the Wigan captain's power, that he drove both defenders backwards over the line with him and grounded the ball for a magnificent score. Botica landed a fine conversion to leave Wigan 14–2 ahead at the break.

In the dressing room, the Wigan's players were quiet and thoughtful, well aware that the game was still far from won, with another forty minutes of gruelling defensive work needed to retain the advantage that their forward power and Hanley's brilliance had created.

If the players were quiet, John Monie was still burning up with tension, pacing the room, talking with an excitement and animation he had rarely shown before. Clutching a fistful of notes and statistics from the first half, he hammered home the need to keep the game tight, make every tackle and pressure Widnes into risks as they strove to get back into the game. While Monie was speaking, none of the players even blinked, their concentration on him as intense as it had been on the game during the first forty minutes.

'Don't take any dummies and don't get caught half-way between two attackers, wondering whether to go in or hold back for the man on the outside,' said Monie. 'Take the man with the ball, let the cover worry about the guy over. Don't let Holliday cut back inside, you know what he likes to do, prop off his left leg and cut back inside.

'You can't relax when the ball's gone past you, keep

(RIGHT) 'Ready for Christmas.' The new cantilever stand, delayed more often than a Sunday excursion train, was not completed until after the end of the season.

(BELOW LEFT) Two assistants cope with the rush in the Wigan Theme Shop on match day.

(BELOW RIGHT) Give 'em a child and it's theirs for life. One of Wigan's youngest fans tries a sweatshirt for size.

(BELOW LEFT) Second fiddle to no-one. Bobby Goulding, still smiling despite a turbulent year. (BELOW RIGHT) 'Buy this chair or I'll put a hit on you.' Rugby League's foremost antique dealer shows that safe hands have a multitude of uses.

OPPOSITE PAGE

(TOP) An apprehensive Dave Myers gets treatment from Keith Mills on an injured knee.

(BELOW LEFT) Champions! Ellery Hanley, Steve Hampson and Ian Lucas celebrate the successful completion of 'Mission Impossible'. (BELOW RIGHT) 'I thought we agreed, no publicity.' Martin Dermott prepares to meet his public.

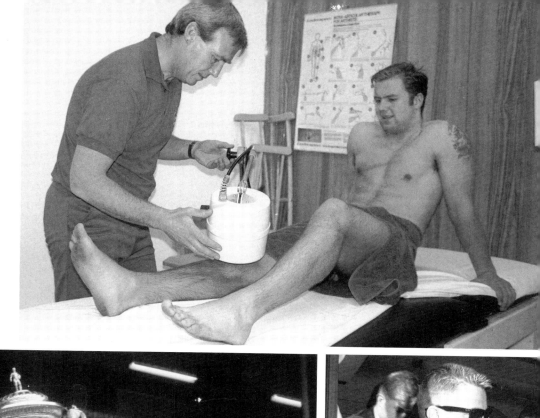

(TOP LEFT) Back-stage heroes. Wigan Secretary Mary Charnock (in blazer) and assistant Mandy Roper look for inspiration or news of a pay rise in the Cup Final programme. (TOP RIGHT) 'With a nose like mine it's bound to get broken occasionally.' Denis Betts, the only ever-present in Wigan's exhausting fixture programme, in reflective mood.

(ABOVE LEFT) The thoughts of Chairman Maurice. Lindsay and friend relax in the wood-panelled splendour of the Wigan Chairman's house. (ABOVE RIGHT) All this and a new stand too. Maurice Lindsay with two of his three expensive acquisitions during the season.

(RIGHT) A diving Andy Gregory arrives just too late to block Paul Bishop's kick for St Helens.

(BELOW) Challenge Cup Final. St Helens capitalise on the rarest thing in rugby league – a Wigan error. Neither Denis Betts' tackle nor the airborne Frano Botica (5) can stop Jonathan Griffiths' floated pass to St Helens winger Alan Hunte (out of shot). Andy Goodway, looking to atone for his loose pass, covers across by the posts, Dave Myers sprints out towards the wing, but arrives too late to prevent Hunte scoring St Helens' only try.

The best feeling in rugby league - victory at Wembley. Coach John Monie, captain Ellery Hanley and substitute Bobby Goulding share the magic moment.

THIS PAGE

Andy Gregory looks for a gap against Hull Kingston Rovers, Phil Clarke sets off in support . . .

(BELOW) Ooof! Instead of a gap, Andy Gregory finds Zook Ema's crunching tackle. Phil Clarke shouts in vain for the ball.

(RIGHT) Defence. Denis Betts goes low on St Helens' Bernard Dwyer, Phil Clarke (in helmet) moves in to take Dwyer high and stop him unloading the ball.

(BELOW) Only the tough survive. Kelvin Skerrett still battling to make the hard yardage, despite the attentions of three Bradford tacklers.

concentrating, keep moving across, keep alert. Don't start forcing the pass in our own 22. Dean tried a bit of a floater in the first half which we got away with, but then Gizz kept it going and gave Kevin a bad ball. Keep it simple in our own 22. You know what you've got to do, get some good drives up the middle and then kick for the corners.

'Let them try and play the football in their own 22, because they will, won't they? Let them do it and we'll capitalise on their mistakes. So it's tackling and it's team work for forty minutes now. We'll start with the same men but then I'll use the subs to give you forwards a spell in turn. OK. I don't want to be watching the last five minutes; I want to already be back in the dressing room, because we've got the game won.'

As the referee's whistle sounded to call the players back out onto the field, Monie turned to Steve Hampson, and said, 'Kick it deep and flat from the kick-off, Hampo, try and get it dead, but kick it flat.'

If Monie was looking to put immediate pressure on Widnes, he got the reverse. Steve Hampson hashed the kick, sending it soaring over the touchline without a bounce, an offence that gave Widnes an immediate penalty kick and six tackles deep in Wigan territory. No-one on the Wigan side criticised Hampson, however, two players running up to give him a few words of encouragement.

Widnes spun the ball to and fro across the field, desperate for an early score, but Wigan's twelve men tackled everything that moved to keep Widnes at bay. The attack was repulsed and as Wigan raised the siege, took possession and brought the ball downfield, there was a second incident that evened the odds once more. Kelvin Skerrett's powerful burst was abruptly ended by a 'coat-hanger' tackle from Emosi Koloto, perhaps seeking revenge for the monster hit that Skerrett had put on him earlier on, but it saw the Widnes player sent to join Andy Gregory in the dressing room.

With twelve men now ranged against twelve, Wigan's grip tightened. Botica kicked another penalty to stretch the lead to 14 points and then, with a quarter of an hour remaining, Hanley completed a magnificent hat-trick with a try worthy of true champions. Shaun Edwards, playing like a man inspired, began the move deep in Wigan's own 22. His pass sent Kevin Iro striding majestically down the touchline. The two exchanged passes again, sending Iro clear once more and as the last shreds of the Widnes cover struggled to cut him off, Iro passed inside to the ever-predatory Hanley, who completed a ninety yard move with a flourish. Botica's conversion, his fifth fine goal of the afternoon, left Wigan an unassailable 20 points clear.

With the game won, Monie abandoned the plan to use his substitutes to give his key forwards a breather, feeling that the starting line-up had earned the right to see it through to the final whistle and receive the well-deserved adulation of their supporters. As Wigan relaxed, certain of victory, Widnes were able to put a more flattering gloss on the scoreline with three tries in the last ten minutes, but neither they, nor their supporters, could dispute that they had been beaten far more decisively than a scoreline of 22–14 would suggest.

On another day, Monie might have been critical of his side's late defensive lapses leading to the Widnes tries. To have done so after such a magnificent win would have been churlish in the extreme and Monie was in no mood to be churlish. He walked round the dressing room, shaking hands with each of his players and with the backroom crew: Taffy, Keith, Bill, Andrew and even Dr Zaman, the team doctor. The win was a team effort, and he was careful to make sure that all felt a part of that team. The room full of laughter, his players shared his mood, all except one, who had already disappeared, for Andy Gregory was too upset by his sending-off to linger after the game. Steve Hampson was quick to notice his absence, 'Where's Gnasher?' he asked, in mordant reference to the alleged reason for Gregory's dismissal.

Bill Hartley handed Monie a piece of paper on which he had scribbled a sporting quote he had come across: *Great teams aren't great all the time; they're just great when they have to be.* Monie's face cracked into an even broader grin, he nodded and pocketed the paper.

Frustratingly, Wigan once more now faced an interruption to their programme, with no game scheduled for the following week. A two-week break was the last thing that Monie wanted, with his team right on top of their form, but all he could do was hope that another team could help Wigan's prospects, by beating Widnes and most of all, by taking some points from leaders Hull.

One rather more immediate worry was Andy Gregory's

appeal against his sending-off. That would be heard by the League's disciplinary committee the next Thursday, and though the allegedly injured party, Kurt Sorensen, was apparently willing to support Gregory's claim that he had not bitten him, both player and coach still faced an anxious week.

A Shitty Night in Castleford . . .

THOUGH born in Wigan, Andy Gregory began his professional career at Widnes. Chased by ten clubs, he still signed for Widnes even though he claims they made him the worst offer of any of the ten. 'Wigan were on their way down to Division Two at the time, whereas when I signed for Widnes on the Wednesday, they were off down to Wembley to play Wakefield Trinity in the 1979 Cup Final that weekend. They had Reggie Bowden as their scrum-half then, but it was a bit of a calculated decision, he was thirty, so I thought if I played well, I'd be able to replace him within a couple of years.

'I played in the 1981 Cup Final, went to Wembley again in 1982 and 1984, went on the Great Britain tour of Australia that summer, came back, played the first game of the season for Widnes and then never played for them again. I went to Ibiza for a holiday and signed for Warrington when I came back. I had a bit of a fall-out with Widnes . . .'

'As you do,' interjected Steve Hampson, who was listening to the conversation from the sidelines.

'Do you mind, Hampo, this is my interview. He'll do you in a minute . . . if he's desperate.'

'I did a year at Warrington, won the Premiership there, but then I had a few words with the coach there . . .'

'As you do,' Hampson interjected, *sotto voce.*

'. . . or rather, he had a few words with me,' said Andy, this time not rising to Hampo's bait. 'That's when I came to Wigan.'

Andy runs a scrapyard with his father-in-law, Tony Karalius, a former professional player. The scrap trade is an ideal training ground for acquiring the skills of hard bargaining, which Andy had put to good effect in his contract negotiations at Wigan and elsewhere, and he had arrived at the ground for training on the Tuesday following his sending-off at Widnes, still chuckling over a day-long round of negotiations for the acquisition of a new drinks machine at the scrap yard.

'I spoke to the company we'd been renting a machine from this morning and fixed to buy one for £1,300. The rep said he'd come round later on to finalise the deal and do the paperwork. So I rang another company, just to check it out, and they said they could do it for £1,000. When the first one turned up, I told him about this, so he said, "Well if it's a cash buy, I can do you one for £500 and throw in a thousand free drinks." He was still sitting there when the rep from the other company turned up. So I told the first one to wait outside while I talked to the other one. I told him the deal I'd been offered, and he said, "Right, we'll give you one for £300 plus two thousand free drinks." They swopped over again and the first bloke said, "Right, I can give you a machine for nothing. It's not quite the model you wanted and you'll have to fill it up manually, but I'll give you that and throw in two thousand free drinks." So I got the other one back in and he matched the offer, but with a proper automatic-fill machine, so I said OK. I called the other rep back in and said, "Sorry, some you win and some you lose" and he started telling me how he didn't really mind because it would have taken them a long time selling the drinks to have made their money back on the machine. He went outside and as he was leaving the yard, he passed the other rep, who was bringing in the box with the free drinks, and he suddenly attacked him. We've got security cameras at the yard, so the lads were watching it on video, they've been watching it over and over again.

'The rep who's been hit comes staggering in, so I said to him, "It's not been your day really. This morning you were coming along to pick up a cheque for £1,300 and now you've got no cheque, you've given us a free machine and two thousand free drinks and you've got filled in as well."'

Gregory avoided suspension after his sending-off and Wigan got back into action with an untroubled 34–4 victory against an injury-hit Hull Kingston Rovers, keeping up the pressure on the First Division leaders. For once there were few injury problems during the build-up to the daunting trip to Castleford in the first round of the Challenge Cup. The only absentees were Andy Goodway, whose broken arm had still not yet healed, and Joe Lydon, who had aggravated a knee injury in the win against Hull Kingston Rovers.

Wigan had not lost a Challenge Cup tie for four years, but Castleford had proved to be among their most difficult opponents in recent seasons and were themselves bang in form, six successive wins propelling them into the top four of the First Division. The game was scheduled for Saturday afternoon, but the worst snowfall of the winter forced a postponement until the following Tuesday night. With Central Park and the adjoining training ground frozen hard and covered in several inches of snow, Wigan were forced to train indoors for the match. Taking advantage of their friendly relations with neighbouring professional soccer clubs, they used the indoor facilities at Old Trafford and Goodison Park.

Castleford's pitch was protected by tarpaulins and tons of straw but a further snowfall two hours before the kick-off forced the groundstaff into frantic efforts to sweep the pitch markings clear of snow before the referee would allow the game to go ahead. It was a bitingly cold night and that, together with the inch of fresh snow on the pitch, guaranteed a crop of handling mistakes; whichever of the sides made less errors would be the winners.

The visitors' dressing room at Castleford's Wheldon Road ground would have been cramped with ten people inside. With thirteen players, two substitutes, the coach, his assistants, the physiotherapist, the first-aider, the strapper, the kit-man and myself all jammed in there as well, it was almost impossible to move without asking three other people's permission first. Joe Lydon, who had come along to watch the match, pointed to a vertical mark on the wall, two-thirds of the way across the tiny room. 'You think it's bad now? That mark was where the wall used to be, the rest of the space then was taken up by the showers.'

Denis Wright, Keith Mills and Andrew Pinkerton were all at work rubbing the 'hot-stuff' into the players' legs, and because of the cold and the snow, they also worked it into their backs. In the close confines of the cramped dressing room, the overpowering smell of liniment caught the back of the throat and stung the eyes. The tension was palpably greater than for a normal game and the players were changed and ready much earlier, forty minutes before the kick-off. Most were quiet, their minds focused on the match, largely oblivious to the human traffic around them as Denis, Keith, Taffy and Andrew scurried around the room, applying vaseline to the players' knees, strapping their fingers, wrists and ankles, and handing out tie-ups, the tapes with which they secure their socks.

Most of the talking came from Monie, Hanley, Edwards and Gregory. All stressed a familiar message – basics. 'Play the way we've trained. Keep it tight. Work hard. If someone makes a mistake, let's not have a meeting about it, let's just get on with it. Keep the middle tight.' The latter remark from Monie reinforced a message he had been delivering at training all week.

In Monie's opinion, Castleford's greatest attacking threat would come close to the play-the-ball, for they were adept at drawing the markers out of position and slipping inside passes to supporting players breaking through around the ruck. Their stand-off Graham Steadman was also a considerable danger; not the best distributor of the ball, but a very dangerous poacher of half-chances with a devastating left foot side-step and explosive speed.

In the Wigan dressing room, Andy Gregory and Shaun Edwards were maintaining their competitive edge. Whenever either of them contributed anything to the pre-match instructions and exhortations, the other would follow up immediately with some advice of his own. The rivalry and tensions between them were as evident in the dressing room as on the pitch. Although this had often been a source of potential conflict in the past and no doubt would be again in the future, it was also a creative tension, driving both to raise their game to heights, both as individuals and as a half-back pairing, to which few others could even aspire.

John Monie offered his final words as the players moved towards the dressing-room door. 'The biggest prize in the game is on offer on a shitty night in Castleford. It's a long way to Wembley, but it starts here.'

Most spectators were probably expecting a tight struggle, with defences dominant and only a couple of points separating the sides, but when the game started, it rapidly became apparent that Wigan did not share that expectation. The lead was again set by props Ian Lucas and Kelvin Skerrett, both all fire and aggression, tearing into the Castleford pack from the start. The 'Cas' forwards struggled to hold their powerful drives, while in defence Lucas and Skerrett were stopping their opposite numbers in their tracks, then driving them back yards towards their own line before dumping them into the snow.

With the other Wigan forwards following their lead, Castleford were pinned in their own territory and pressured into a string of mistakes. By contrast, whenever Wigan had the ball, they were virtually error-free, despite the complexity of moves that left their opponents leaden-footed as the ball was switched with bewildering speed.

The game was effectively over inside the first ten minutes. A Castleford fumble in their own 22 was pounced on by David Myers. Just before he was tackled into touch, he flipped the perfect inside pass to Kevin Iro, leaving the powerful Kiwi centre to bruise his way past two defenders to the line. Five minutes later, Frano Botica was over after a magnificent move. Andy Gregory was the initiator, Shaun Edwards carried it on, making a dazzling break and then floating a huge pass out to the left, where Iro collected, drew his man and sent Botica clear for the score. Frano added the conversion to his own try and Wigan were 10 points ahead.

Edwards was soon across the line himself, only to be recalled for a forward pass and Myers twice could not hold scoring passes, but such was the Wigan pressure that further tries were inevitable. Edwards and Gregory were again the key participants in another dazzling move that led to the stand-off scoring under the posts. Gregory offered at least half-a-dozen dummies before picking out Andy Platt with a ball that sent the second row surging clear. He transferred to Edwards, who left the Cas full back floundering with a perfect side-step to score without a hand laid on him. After thirty-six minutes Castleford finally entered the Wigan 22 for the first time in the game, but as if to punish them for their impudence, Wigan immediately scored a length of the field try.

Castleford stand-off Graham Steadman, who is probably still waking up screaming in the dead of night with dreams of four or five Wigan forwards in his face, threw a hopelessly over-ambitious long pass. As it hit the ground, Frano Botica nipped in, booted it clear, kicked on again from the half-way and held off the covering defenders to scoop up the ball and plunge over the line. His brilliant conversion from the touch-line almost seemed to be gilding the lily.

As the half-time siren sounded, the Castleford players shook themselves as if waking from a collective nightmare and shambled from the field. On a dry pitch and a sunny afternoon at Wembley Stadium, the quality of Wigan's football during a first half of total dominance would have been impressive enough; on a bitingly cold February night at Castleford, with a couple of inches of snow on the pitch, it was simply unbelievable. There were no premature celebrations in the Wigan dressing room, however. They knew that the game was won if they held their discipline and maintained their control and they were not about to do anything as unprofessional as surrender a 22 point lead.

Ian Lucas did not take the field for the second half after injuring his shoulder, but his display over the first forty minutes alone had confirmed him as one of the best props in the game. John Monie's complaints earlier in the year about a lack of aggression, though correct at the time, now seemed ridiculous, as Lucas dominated and subjugated his opposite number. His right to be considered the first-choice Wigan prop, even ahead of the now rejuvenated and almost equally impressive Kelvin Skerrett, looked indisputable.

Andy Platt joined him on the bench early in the second half after breaking his left hand making a tackle, but Wigan's hold on the game remained relentless. David Myers added their fifth try, after Ellery Hanley had been held just short following a typically barnstorming run and only an outrageously one-sided penalty count kept Castleford in the game at all. After one of their sixteen penalties – Wigan were awarded three – had established them in the Wigan 22, they scored their only points when centre Shaun Irwin dived over.

That was a more positive contribution to the game than their attempts to nullify one of their chief tormentors, Andy Gregory. Three times during the match, he was flattened long after the ball had gone, the most dangerous time, for the player is relaxed and not braced for a hit. On the first two occasions, the hits came so late that neither the referee nor the touch-judges noticed them, but the third time proved unlucky for Castleford wing David Plange, who was deservedly sent off.

Dean Bell also had to cope with the effects of a hit made long after the ball had gone. 'Mean Dean' is normally one of the most fiery and feared backs in the game, but on this occasion he restrained his natural instinct to exact instant retribution, earning a post-match tribute from his coach. 'In view of the fact that Dean was hit off the ball and received little protection from the referee or linesmen, I thought his behaviour was extremely professional and mature. He didn't lose his head and wipe out about six or seven of the opposition, which he's perfectly capable of doing, he kept his cool. I appreciate that kind of mental toughness.'

As the final hooter sounded, the shivering spectators streamed from the terraces and the players ran for the dressing rooms and the waiting hot baths. Ellery Hanley was the last to reach the dressing room, having stopped to undo his tie-ups and give them to a little boy who shyly approached him for an autograph as he was leaving the pitch. It was a brief but revealing moment; the suggestions that Hanley is just an aloof and remote superstar are obviously far from the whole truth about him.

The demolition of Castleford had been clinical and professional; it had also been quite brilliant. The first half display was the best I had ever seen on a rugby league field. John Monie did not go quite that far, but he did describe it as 'our best display since I came to Wigan'.

As the Wigan bus pulled out of Castleford, following the trail of red tail-lights from their army of travelling supporters back through the snow to Wigan, Maurice Lindsay was hoping for a less demanding challenge in the second round of the Challenge Cup. 'That was a magnificent performance, but I think we've earned a nice soft home tie in the second round.' He was to get 50 per cent of his wish. The tie was a nice soft one against the bottom club in the First Division, Rochdale, but Wigan were drawn out of the hat second and had to travel.

Rochdale had been having a dismal season. They had won only one League game and were firmly anchored at the bottom of the table, already certain to return to the Second Division after just one year in the top flight. Their one hope of salvaging anything from their traumatic year was to make progress in the Challenge Cup, but against a Wigan side now approaching their best form, that was a very fragile hope.

Just how fragile quickly became apparent as Wigan set about destroying them with football of ruthless, chilling efficiency. Ellery Hanley had been switched to the centre in place of the injured Kevin Iro and he revelled in the return to his original club position, scoring six superb tries, a hat-trick in each half. Even so, he was outscored by Frano Botica, who kicked twelve goals from thirteen attempts and also scored a try. As Rochdale disintegrated, there was even a rare try for Ian Lucas, who was immediately engulfed by his delighted team-mates. A final score of 72–4 was even more remarkable considering that Wigan had played the second half a man short after Shaun Edwards was sent off.

He faced the usual worrying wait until the following Thursday, when a suspension of more than one match would rule him out of the next round, the quarter-final. Wigan finally drew the home tie they wanted, but it was against far tougher opposition, Bradford Northern, who had already removed them from the Regal Trophy at Central Park.

Trouble at t'club

BEFORE they could turn their attention to the Cup, however, Wigan had to maintain their momentum in the Championship, meeting Wakefield Trinity at Central Park, seeking revenge for Trinity's shock win at Belle Vue in November. Wigan's chief tormentor that night, Ged Byrne, was again at stand-off for Wakefield, relishing another opportunity to embarrass the club that had sold him. Wigan lacked Shaun Edwards, who had received a one match suspension for his sending-off at Rochdale, Kevin Iro and Joe Lydon, as well as the long-term absentee Andy Goodway.

Wigan trained poorly during the week and looked jaded against Wakefield, an ominous sign with a crushing burden of fixtures to be fitted in before the season's end. They did manage the win, 16–8, but it was a far from impressive performance. John Monie was not unduly worried by his side's lacklustre display, however. 'In retrospect, we probably trained them too hard last Thursday. We ran the guts out of them and I think it showed in Sunday's game.'

At the team meeting on the following Tuesday, Monie had the daunting programme of fixtures through to the end of the season in front of him. 'We're going to have to play seven games in March and eight games in April, so we're playing at least twice a week from now to the end of the season. The only time we won't have a midweek game is when we're playing a Cup tie the following weekend, and we've got four games scheduled the week of Easter, including Widnes on the Tuesday. So the important things for the next few weeks are rest and rehabilitation – doing the right thing after the games. It's vital that after each game you have twenty-four hours rest.

'I still state that the number one aim is to win this Championship. We've got a lot of games to play but we can win it, providing that we look after ourselves after the games. So if you've taken a knock, you must ice up on the Sunday night and get straight in to see the physio on Monday. We won't be doing much training for the next seven weeks, we'll be playing Sunday, getting together Tuesday, playing Wednesday, getting together Thursday and so on. I'm not going to run hell out of you in training but your commitment to the team is that you're going to look after yourselves and that means rest and rehabilitation.

'My idea differs from Maurice's about how we're going to win this Championship. Maurice thinks that because we've got a big squad we should use it, but my idea is to use the fifteen players who are the best – who are showing the best form. If one of them gets injured, we bring in the sixteenth best and so on.'

For the Challenge Cup quarter-final against Bradford Northern, the 'money was on' as the old players say. Monie told the players the size of the very substantial winning bonus the board had authorised, reflecting the fact that getting to Wembley this year was perhaps even more important to the directors than the players. Wigan's multi-layered financial structure depended on a trophy-winning team. Without the Challenge Cup and the Championship, Wigan's sponsorships would be less lucrative, the ground advertising lower and season ticket sales would drop. In a season where the costs of contracts and financing the new stand had stretched even Wigan's resources to breaking point, the cash flow from a share of the Challenge Cup semi-final and final revenues was also not just welcome but essential.

As Monie sent his players out to train, the weekly board meeting was beginning next door. The directors had assembled in the boardroom for the first time for some weeks, for according to Maurice Lindsay an architect's error had forced the contractors to slice off the outer wall to accommodate part of the steel skeleton of the new stand. The damage had now been made good and with the smell of fresh plaster still in the air, Jack Robinson took temporary charge of the meeting, pending the arrival of Maurice, who was busy commuting from one local television studio to another, doing interviews about the present and future state of Ellery Hanley's contract with the Wigan Club.

The week of the Challenge Cup quarter-final was already going to be a pretty momentous one for Wigan, but two events made it even more significant. The rift with Bobby Goulding that had been steadily widening since John Monie's prescient pre-season remark, 'We're going to have trouble with Bobby this year' had now widened to the point where it seemed unbridgeable. Already resentful at being passed over in favour of Andy Gregory, who was now playing at a new peak of his form, Goulding responded to the news that Gregory was being offered a new contract by staying away from training. He was immediately dropped from the 'A' team. With his own contract due to expire at the end of the season and showing the worst complaint in the coaching manual – bad attitude – the once undisputed heir to Andy Gregory seemed on a collision course with his coach that looked certain to end in his transfer. The exasperated Monie and the Wigan directors were in complete agreement; without a major change in his attitude, the time had come to sell Goulding to another club.

Leeds were interested and a price of around £150,000 was discussed, with Wigan willing to take a player valued at £30,000 in part exchange, to boost their squad for the tough run to the end of the season. The potential stumbling-block was Leeds' insistence that Goulding must agree to move there. Wigan had been unsuccessful in trying to pry him loose of the influence of his family and friends in Widnes. Despite his original assent to the idea, Bobby had never moved to Wigan, and without his agreement to move to Leeds, the transfer would be off.

Wigan were eager for the deal to go through, both to rid themselves of an embarrassment and to add a healthy six figure sum to the bank balances. For Goulding it looked likely to be the sad end of a Wigan career that only six months before had seemed certain to be a long and glittering one, but he was not the first and will certainly not be the last sportsman to have a natural talent blighted by a lack of maturity.

The transfer to Leeds did not occur, however, talks between the player and the club breaking down. Leeds contacted Maurice Lindsay to say that they were no longer interested 'at any price'. That evening Goulding made his first appearance at training for some time, asking Lindsay about the possibility of a new contract with the club. 'Just get stuck into training for a while, Bobby,' said Maurice, 'and we'll talk about a contract a little later in the season.'

In a normal week, Goulding's impending transfer would have made massive headlines in the local press. As it was, the story broke as a rather low-key follow-up to a far bigger story, the possible involvement of Ellery Hanley with American football.

The newly-formed World League of American Football had a seven figure promotional budget for their new team in Britain, the London Monarchs, and Ellery had been targeted as a key part of the publicity campaign, the high-profile capture that would generate massive publicity for the new club. The Wigan players and officials had known of Ellery's possible involvement since the previous week, when the dressing-room chat at the Tuesday night training session had all been about his planned flight to Orlando, Florida, for trials with the Monarchs squad. The Wigan board had vetoed that idea, stressing that the trip would conflict with his first contractual duty to his rugby league club, a decision that he accepted without rancour.

That was far from the end of the matter. The following Monday's *Daily Mirror* splashed a three page scoop, a 'world exclusive' interview with Ellery, revealing his plans to play for the Monarchs, with a debut set for Wembley Stadium on Easter Sunday. There were also quotes from the chairman of the Monarchs, claiming that Wigan had agreed to share their star player with them, and that Hanley would be playing for the Monarchs whenever this did not clash with a Wigan game.

Since Wigan had fixtures on both Good Friday and Easter Monday, it was scarcely possible that they would agree to allow their captain to play in a game of American football on Easter Sunday as well, but the club had to tread carefully in their public reaction to the story. Hanley's contract expired in October, and the board were well aware that even if Hanley chose to leave the club, the amount of financial compensation they would receive would be negligible. In fact, Ellery's advisers had always made clear to the Monarchs that rugby league was his first priority. If there were to be any conflicts of interest, they would be decided in favour of rugby league, but that was not the message that the Monarchs chose to highlight in their carefully-orchestrated media campaign, and the Wigan board can be forgiven for fearing the worst. In the first blaze of publicity, nobody had the time or inclination to query whether it reflected reality or just hype, like much else in the story of Hanley's flirtation with American football.

While they waited for Maurice Lindsay to arrive, his three co-directors worked their way through other, less contentious parts of the agenda than their captain's role in the Monarchs' publicity. The 'phone in the boardroom rang constantly, anxious fans plaguing the life out of Tom Rathbone, as usual in his role of honorary telephone receptionist, demanding to know if Hanley would be staying or going. One call was from a blind supporter who said that he had been a Wigan fan all his life, although he had obviously never seen them play. Instead he listened avidly to the local radio commentary every week, and begged them not to let Hanley go.

They worked their way through the annual pay review for the staff, interrupted every few minutes by the ringing of the telephone and by the arrival of a string of players with worries or grievances to put. Wingman Mark Preston wanted to know whether his contract would be renewed. The board made soothing noises about his value to the squad, though these were in contrast to the opinions that John Monie had expressed about Preston's ability in frequent discussions with the board. Preston left, partly mollified, to be succeeded by the 'A' team hooker, Augustine 'Ducky' O'Donnell.

The circle of consequences from the earlier efforts to keep Bobby Goulding happy and on the Wigan playing strength was still widening. O'Donnell had been driven to put in a transfer request a couple of weeks before, because of his frustration at being passed over in his natural position, not in favour of another hooker, but of Wigan's disaffected second-string scrum-half. A couple of the senior players had talked to O'Donnell and persuaded him to come back to the board to withdraw his transfer request, although he first wanted some reassurance about his future prospects. The use of his nickname lent a slightly surreal air to the discussions.

'Do you see a future for me at Central Park?'

'Well it's up to you, Ducky, that's all we can say really,' said Jack Robinson. 'If you play well enough, you'll be in the first team.'

'But John's been putting Bobby in at hooker ahead of me.'

'Well I think John's been under a lot of pressure there, Ducky, with Bobby being the Great Britain scrum-half last summer, but I think he's now decided that Bobby just hasn't got the right attitude.'

'Yeah, his heart's not in it, is it?'

'No. We definitely think you're first team material, Ducky, but over the last twelve months you haven't been playing quite as well as you can, even though we know you've had some injuries. You've a big chance between now and the end of the season though. We've got to play eleven games in five weeks and Martin Dermott's struggling with a groin injury, so John is going to be looking for players to bring in.'

'If I come off the list, would you consider a new contract for me, even though there is still a year to go on the present one?'

'We'll always look at proposals, Ducky, but what have you in mind?'

'I don't know really.'

'Well have a think, come back to us with something and we'll look at it.'

As O'Donnell was leaving, Lindsay arrived, immediately bringing his colleagues up to date on the latest news from the Hanley front. Maurice had been closeted with the club's legal advisor for most of the day and passed on the gist of their discussions. 'His advice was not to be too hawkish, but to point out quietly but firmly that Ellery Hanley is a Wigan player until the end of the season. He says that if we're too hawkish about it, we may just alienate Ellery and he's got such a tiny portion of his contract to go that we may create difficulties for ourselves if we lay down the law to him.

'In fact, I'm sure the thought of walking out on Wigan would never enter Ellery's head, but I'm anxious that he doesn't wear himself out or get injured playing American football. He's too important to Wigan for that. I knew the story was in the offing, after talking to Ellery last week, but I nearly crashed my car tonight, when I heard the boss of the London Monarchs on the radio, claiming he'd reached an agreement with me; I've never spoken to the bloke in my life.

'I hope that kind of thing isn't believed by the players in the dressing room though, because we're asking them to play eleven games in the next five weeks and everybody's got to share the workload. It would be different if we were 15 points ahead in the title race, like we were four years ago, but we're not. We're 5 points behind and I can't see any game at all that we'd be able to let Ellery miss. Otherwise, to be honest, it wouldn't bother me if he played a couple of games of American football and then it all just faded quietly away. It's going to be hard enough for us to win that Championship now, especially with this Ellery business.'

The Monarch of Central Park

IN FACT the Wigan captain had stunned the rugby league world twice that week; first by announcing that he wanted to play American football for the London Monarchs, and secondly by actually agreeing to talk to the media about it, something he had been singularly unwilling to do as captain of both the Wigan and Great Britain rugby league teams, though he claims this is because of misrepresentations of his views by the media in the past.

After several years of total media silence, broken by occasional exclusives in the tabloid newspapers when he felt he had a story to tell, Hanley's appearances on BBC TV's Sportsnight, Radio One's Breakfast Show and the Jonathan Ross chat show on Channel Four, all in the same week as the three-page exclusive in the *Daily Mirror* which launched the whole circus, was as unexpected as a string quartet providing the half-time entertainment at Central Park.

Hanley claims that having given his involvement with the Monarchs' publicity careful consideration, he had decided that it would in no way damage his first love, the game of rugby league. His contract with Wigan made it unlikely that he would even lace an American football boot in anger until the Monarchs' season was already three parts over, but his value to the Monarchs was primarily as a publicity weapon, and in that he had been hugely successful.

A week before Hanley's announcement, it would have been doubtful if more than one person in a thousand had even heard of the London Monarchs. Now anyone with even a passing interest in sport not only knew all about them, but also knew that they would play their first home game at Wembley Stadium on Easter Sunday. The fact that Hanley would not be playing no longer mattered. The Monarchs had already achieved their primary aim from the use of Hanley's name – a massive burst of publicity.

139

Hanley's deep-seated and long-standing antipathy to the media is partly due to what he sees as the tabloids' scandalous attempts to breach the privacy to which he feels entitled in his life off the rugby field. By his continuing refusal to make any comment, he has now largely achieved his desire to be left alone by the media, yet he does not help his own cause by his refusal to speak to the press at all, even when approached in his role as captain of Wigan and Great Britain. He argues that his stance is justified because of earlier press attacks on him, but his refusal to talk to the media ensures that, in the absence of any evidence to the contrary, even inaccurate stories about him remain widely believed.

Hanley has become the game's greatest practitioner, a status reflected in the MBE he received from the Queen in 1988 for services to rugby league. It was an award that delighted many people in the game, who were pleased at the recognition of his rise to the pinnacle of the game – 'one of the major achievements in sport' according to Rugby League spokesman David Howes – but some journalists were disappointed that a rare public honour for the sport had gone to Hanley. They argued that while a tremendous example of athleticism, skill and determination on the field, off it, he was at best a reluctant ambassador for the game. Hanley's view is that the journalists who were aggrieved had adopted a churlish and spiteful stance. He was deeply touched by the honour and grateful to those who had made it possible.

To suggest that such an honour would ever come his way would have seemed a remote possibility as the young Hanley began his rugby league career, although the iron will and determination that were ultimately to make him the world's greatest player were already in evidence. 'His will was unbreakable,' recalled a contemporary, 'he just wouldn't give in.'

A local lawyer, John Fitzpatrick, became Ellery's manager and confidant, and today remains one of the few people that he trusts completely, though Hanley trusts his own judgement and is not afraid to reject advice from any source if it conflicts with his principles or instincts. He is definitely not a subscriber to the view that all publicity is good publicity and his general rule of not talking to the media is a long-standing one. Such a policy adds rarity value to Hanley's very occasional tabloid 'exclusives', such as when he was in dispute with Wigan's former coach Graham Lowe, or when breaking the news of his involvement with the London Monarchs, but his refusal to grant the interviews willingly given by every other participant in the sport has caused resentment inside and outside the game.

The award of the Adidas Golden Boot to Hanley as the world's greatest international player – the first time the award had ever gone to a British player – was virtually snubbed by some sections of the media because of their antipathy to him, though Hanley would argue that such an important award deserved much wider media coverage in any event. His refusal to use the media to boost his image as one of Britain's finest sportsmen may also prevent him from cashing in on his talent through advertisements and personal appearances in the way that other sportsmen have been able to do, but he has made his choice and is happy to live with the consequences.

Like his club colleague Denis Betts, Hanley's youthful preference had been for association football; it is an often-told tale that he was only persuaded to play rugby league because of the threat of a slippering from his teacher if he didn't. He soon grew to like and excel at rugby league, however, and was signed by Bradford Northern while playing for the Corpus Christi Boys Club in Leeds, becoming a massive star in a declining Bradford side. Such was his extraordinary power and pace that his then coach Peter Fox confesses, 'I gave instructions to the rest of the team that whenever Ellery called for the ball, whatever move was on, or planned, they were to give it to him straight away.' Their generosity to him was repaid in full, Hanley scoring a phenomenal number of tries for them, including 55 in the 1984–85 season, a First Division record, keeping Bradford from relegation almost single-handed.

His contract expired at the end of that season, however, and Bradford's directors complained that he was demanding a disproportionate increase in his earnings, even allowing for his star quaity. Hanley claims that, in fact, Bradford never offered him terms at all. While he and the club exchanged recriminations, Wigan saw their chance and moved swiftly to sign him in a player-exchange-plus-cash deal worth a world record fee. It is entirely possible that it actually suited Bradford to sell Hanley at the time, but that is not something their board would have wished to admit to their supporters and, in the customary absence of any statement from Hanley, the Bradford board's version of events has been perceived to be correct.

His talent blossomed even more at Central Park, where he was surrounded by high-quality players, and he broke his own First Division record by scoring 63 tries in his second season at Central Park. His try-scoring rate has diminished since he made the switch from the backs to the forwards and had to cope with the extra defensive duties of the loose forward role. If he has lost a little of his pace, however, he has increased still more his extraordinary power to break tackles and fend off defenders and is now almost the complete player.

There are better passers and kickers of the ball, but Hanley's defence is flawless and his understanding of the tactics and strategies of the game so good that he qualified for the national coaching certificate with one of the highest marks ever recorded. He seems to be being groomed as John Monie's successor at Central Park, with the Australian opening his coaching books and his methods to Hanley, who is also being talked of as a possible Great Britain coach of the future. Both prospects fill many journalists with dread, but journalists will not be making the coaching appointments and Hanley is interested only in the judgement of his peers in the game.

Apart from his defence and his tactical appreciation, Hanley is without question the most devastating runner in the game. Martin Offiah, a close friend, is faster, more elusive and an even more prolific try-scorer, but no-one breaks tackles or makes 'busts' through the heavy defensive traffic in midfield with the frequency or flair of Hanley. Some opposing supporters feel that he gains an unfair advantage for his team by 'professionalism' such as excessive questioning of referees' decisions, but even the most one-eyed opposing supporter would also agree that Ellery is not remotely a 'dirty' player. In a long, high-profile career, his only sending-off has been for allegedly abusing a referee, a charge he vehemently denied.

His international career, begun as a Bradford player, has also blossomed, while an outstandingly successful stint as a guest player with the Australian club Balmain cemented his reputation as one of the world's greatest players. His pre-eminence as the finest British player of his era was confirmed when he took over the captaincy of the Great Britain side, a role he continues, despite the problems caused by his media silence. The Great Britain management have shown no more inclination to force Hanley to accept the traditional captain's role of public spokesman for the team than have Maurice Lindsay and his directors at Wigan.

While his dislike for the media may be understandable, it is unfortunate that the Wigan captain, like many fellow-players, fails to make any distinction between the tabloid news hacks carrying on their sordid trade of cheque-book journalism, innuendo and kiss-and-tell revelations and the sports reporters who have often gone out of their way to protect players from some of the consequences of their misjudged actions. Certainly there were years of accumulated frustration in the complaint of a rugby league official that while plugging American football, Hanley had appeared on the very television programme that he had refused, when invited as Great Britain rugby league captain, during the Ashes series against Australia a few months before. Promoting the sport that had supported him throughout his career was apparently a less high priority than promoting American football. Hanley considers this to be unrealistic, because, by virtue of his appearances, rugby league received massive national television publicity.

Hanley's trappism extends to even the most trivial occasions. A magazine which had booked him for a modelling session of some new clothes, tried to interview him as well. The questions concerned minor areas of his private life, such as his preference for boxer shorts or briefs, or his favourite sandwich-filling, but Hanley refused to answer even such trite questions, stating that the contract had been only for a photo-session and that the magazine was trying to take unfair advantage of that to obtain an interview that they knew he would have refused if approached directly.

When the *Observer* newspaper's *The Experts' Expert* series profiled rugby league players, Hanley was the unsurprising choice of his peers as the outstanding present-day player, but the picture of him was unaccompanied by any copy. Of all the people in all the various fields of human activity profiled in the series, Hanley was one of the very few whose picture was unaccompanied by any comment.

If Hanley's media silence on his own sport annoys and frustrates officials and journalists, it has no effect on his standing amongst his fellow-players. 'You can't be in awe of anyone in this game,' according to Denis Betts, 'but when you look back on your own career and see who you've played alongside,

Ellery Hanley will be one of the greatest. He leads from his actions not his mouth, he never backs down and he's totally dedicated to the game. He's a great rugby league player, a great person to play alongside and a great person to know. He speaks for all of us on the pitch; he doesn't need to say another word to anybody.'

The image of Hanley as an aloof and hostile superstar, brushing aside the attentions of fans and autograph-seekers is also wide of the mark. For every allegation that Hanley was aloof or brusque, there were several stories of him taking time to talk to young fans and sign autographs. He also does unpublicised work for the Fight for Sight charity and in the week before the Cup Final, he donated £2,000 each to Fight for Sight, the Wigan Scanner Appeal and to the Rugby League Foundation, which aids the development of the game at junior and amateur level. He also made an unpaid appearance at a press conference to announce the donations. That money was the sum received in damages from a libel action. Journalists who write about Hanley despite the obstacles posed by his media silence should check their facts carefully.

My relationship with Hanley during my year with Wigan was based on an unspoken agreement: I would not ask him any questions and he would not give me any answers. My arrangements with the Wigan club gave me complete access to everything and everyone at Central Park, but I was not so naive as to imagine that would include access to their reclusive superstar.

For nine months we maintained an uneasy truce, broken only by Hanley's occasional complaints to Maurice Lindsay about my presence in the inner sanctum of the dressing room. Eventually Ellery confronted me. 'The players don't want you in here any more. You make them uncomfortable, they can't relax when you're here.'

Though I was aware of the players' reluctance to share their dressing room with a journalist when the idea of the book was first raised, I had thought that I had overcome their initial misgivings by this stage of the season. I was well aware that my welcome at Central Park depended on me keeping anything I saw or heard there absolutely confidential. While the often-scurrilous chat indulged in by the Wigan players, like any group of young men, was often entertaining, it was not what interested me for the account of Wigan's year.

While the rest of the team undoubtedly shared their captain's reservations, Ellery was the one to express them, though he would no doubt have argued that, as captain, he was merely fulfilling his role of players' spokesman. 'I'm disappointed that you feel like that, Ellery. I would have thought that I had proved that I could be trusted by now. I mean I knew about the London Monarchs story a week ago, because the players were all talking about it at training last Tuesday. If I'd been interested in betraying confidences, I could have done so.

Arguing with Ellery once his mind is made up is a waste of time, especially if a journalist is doing the arguing. 'I'm not interested in that. We don't want you in here at all really, but you can come in on match days.'

Those were virtually the first and last words he addressed to me that year. He wasn't outwardly angry or emotional about it, but I got the message. I accepted reluctantly that there were problems with any journalist being in a dressing room, and I agreed to leave the players to it.

Ironically, Hanley's Wigan commitments, coupled with a hamstring injury, ensured that he has yet even to set foot on the field for the London Monarchs. If he is ever to make his bow as a gridiron player, it will have to be in some future close-season. Their attendances boosted by his publicity work on their behalf, the Monarchs will not be too troubled by his non-appearance on the field.

There could scarcely be a stronger contrast between the public persona of Hanley and the man widely regarded as his probable successor as captain of both Wigan and Great Britain, Phil Clarke. John Monie has no doubts about Phil's future. 'He's certainly captaincy material and he looks to me like an automatic choice to succeed Ellery, whenever he decides to call it a day.' Personable and intelligent, articulate and handsome, Clarke has the personality that any sport would welcome in the captain of its national side. He is also one of the most gifted young players in rugby league.

Phil's father, Colin, played for Wigan from the mid-1960s to the mid-1970s at hooker and went back to coach them in the early 1980s, losing the job when sacked by Maurice Lindsay to make way for Graham Lowe, despite taking the side to Wembley that year. That could have made Wigan's interest in signing his son a few years later very difficult, but according to Phil, his father made it very easy for him. 'I felt a bit like that really but he was great. He told me that if I wanted to sign for my home-town club, then fair enough. I think inside he's Wigan through and through. Even when he got sacked, he still wanted Wigan to win everything.'

The fact that Colin never harboured a grudge against the club was also a considerable relief to Maurice Lindsay. 'It was a very satisfying night for me when I met with them both to discuss a contract for Phil. I'd parted company with Colin under sad circumstances, because obviously he didn't agree with my assessment of our coaching needs at Wigan, so it was very generous of him to conduct himself in such a gentlemanly manner. No memories haunted the night I met them, so much so that I told Phil that if things went well for him, I would tear up his contract and give him a new, improved one. I did that before he left for Great Britain's tour of Papua New Guinea and New Zealand, giving him a new four-year contract.'

In contrast to Shaun Edwards's development under the hawk-like eye of his father, Phil's rugby league apprenticeship was a much more relaxed affair. 'He never pushed me, never even suggested I play rugby. I decided to play myself. When I was sixteen he said that if I was going to take it seriously, then he'd help, watch and give advice whenever he could, but he was never pushy or anything like that, he was brilliant with me. Now he just comes and gives advice when he can. He always picks up one point after every game, he's like a personal coach really.

'I never thought about being a professional when I was playing as a kid. It was only when I was playing for St Patrick's under-17s that a scout from Wigan approached me and asked if I wanted to go and have talks with them. Up to that time I had never really thought about being a professional, it was never in the forefront of my mind. It wasn't something I worried about really, though a lot of young lads do.

'After Wigan came in for me, there were one or two other clubs interested as well, but it was my home-town club and I'd been watching them since I was about one, because my Dad was playing for them when I was born and my mother used to take me to all the games. So it's been my team all my life.'

Phil is also laid-back about the speculation that he is already earmarked for the captaincy of his club and his country. 'I try and play it down as much as possible because it only takes one injury or a bit of bad luck and you're out, you might never play again. Rugby's just a game, it's not the be-all and end-all in life. As long as I keep enjoying it that's all that matters, it's just adding pressure if you start thinking about how good you're going to be.

'It was a really big shock, the first time I went into the dressing room as a first-team player. I played alongside Graeme West on my debut and only a couple of years earlier I had gone to Wembley as a supporter to watch him lift the Cup. I was a little bit in awe at first, but you soon get over that when you start to play. The jerseys are laid out in a certain order in the dressing room and it's probably been done in that way for twenty years, but it can be a bit confusing when you're new to the team, because you don't really know which peg to use and some people can get really upset if you take their peg. Even when Nicky Kiss lost his place in the first team he still kept his peg, so there was a lot of conflict between him and Martin Dermott just about this peg. The one wall that's left for substitutes is where the young players go and I suppose the sign that you've really made it into the first team is when you get your own peg.

'The existing first-team players are never nasty or anything like that when a new player comes into the team, but I suppose they're looking over their shoulder, thinking, "This player is going to try and take my place." It's a professional game and that's what everybody is concerned about – getting themselves in the side.'

Phil earned selection for the Great Britain touring party at the age of 19, just a few months older than Bobby Goulding. Despite that and an already sizeable collection of winners' medals, there is no likelihood of him getting complacent. 'Having toured with Great Britain, I often find I can't get into the Wigan first team, but I hope I'm a much-improved player as a result of the tour and I'm more determined than ever to fight my way into the Wigan side. In a way I've not really achieved anything yet. I haven't played at Wembley and there's a lot of other things for me to do in the game.

'I wouldn't carry on playing if I stopped enjoying the game

though. For some people it possibly is a business, but personally I'd say it's got to be a pleasure, otherwise you couldn't do it, you couldn't carry on. When it stops being a pleasure that's when you stop playing.'

A Pretty Cheap Trick

THE PROBLEMS with Hanley and Goulding were put firmly on the back-burner as Wigan began the preparation for the Cup quarter-final against Bradford. The York-shiremen had spoiled Wigan's Christmas with their Regal Trophy victory at Central Park and neither Monie nor his men were in any mood to allow them a repeat. Bradford's game was based around a big, hard pack of forwards, battering their way down the middle. They produced little in the way of open football but were always difficult to beat, as Wigan already knew to their cost.

As expected, the first forty minutes proved to be a grim, unrelenting forward struggle, with defences well on top and ferocious hits repeatedly sending the ball carriers spinning to the ground. Bradford took first blood with an early penalty, but that advantage was nullified by Frano Botica's successful kick after twenty-five minutes. The big crowd's collective anxiety as Wigan repeatedly failed to breach the defence was obvious, but with just seconds to go before the half-time hooter, Wigan scored the try that signalled the end of Bradford's resistance, Martin Dermott wriggling over from dummy-half after Ian Lucas had been held just short of the line. A brilliant touchline goal from Frano Botica sent Wigan in at the interval with a useful 8–2 lead.

Andy Platt left the field with a torn stomach muscle shortly after the restart, but it was soon evident that Brad-ford's desperate first half defensive efforts had taken too much out of them and, just four minutes into the half, Wigan put the issue beyond doubt. Shaun Edwards collected a Steve Hampson 'bomb' and quick passing between Gregory, Iro and Bell gave Botica just enough room to squeeze in at the corner. Another superb conversion added to Bradford's discomfort.

Andy Gregory, back at the peak of his form, tormented the

visitors as Wigan relaxed and began to play open expansive football. Gregory scored the next himself, going on a curving run to the line as the defence held off, waiting for him to unload. It was only his third score of the season and brought him a standing ovation from the delirious crowd. Gregory again initiated the next try, a 'Beast' special, as Kevin Iro took off on a storming eighty yard scoring run, leaving defenders floundering in his wake. Bradford's lightweight fullback, Roger Simpson, was simply trampled underfoot as Iro tore to the line. In the final minute American football's newest recruit set off on a typical surging break to give Dean Bell a clear run to the corner. Botica again goaled, again from the touchline, to give himself half of his side's points in a 32–2 thrashing.

The Wigan fans were ecstatic as they streamed from the ground and even the normally restrained Monie was full of praise. 'I thought we put in a great performance. We were made to work hard and although it took us a little time to get going, that was down to Bradford's forward strength.' Monie allowed his players little time to dwell on the achievement, however. 'Now we must concentrate our minds on Wednesday night's Championship game against Hull.'

While they did that, the Wigan fans' prime concern was with which side their heroes would draw in the Challenge Cup semi-finals. Widnes, St Helens and Oldham had joined Wigan in the last four, Widnes looking particularly strong in their demolition of Warrington. In common with Wigan and Widnes fans, most neutrals hoped that the two giants of the sport would not meet until Wembley, giving the game's showpiece occasion a match to savour and guaranteeing a competitive final after three years of effortless Wigan dominance.

Of the other two sides, Oldham were probably the easier tie, but with one eye on the possible revenues from the semi-final, Maurice Lindsay was hoping for St Helens, who would be certain to draw a massive crowd to the neutral ground chosen for the semi-final. Lindsay was to be disappointed, for when the draw was made, Wigan came out of the hat with Oldham, the last side to beat them in the Challenge Cup four years before.

Just three days after the Cup victory against Bradford, Wigan were back in action in a vital Championship match against Hull. The once runaway leaders had been hauled back to the pack and the Humbersiders knew that their title chances rested on winning at Central Park. Wigan could theoretically afford to lose one more game on the run-in to the title, but beginning a gruelling programme of 11 matches in 32 days – 'Mission Impossible' in John Monie's opinion – they scarcely wanted to slip up at the first hurdle.

The players sprawled around the meeting room a couple of hours before the kick-off, until John Monie called them closer to the front to watch a videotape. Fourteen of the fifteen-man squad obediently moved their chairs up to the front, forming a semi-circle around Monie. Only one, Andy Gregory, ignored the request, remaining sitting on his own, towards the back of the room.

Monie did not rise to the bait, instead switching on the tape of the Sydney Grand Final between Canberra and Penrith and drawing the attention of his players to the solid foundations that Canberra laid for their flowing football later in the game. 'They played some good football to win this game, but for the first twenty minutes they just drove it up the middle, one and two off the ruck, made the yardage first and then started to move it around. That's how Hull strung together eight or ten wins at the start of the season, because their props were making good yardage up the middle. So we've got to stop them from doing that tonight.'

Just before Monie sent them down to the dressing room to get changed, he put on a second tape, an interview with the then Hull coach Brian Smith, recorded after Hull had beaten Wigan at the Boulevard the previous autumn.

'You've beaten some pretty big sides, haven't you?' asked the reporter.

'Yeah,' said Smith, 'big sides on paper, media teams.'

Monie played it a couple of times, then turned off the tape. 'O.K. So we're a big side on paper, let's see what you can do out there on the pitch. Let's go.' As the players filed out, Monie turned to me and winked, saying, 'That was a pretty cheap trick, wasn't it, using that tape, when Brian Smith is back in Sydney and not even in charge of the side?'

'Yeah, but the old ones are always the best, aren't they?'

Out on the pitch, whether because of Monie's cheap trick or not, Wigan were again in awesome form. Andy Gregory may have been a lonely onlooker in the team meeting, but out on the field he was at the heart of everything, in peerless form, displaying his full range of sleight of hand, barefaced cheek and football vision. Hull didn't look a bad side and in the French international Patrick Entat, they had probably the second-best half-back playing in Britain. His and Hull's problem was that they were facing the finest half-back in the world.

Hull had taken an early lead with a penalty goal, but on the quarter hour, Gregory made his first telling intervention, a glorious pass fully thirty yards to his left setting Dean Bell free. His pass to Frano Botica was sweetly timed and though the ex-All Black still had his winger to beat, he feinted to the inside and then swept past him to the corner for a fine try, to which he added a towering touchline conversion. Ten minutes later Joe Lydon scored with his first touch of the ball after coming on as substitute, as Phil Clarke, Hanley and Edwards combined beautifully to put him away. Lydon's second from a shrewd Andy Gregory kick through and a score for Denis Betts after a masterfully delayed pass from Gregory, left Hull high and dry despite Lee Jackson's try for them in first-half injury time.

Wigan inevitably eased off a little in the second half, 22–6 ahead, perhaps with one eye on their daunting fixture schedule, but they still added two further tries, Frano Botica completing a fine hat-trick to go with his five goals. His second was a walk-in at the corner, the third a beauty provided by Shaun Edwards after intercepting a stray Hull pass, with Botica jinking past two defenders to score at the posts. Monie had had reservations about the ex-All Black earlier in the season, darkly muttering about, 'Having to do a hell of a coaching job on him,' but it had clearly been very successful. Botica's defence had improved out of all recognition, he was scoring tries regularly, reading the game well and kicking goals from all over the field, plugging a gap that had been one of the few weaknesses in Wigan's game in recent years.

One down and ten to go for Wigan, and after a refusal by the Rugby League to consider extending the season, four of those ten would have to be played in the final week of the season, including the vital clashes against the teams that were now Wigan's closest rivals for the Championship, Widnes and Castleford.

The next opponents to face the Wigan mincing machine were far less daunting, however, the bottom club Rochdale Hornets. They were duly despatched 44–16, despite their recent discovery of the most effective ploy they had used all season, reducing the width of their pitch by moving the touch-lines in a few yards. Even on the narrow field, Wigan found plenty of try-scoring opportunities, the most heartening that leading to an Andy Goodway score on his return from a long injury absence with a broken arm.

Less cheering was Kelvin Skerrett's dismissal, his old in-discipline resurfacing in a clash with Rochdale's hooker. To lose a player sent off in a 'nothing' match with the points already securely in the bag, was particularly galling for Monie. The Challenge Cup semi-final against Oldham was the follow-ing Saturday and Skerrett had jeopardised his chances of playing with a moment of hot-headedness.

Trial by Ordeal

S KERRETT was duly suspended for two matches, ruling him out of the semi-final against Oldham, the last team to beat Wigan in the Cup four years before. There was to be no repetition of the Oldham heroics this time however, as Wigan cruised to victory, earning an unprecedented fourth consecutive visit to Wembley while scarcely seeming to break sweat.

The Oldham defence appeared mesmerised by Andy Gregory, who made early tries for Shaun Edwards and Ellery Hanley with a grubber kick and a short pass. When a dreadful mistake let substitute Andy Goodway in for a third first-half try, the match was over. Already 20–0 up at the interval, Wigan cruised through the second half, allowing Oldham to regain a measure of self-respect with two late tries, in a 30–16 defeat.

John Monie was far from pleased with the overall display of his side, but as he himself said, 'It's a miserable coach who complains too much about his side when they've just won a Challenge Cup semi-final by 14 points.' Whether blase by now about the achievement of reaching Wembley or just depressed by a careless second-half performance and the low-key nature of a semi-final that never generated any tension at all, the atmosphere in the Wigan dressing room was strangely flat.

'It was a bit of an anti-climax after the way we started,' said Dean Bell. 'We can play a lot better than that, and we'll have to at Wembley'. Shaun Edwards described it as Wigan's worst performance of their cup run, 'But when you fall short of your potential and still get to Wembley, it can't be too bad.'

Perhaps the other reason for Wigan's low-key performance and even lower-key post-match celebrations was the knowledge of the awesome task facing them in the next three weeks. Beginning on the Tuesday night with a game against their hated opponents Warrington at 'the zoo', as the Wilderspool ground is often unkindly known, Wigan had to fit in eight games in nineteen days to complete their league programme. Most grotesque of all, they had to play four games in the final six days of the season. On their form in the previous few weeks, no team in Britain could live with Wigan, who had won every game since the New Year's Day defeat by Warrington, but, debilitated by an incessant programme of tough fixtures, it was possible that battle fatigue would deprive them of the title.

Wigan came through against Warrington by the surprisingly comfortable margin of 25–6 and survived tough battles at both Featherstone and Oldham, the latter their thirteenth consecutive win. It was certainly an unlucky thirteen for Kelvin Skerrett, who was again sent off, just one match after returning from suspension for his previous dismissal. With so many fixtures in so few days, Monie needed all his players fit and available, not sidelined because of their ill-discipline. Whatever calming influence Ian Lucas had previously exercised on his prop partner seemed to be waning rapidly.

Wigan were now on the home stretch, but an intimidating run-in to the title awaited them. St Helens had surprisingly but convincingly beaten Widnes to earn the right to face Wigan in the Challenge Cup Final at Wembley and the two sides would now meet in a dress rehearsal at Central Park on Thursday 5 April. On the Sunday, Wigan would entertain Castleford and on the following Tuesday they would meet their chief rivals for the title, Widnes. On the Thursday they were then due to meet Bradford Northern, followed by their final Championship fixture of the season, away at Leeds on the Saturday.

Five games in ten days, all against sides in the top eight in the First Division, and including the Championship decider against Widnes; if Wigan could come through that trial by ordeal and retain their title, they would truly have earned the right to be recognised as the greatest team of the greatest game, perhaps of all time. The players grabbed what rest they could, in between playing every couple of days and fitting in light training and heavy treatment sessions. The treatment room at the other end of the corridor from the dressing room was increasingly coming to resemble a MASH unit as more and more casualties of the fixture pile-up sought relief from their injuries. 'There's scarcely a member of the squad who hasn't had to have treatment in the last couple of weeks,' said Keith Mills, turning back to begin work on yet another injury.

If the trainers and players were working flat-out, however, so were the office staff, in particular, the Wigan secretary Mary Charnock and her assistant Mandy Roper. In addition to the normal administrative workload, they were selling tickets for games that came round every two or three days and also preparing to cope with the annual stampede for Wembley tickets. The Wigan fan-club on the stairs by the office were also preparing themselves, like several thousand other Wigan fans, for an all-night vigil on the car park, or a desperate scramble to claim a precious ticket for the Cup Final.

Mary Charnock has worked at Wigan for ten years. Apart from a brief spell on a YTS scheme, it has been her only job since leaving school. She is in complete contrast to the normal run of club secretaries, who are usually middle-aged, male jacks-of-all-trades to the clubs that employ them. Maurice had recruited her on the advice of his secretary in his previous business. 'She kept telling me what a lovely girl she was, but couldn't find a job. I arranged to see her at Central Park one evening, but I forgot all about it. I was working late and Mary waited outside for ninety minutes and never opened her mouth. When I came out, she was still there, so I apologised and offered her the job. It's proved to be the biggest winner I've ever backed. She's as intelligent, if not more so, than any male club secretary I've met in rugby league and she has a great temperament.'

Tall, slim and attractive, Mary is also dauntingly efficient, using the coolness under pressure she had to acquire in her early days at Central Park, when she and Maurice were almost the only full-time staff. 'As well as all the office work, I used to do the sponsorship, sell the advertising for the programme and we even had the club shop in here as well, the one across the road wasn't even thought of then.

'It was a bit of a madhouse at times. I remember a year we got to Wembley, I think it was 1984, when we lost to Widnes, I didn't travel down with the club, I went down later with my family, so they all set off at lunchtime on Friday and I was here on my own. Maurice had told me to lock up and get away about three o'clock, but I couldn't get out of the place.

If I locked the door, they were banging on the windows shouting, "Just sell me a Wigan scarf," and that sort of thing. Jack Robinson turned up in his car to load up some stuff we'd arranged to have on sale at the station the following morning for fans going down by train, and people were surrounding him trying to buy stuff as he was loading it into his car. He finished up selling it out of his car boot on the car park.'

Mary is single, but like her assistant Mandy, she sees the players in a different light from the star-struck teenagers who line the stairs every training night. 'You don't see the players that way, when you spend a lot of time around them, do you? The players are superstars to the girl fans, but to me they're just ordinary blokes. Only the really great ones will be re-membered after they finish playing, the others will soon be forgotten.'

Four of Wigan's single players were sprawled around the office as she was talking, comparing raunchy and extremely explicit notes on their weekend's activities, but Mary affected not to notice, carrying on working imperturbably. At five she put on her coat, pointedly opened the door wide and after the players had filed out, she locked up and headed for home. Her assistant Mandy Roper, is younger, equally attractive and equally dismissive of my attempts to portray them as the most-envied women in Wigan. 'It's their life to some fans, they come in and tell you their problems. You get lots of girls trying to get this and that signed by the players and we get a lot of cards and messages to pass on to them . . . most of them printable too. We have a lot of contact with the players, because most of them are bobbing in and out every day. But socially? I go out with Mary, but I don't go out with the players. I see them out sometimes, but I don't go out with them. I know too much about them.'

She laughed when I asked if the office staff got an end-of-season bonus like the players, saying, 'Does that answer your question? I enjoy the work and meeting people though, apart from the ones on match days, when you get loads of people coming in saying that someone was going to leave tickets for them. If there aren't any for them, they don't get any and if they get stroppy I just walk away.

'When the Cup starts people shove notes through your door, total strangers some of them, trying to get tickets for Wem-bley. We could sell a lot more Wembley tickets than we actually get. The season ticket holders get first pick, but a lot of Wigan fans last year just nipped down to Warrington and bought tickets there. St Helens are a lot better supported, though, so there won't be any spares anywhere this year.'

Of the countless messages and tearful entreaties to players received in the office, Joe Lydon undoubtedly receives far more than his fair share. He works for the club's promotions department in offices above their shop, and as one of the biggest names in a Wigan side full of stars he is a considerable asset to them, a publicist's dream. In any poll of Wigan's army of female fans, he would probably be voted most wanted man by the length of a street. Tall, dark and handsome, articulate, educated and full of charm and humour, he is a world away from the neanderthal stereotype that rugby league players have been unfairly saddled with for years. He is also as popular with his team-mates as he is with the opposite sex.

At 27, one of the elder statesmen of the Wigan team, Lydon has won virtually every team and individual honour in the game during his two-club career. He made his first appearance at Wembley in 1975, playing for Wigan's under-11s in the traditional Cup Final curtain-raiser, and has returned there several times as an adult player.

Despite being born in Wigan, Joe began his career with Widnes, on the eminently respectable professional grounds that they had offered him the best contract. He was actually playing rugby union at the time and had appeared for England Schoolboys, but there was never any doubt that his ultimate destination would be a top rugby league club. Unlike several of the Wigan players, however, playing for his home-town team was never uppermost in Joe's mind. 'To be honest, it wasn't, no. I would have been just as happy to carry on playing union for a while, but when the offers came, it was a matter of accepting the one that gave me the best terms and that was Widnes.'

Joe stayed with Widnes for four-and-a-half years, establishing a reputation as one of the fastest and finest three-quarters in the British game. His speciality was scoring improbable long-range tries and his devoted female following – as extensive then at Widnes as it was to be at Wigan – would begin an orgasmic wail of delight every time he touched the ball. Given that level of adulation, Widnes' decision to sell him to Wigan was either brave or foolhardy, but Joe believes they had little choice, faced with a severe financial crisis. 'I think they needed the money badly. I believe myself and Tony Myler were offered and Wigan came in for me.' Joe himself was almost the last person to know about the transfer. 'I remember saying that I didn't think I'd find out if I was going to be sold until it had happened, and sure enough, a few days after that, they said, "We're selling you to Wigan."'

Since his transfer, Joe has increased the size of his fan club still further and added yet more medals and honours to his already impressive haul, including the Man of Steel award for the player voted the best in the country by the hardest jury to impress – his fellow professionals – and the Lance Todd trophy for the outstanding player in the Challenge Cup Final. He has more medals than a Chelsea pensioner, and the only thing he has so far failed to achieve in the game is to finish on the winning side against Australia, an omission he hopes to rectify during the 1992 Great Britain Tour.

Lydon's versatility has seen him occupy every backline position including scrum-half for Great Britain, and though he would prefer a settled position with Wigan, his regular switches between wing, centre and full-back for his club don't really bother him. Injuries are becoming an increasing problem for him – 'I'm old enough to have seen Joe Lydon play two consecutive games' is a popular press-box joke – but Joe will undoubtedly be recognised as one of the great talents of his own era, though he feels that just as the gap in standards between the clubs is constantly narrowing, so the greater dedication and fitness of modern players is narrowing the gap between the best and the rest.

'There's a different attitude to the game now. It hasn't totally changed, but all the players today have the same attitude that just the great players of the past showed. Everybody now is fitter, faster, wants to win 100 per cent and looks after himself. People used to play it mainly for enjoyment, whereas now – I don't say we don't enjoy playing now – but it is a profession, a business first and foremost for many players. The reason I signed to play rugby league was not for the love of the game, it was for the money. I wouldn't say I was totally professional, but it was the deciding factor.'

In return for the money these professionals earn, their bodies take a pounding every game that would put me in traction for twelve months. The ferocity of the hits each player takes and makes forty and fifty times a game cannot really be understood from the stands or up on the terraces. Get down to pitch level and close to the action, however, and you will not only hear but almost feel the impact, as a fifteen stone prop, legs pounding like pistons, is hit and smashed to the ground by the ferocious impact of a two or three man gang tackle. After the game the players will use ice to bring down the worst of the swelling on bruises and torn and battered muscles. The next morning they will often be so stiff that even getting out of bed will be a major achievement, but by the time they have finished training the following day they will be back in shape and ready to face the punishment again.

Joe Lydon plays down the physical hardness that players must have to play the game. 'I think you get used to the hits and the pounding your body takes. At the start of the season, when you're a little bit soft, you bruise more easily, but then you get hardened to it again, though the bruises get harder to shake off as you get older. Every player has a different pain threshold though. I remember Glyn Shaw getting up and playing the ball with a broken leg here and Mick McTigue at Salford, you could have pulled his leg off and he wouldn't have noticed!'

Just as the impact of the tackles and the speed that the ball travels are not always evident from the stands, the finer points of the game may often elude spectators. Most players probably suspect that the majority of spectators and certainly the majority of journalists, know little about the game. There is a widespread and perhaps justifiable belief that if you have not played the game at the top level, you cannot understand it. Although Joe subscribes to the belief, he is charitable enough to allow the spectators the benefit of the doubt.

'I think a large percentage of the crowd probably understand more about the game than we perhaps think they do, but it's hard to do if you've never played it. You hear a lot of rubbish talked as well of course. The game looks very different from up in the stands too, there's lots of talk goes on out on the pitch that you'd never hear and there are things that might look nasty and aren't and those that don't and are.'

Apart from getting used to the physical battering taken during a game, like all the other players, Joe also stressed the mateship, the loyalty to your team-mates, that kept players on the field, even when injured. 'You tend to stay on the field with injuries because you don't want to let yourself or your mates down. People used to carry injuries into games as well, but that has changed, you don't do it as much now, for two reasons I suppose: there is more pressure on you to perform at your peak and the squads also tend to be bigger. You want to keep your place, but if you play when you're not properly fit and play badly, you will lose your place anyway, perhaps permanently, so it's better to stand down for a week than turn out and play badly. It's very tough to watch the games when you're not playing because of injury though, I've tried sitting everywhere, down on the bench, up in the stands, on the terraces and it's hard to do.'

Joe has suffered at the hands of the tabloids as much as Ellery, but though his private opinion of journalists might not be too different from that of his captain, in public he is open and accessible to them, and a popular interviewee because of his articulacy and wit. He also differs from Hanley and from many of his contemporaries in his plans for after he retires from the game. He has a degree in graphic design and intends to make that his career. 'I'm not planning to go into coaching when I finish. I work in the promotions department for Wigan at the moment, but when I finish playing I'll go into graphic design. A lot of players do go into coaching straight away, but I think they should stand back from it for a while. It's very hard to be a player on Monday and a coach on Tuesday; you might have the respect of the players as a player but you won't have the authority you need as a coach.'

Mission Impossible

WIGAN'S games against St Helens are normally among the highlights of the season, but jammed amongst so many other fixtures, neither players nor fans had time to devote to their normal build-up to the game against St Helens. Saints were almost as battle-weary as Wigan, having played their Challenge Cup semi-final against Widnes on the previous Saturday, followed by a Championship match against the same opponents two days later.

Though Wigan-Saints derbies are never less than fiercely fought, there was no great incentive for St Helens to really pull the stops out for this one, the result mattering little to their final league position. Just the same, after squandering a string of early chances, Wigan were grateful for the boot of Frano Botica, who landed five fine goals and for an astonishing power-burst from Kelvin Skerrett, who wrenched himself free of four or five tacklers before plunging over the line, to keep them in front. A spirited Saints challenge finally subsided late in the game, as two Wigan tries in the last five minutes wrapped up a 28–14 victory.

Once again there were injuries to add to the already crippling toll. Andy Platt limped off after only a few minutes, clutching his hip, Kevin Iro injured his knee, Kelvin Skerrett collected a knock and Martin Dermott finished out on the wing after damaging an arm. Despite his injury, he was able to score a try from that unaccustomed position, pouncing on Andy Gregory's grubber kick. As he swaggered back to the half-way line, collecting 'high fives' from his exultant team-mates, Dermott called out, 'Martin Offiah eat your heart out!'

With Shaun Edwards, Steve Hampson, and Ian Lucas missing from the starting line-up too, Wigan had more reason than usual to be grateful for the brilliance of Andy Gregory and Ellery Hanley, who inspired them to the victory against Saints and then repeated the dose with an even more patched up team three days later, to send Castleford packing 24–4.

The fixture congestion was obviously beginning to affect the directors almost as much as the players. Jack Robinson turned up at Central Park at 2.00 p.m. on the day of the Castleford match. He looked round the deserted car park in astonishment, before remembering that the game was not scheduled to kick off until 8.00 p.m. that evening. 'We were all waiting for him to say he was disappointed with the crowd,' laughed John Monie, who was watching from the office at the time.

As a result of the mounting injury-toll, Monie had chosen Andy Goodway at centre, Phil Clarke was at stand-off and 'A' team coach Graeme West started his first game in eighteen months at prop. There was also a surprise recall to the substitutes bench for Bobby Goulding, now back in training and down in weight after eating nothing much more filling than humble pie since the collapse of his transfer to Leeds. Despite their makeshift side, Wigan dominated from first to last. Led by the incomparable Hanley, the defence was absolutely impregnable, while Gregory again prompted the attack to create the tries that won the game. Andy was playing the best football of even his outstanding career and it seemed that he and Hanley by sheer example and effort of will could drag themselves and their team-mates to another title. Not that any of their team-mates was shirking the effort needed.

The stop-gaps all did their job admirably, Goodway fashioning a try for Myers with a pass that no regular centre could have bettered, while Goulding came on to lay on a try for Hanley. West got through his share of the defensive workload and then returned after a spell on the bench to score the final try of the night from Gregory's pass, earning a standing ovation that was still continuing as the final whistle sounded. Monie ran on to the field punching the air, an extraordinary display of emotion from the normally reserved coach.

'I was as moved with emotion as the crowd when Graeme scored in the dying seconds. I don't think I've ever witnessed a happier scene at any ground; the sea of raised, clapping hands on every section of the stadium was truly a sight to see. The players clearly felt the need to thank all the fans for their tremendous support and I too joined in. I didn't come on to the pitch to celebrate, the win was splendid, but the battle isn't over yet. I came on because I too wanted to thank the fans for their dedication and their loyalty.'

During the frenzied run-in to the Championship, Monie had been enforcing a rule that those players with injuries automatically missed the next match, allowing time for their battered bodies to recover a little, but the next game, only two days later, was the most crucial of all, against Widnes. For that game Monie selected his strongest available team, after carrying out late fitness tests on no fewer than six injured players.

The Tuesday night match against Widnes was for the Championship. If Wigan won, they had only to win one of their remaining two games to take the title. If they lost, Widnes would be champions, providing they won their final game at home to the relegated bottom club Rochdale, a formality if ever there was one.

Despite the battering Wigan had taken over the previous few weeks, when John Monie picked his side, only one player, Kevin Iro, was missing from his first-choice line-up. The chosen team was: Steve Hampson; David Myers, Dean Bell, Joe Lydon, Frano Botica; Shaun Edwards, Andy Gregory; Ian Lucas, Martin Dermott, Kelvin Skerrett, Andy Platt, Denis Betts, Ellery Hanley. The substitutes were Andy Goodway and Phil Clarke.

The most surprising inclusion was Shaun Edwards, who had been troubled by a groin injury which was sufficiently serious for him to consult a London specialist. There were worries that Shaun would even miss the Cup Final, but he returned from his trip to London on the day of the Widnes match, to announce that the specialist had found no major problem. Shaun had been for a training run, felt no ill-effects and was completely confident that he could both play and last the full eighty minutes. One or two of his team-mates expressed amused cynicism about Shaun's miracle cure. 'I wish I could find a train that would get me to Lourdes and back as quickly as that,' said Martin Dermott. 'He'd have played against Castleford on Sunday,' said Andy Platt, 'except that there was a blind man and a leper in the queue ahead of him.'

The team met as usual ninety minutes before the 8.00 p.m. kick-off and John Monie showed a videotape of five minutes from Widnes' last game against Sheffield, highlighting a couple of weaknesses he had spotted, before going on to talk about the night's game. 'We want to have had more time in possession at the end of this game than Widnes. We want more of the ball than them. If we do that, we'll win, it's that simple. This is a team that don't play the advantage line very well. They tend to throw the ball back and back and back, so if we meet them at the advantage line we can hit them for a loss.

'Now there are two things we have to concentrate on. Number one is Phil McKenzie. McKenzie is the one that makes them tick. McKenzie makes the run before they score the try. McKenzie calls the shots. So the first priority is: Get McKenzie. Markers one and two at the play-the-ball, don't go chasing off across the field, get McKenzie. If he tries to get out of there, put him on his arse. I want plenty of name-dropping out there, drop his name all the time and get him.

'Number two is Jonathan Davies. He's got a left-foot step. If you're lining him up, move your left hand before you move in and that's the way that he'll step. He does their downtowns, but what he often does on the sixth tackle is to fake the kick, step to the left and then take off. Stay on McKenzie first on the sixth tackle, though, don't leave him until he's passed the ball, otherwise he'll go himself and then kick. The first thing is get McKenzie. Then when he's passed it, go for Davies. Don't try and charge the kick down, go to tackle him. If he steps the first marker, the second gets him.

'They've got a few players in the team that aren't so keen on tackling. They just want to get a big hit on you, so you can spin off them or step them. Now you've had two days' rest, but we've just got to play on enthusiasm and because we're all mates. So all your strength has got to go on being one. We've got to help each other and feed off each other. One person can get tired, but the whole team can't get tired. OK. Don't worry too much about the pictures on this last tape. It's the words that are important.'

He showed them a brief videotape centred on the Australian rugby league player Ray Price, a man who 'never took a backward step' in one of the favourite clichés of rugby league coaches, and who gave his all every time he stepped onto the field. The theme of the tape was the mateship, the friendship, the loyalty, that he inspired in others around him. When the tape finished Monie turned up the lights, saying, 'Stick together and nobody can beat us. Let's get 'em. Let's go.'

The Central Park stands and terraces were packed long before the kick-off. The gates were shut against a few thousand more who couldn't get in, many of them transferring to the only free spectators' area at Central Park, a section of the ring-road with a view of a quarter of the pitch. A press-box humourist pointed at them. 'Look, there's Maurice Lindsay selling them tickets to stand there.' About 2,000 people lined the pavement and stood on the grassy mound on the far side of the dual carriageway, desperate to see what they could of the game, but just as important perhaps, to be part of the biggest night of Wigan's year so far.

In the dressing room, divorced from the noise and mounting excitement on the terraces, the players were going through their usual pre-match routines, taking turns on the treatment table to be rubbed down, stretching and jogging on the spot to warm-up, getting strapped-up by Denis and Keith, or hassling Taffy for tie-ups, shoulder pads and electricians' tape.

The tension in the dressing room even affected me; I could feel my stomach knotting and my jaw clenching. There was a cold determination about the players. The long winning run and the shared hardship of battling against a cruel fixture pile-up had seemingly fused these very disparate individuals into an unified whole. If there was any resentment, it was against the events conspiring to take their title away from them. The tension was still very evident, of course, but the dominant impression was of grim confidence, controlled anger, even fury. I began to feel rather sorry for Widnes; it was their big night too, but from the look of the Wigan players, the Chemics didn't have a prayer.

Andy Gregory and Joe Lydon were having their strapping applied in the boot room. 'This is our room,' said Joe, 'all the ones who've been banned from the other one for laughing before a game come in here.' Sure enough both were cracking a constant stream of jokes, to each other and to anyone else wandering in.

'Just run at Davies,' said Gregory to Andy Goodway, as he came in to get some tape. 'You saw what he's like the other day. He was that low going into the tackle I thought he'd dropped 10p. Olga Korbut couldn't get that low.'

'Yeah, it doesn't matter if we don't get through,' replied Goodway, 'just keep running at Davies, make him work and then he'll drop out of the line. Anyway, if they can't be bully-boys, they're a shower of shite this team.' A very nervous-looking Phil Clarke wandered in, saying, 'It's once more into the breach then.'

'William Shakespeare, who does he play for?' asked Joe. Martin Dermott, looking for headache pills, was the next victim. 'What is it Derms?' said Joe. 'PMT – pre-match tension?'

The walking wounded had their injuries padded or treated to get them through the game. Dr Zaman, the team doctor, gave Andy Platt a pain-killing injection in the hip that he had injured against St Helens, Ian Lucas had a sore elbow strapped to minimise lateral movement of the joint, others had the regular strapping needed to protect ankles, wrists and fingers from future damage or prevent old injuries recurring.

The players were due to go out and warm-up fifteen minutes before the kick-off. By 7.40 p.m. all were changed, strapped and ready. The touch-judge had already been in to inspect their studs and check for rings on their fingers. As the tension built even higher, more and more players were talking and exhorting each other; at times four or five would be talking at once.

Ellery spoke for the first time, silencing his team-mates. 'I'll tell you now, you've got to be squeaky clean with this ref. If you're even an inch offside he'll pull you up for it.'

'I don't want you to try and cheat to win penalties,' said Monie. 'We just want to play this game and win. Just give 100 per cent all the time, and if we get a fair shake from the referee, we'll blow them off the park.'

Bill Hartley led the players out for the warm-up, to a huge reception from the capacity crowd. Monie stayed in the dressing room, studying his notes, while the other members of the back-up crew stood around, waiting to complete their last minute tasks when the players returned. 'How long will Andy Platt last?' Monie asked Dr Zaman.

'The injection should last ninety minutes, Joe had the same one before the Cup Final last year. Unless Andy does something stupid, he won't have any pain.'

'I'm hoping to get him off after sixty minutes, if I can.'

Graeme West was joking to Keith and Denis about the last minute try he had scored against Castleford. 'Old ladies have been coming up to me in the street saying "We're proud of you." It's unbelievable.' The players returned, sweating from the warm-up. Kelvin Skerrett, breathing heavily, headed straight for his peg to use the inhaler for his asthma. There were now just five minutes to the kick-off. Ellery began his brief address to his team, punctuated by dull thuds from the next dressing room as one of the Widnes players psyched himself up by punching the wall.

'All those wins in the past mean shite if we don't win tonight,' said Ellery. 'Basics, that's what we've got to do – good tackling.'

'Fundamentals,' interrupted Monie. 'Keep thinking "I must move up in defence." You attack in defence, you attack in defence.'

'We can't come back next week,' chipped in Andy Gregory. 'We do it tonight.'

The referee's whistle sounded from the corridor, calling the teams out. The Wigan players stayed in the dressing room, waiting for Widnes go out first. As the sound of the Widnes players' boots receded down the corridor, the Wigan players formed a circle around the treatment table and all began jogging on the spot. At a command from Ellery they began to sprint on the spot, their studs beating out a staccato tattoo on the floor, all the players yelling out 'ONE-TWO-THREE-FOUR-FIVE-SIX-SEVEN-EIGHT-NINE-TEN.' Then all put their right hands together into the centre of the circle, turned and filed out of the dressing room. A television crew, two or three hangers-on and a few stewards and club officials hovered in the narrow passageway, but the players ignored them, their eyes fixed on the pool of light at the end of the tunnel leading to the pitch.

The storm of cheering and booing that greeted Widnes had subsided. Every eye was now trained on the gap in the wooden screen surrounding the new stand, from which Wigan would emerge. The crowd erupted as Wigan came out of the tunnel, led by Ellery Hanley, MBE. He walked with a slow, measured tread, a gait suited to his exalted position as the sport's most highly-paid and gifted practitioner. Former Wigan wing Henderson Gill used to swagger across the Central Park pitch as if crossing the floor of a disco, but Ellery walks with the demeanour of a businessman entering the office to start work for the day.

Past the posts, Ellery turned his back to face his players and tapped hands with each one as they broke into a trot and fanned out past him in a V-formation, catharsis for the crowd, who cheered themselves hoarse at the sight of their heroes advancing to destroy their most-hated rivals. Handfuls of torn paper tossed in the air by the fans to greet their team, drifted down to the ground like snow.

John Monie and Harry Pinner ascended to the 'crow's nest', the television gantry overlooking the pitch which is Monie's preferred place from which to watch the game, while the rest of the coaching staff, the two substitutes and the other members of the squad, Ian Gildart, Gerard Stazicker and the reprieved Bobby Goulding, filed out to the trainers' bench in front of the stand. The crowd fell silent as the teams lined up for the kick-off, then, as referee Ray Tennant blew his whistle, a deafening roar went up from 30,000 throats, echoing off the roofs of the stands and drowning Central Park in noise.

Wigan began with assurance, Andy Platt almost crossing the line early on, only to fall to a despairing tackle by the Widnes full back Stuart Spruce, while an Andy Gregory grubber kick into the in-goal area was just seized by Martin Offiah as the Wigan attackers closed in. The intense pressure to which Widnes were being subjected finally told as they conceded a penalty for offside, which Frano Botica converted to put his side ahead.

A few minutes into the game, Wigan already looked in complete control, only to be stung by a try out of nothing. Widnes centre John Devereux side-stepped a floundering Joe Lydon and burst clear. His pass inside sent his fellow Welshman – Widnes danger-man number two – Jonathan Davies, haring for the posts. Though David Myers got back to knock him down just short of the line, Myers's momentum carried him past Davies and unhindered, the Welshman struggled to his feet to score, adding the conversion to put Widnes ahead 6–2.

Wigan merely stepped up their effort, pinning Widnes back in their own territory through the power of their running and the astute kicking of Gregory and Edwards. They were making good yardage up the middle through the forwards and threatening danger out wide when Gregory and Edwards linked to set the predatory Dean Bell loose. A try appeared certain as Martin Dermott broke round the ruck and looked to off-load the scoring pass to Kelvin Skerrett, but the big prop had been illegally held back and Wigan were forced to accept the penalty goal instead, again kicked by Botica.

Five minutes later, another 'professional foul' by a Widnes player, who held down Myers to stop a quick play-the-ball and an almost certain score, escaped its just punishment when Botica's kick rebounded from the post, but rough justice was administered by the New Zealander when he squeezed over in the left corner from Edwards's pass a few minutes later. Widnes protested vehemently that Botica had flattened the corner-flag as he dived in through two tackles, the referee disagreed. The whistle blew for half-time with Wigan ahead by 8 points to 6.

The first half had been played at a ferocious pace with only three scrums and a handful of penalties to disrupt the flow of the game, but if Wigan were feeling the pace after so many tiring games in so short a time, they showed no sign of it. Widnes' reserves of strength must also have been sapped in a first half in which they had been under constant pressure. John Monie confirmed that impression when he entered the dressing room.

'OK. Now just sit down, drink some liquid and get some air. Anybody hurt, anyone carrying a knock?' No one replied. 'We've had to make 111 tackles, but they've done about 150 next door. So we're looking at six tackle football this half, field position, good defence and they're gone. The score's close because Joe missed a tackle badly. When you line up a tackle, don't put your head down on the grass, stay upright, get in close first and then, bang, hit him. Now its commitment, it's enthusiasm and it's all about tackling for the next forty minutes. What's the good of me coming in here talking though? I'm not going to say something clever. You all know what needs to be done already.'

Monie left the dressing-room to return to his eyrie, leaving Ellery to complete the interval speech-making. He spoke with hushed urgency, trying to infuse his players with his own unbreakable will. 'I need the commitment of everyone here. Forty minutes, that's all it is. Good defence, but by commitment I mean most of all good talk out there. Keep talking, keep name-dropping McKenzie, keep geeing each other up. We're not going to throw away all those matches we've won now.'

He broke off to go and give Joe a quick word of encouragement, the man singled out by Monie for the error that had led to Widnes' try, then turned back to the team. 'Right let's have a "ten" before we go back out there.' Again the players formed a circle, chanting from one to ten as their studs thundered on the floor. As they clasped hands in the centre, Ellery shouted 'After three – Wigan. One. Two. Three. WIGAN.' They roared it in unison, then followed him back down the tunnel to the pitch.

The second half began the way the first had ended, with Wigan applying relentless pressure to a creaking Widnes defence. Another professional foul cost Widnes a further 2 points, as Botica punished them with his third goal of the night. Five minutes later, Wigan put daylight between themselves and their challengers as Edwards sped in at the corner, with the Widnes defence in disarray after just keeping Myers out under the posts. Botica's brilliant touchline conversion put the champions ahead by 16–6.

Widnes were finished. Hanley was recalled as he crossed the line for a borderline forward pass from Skerrett, but it made no difference. Denis Betts capped a towering game for Wigan with a good try shortly afterwards and Phil Clarke completed the scoring two minutes before the final whistle, forcing the ball down despite the attentions of four Widnes defenders. The scoreboard read: Wigan 26 Widnes 6, and the crowd stayed to cheer the Wigan players to the rafters as they lapped the pitch, waving and applauding the fans who had willed them to victory.

Once back in the dressing room, the first words from Wigan's ultra-professionals were predictable. 'We've won nothing yet, one more and then we can celebrate.' Just as predictable were the cautionary words of their inspirational captain. 'Be careful of all the back-slappers,' said Ellery. 'Don't go silly, do the sensible thing, get plenty of rest before Thursday.'

'Mission Impossible', said Shaun Edwards, quoting a press comment by his coach when Wigan began their eleven games in thirty-two days. 'One more and we'll have done it.'

'What do you want to do?' asked John Monie, slightly tongue-in-cheek. 'You can either have Thursday off and win the competition at Leeds on Saturday, or you can beat Bradford here on Thursday and then have Saturday off.'

'Thursday' they all shouted, 'and then we'll win on Saturday as well.'

'Glad to hear it' added Maurice Lindsay, 'and we'll be absolutely delighted to have to pay you a winning bonus of

£1,250 on Thursday night.' The cheers that greeted his remark showed that Wigan are ultra-professionals in every way.

A Test of Character

EVEN in a town as satiated with rugby league success as Wigan, the achievements of the team in overcoming the almost insuperable mental and physical obstacles to put the title within reach, inspired the Wigan public. John Monie was deluged with letters expressing admiration for his staff and his players.

Among them was a letter from a couple writing to praise not only the performance on the field, but the 'caring nature of the players, especially Ellery Hanley and Andy Gregory, for acknowledging the people in wheelchairs.' Those included the couple's son, facing eighteen months with both legs in plaster because of a rare disease. 'They have helped him cope that bit better and have made our job of looking after him that much easier. When he gets upset and down-hearted, he can be reminded of that "Special Night" when he met two of the players.'

An 83-year-old woman, who had watched Wigan since the age of four, also wrote praising the team and asking to meet the players to express her admiration in person, though she had already made the acquaintance of one of them. 'I gave Ellery a hug when he came over to the disabled fans after the match on Tuesday.' That gesture by Hanley and Gregory was spontaneous, with no thought of publicity or reward. If the attentions of the fans can sometimes be wearisome for players in search of a quiet night out, there is nonetheless a genuine warmth and loyalty towards the supporters who follow them so devotedly.

Another fan wrote enclosing £5 for the 'players' pool'. 'I know it's not much, but it is to me. I just feel compelled to send a little something as a token of my admiration for the lads' heroic efforts of late. I'm just so proud it's unbelievable. It's two days since I last took my Wigan "bobble" hat off my head. I'm so high that if I get any higher, I'm going to need oxygen.'

Two days after the Widnes game, Central Park was again packed with those, and another 20,000 expectant supporters, as Wigan faced Bradford Northern, seeking the win that would give them the title. The Championship trophy had already been brought to Central Park, to the superstitious fear of one or two of the office staff. 'I don't like it being here before we've won it, it might be unlucky,' said one. The trophy sat on Maurice's desk, discreetly, if ingloriously shrouded in a black bin-liner.

Kelvin Skerrett and John Monie arrived shortly before the team meeting, having attended the disciplinary hearing into Kelvin's sending-off at Rochdale. Both were in filthy moods, for Kelvin had been handed a four match suspension, which, if sustained on appeal, would rule him out of all Wigan's remaining games, including the Challenge Cup Final. Monie took Graeme West on one side for a word, fearful of the hot-tempered Skerrett's reaction out on the pitch. 'Keep your eye on Skerrett, Graeme. If you think he's only going through the motions or if you think he's going in too hard, we'll have to do something about it.'

In the team meeting Monie went through his familiar routine, highlighting a few opposition strengths and weaknesses and stressing the qualities that would take his side to victory. He had a particular warning about Bradford's loose forward John Pendlebury. 'The worst memory I've got from when they beat us in the Regal Trophy is of Pendlebury stepping past a Wigan player waving an arm at him, before strolling in for a try. I still get nightmares about that. Don't let it happen again. He's got a left-foot step, don't miss him. He's not that good, get into his ribs. We've come too far not to get it tonight. Tonight's the night boys, let's get it.'

Later, in the dressing-room, Monie paced the room, delivering his now familiar lecture. 'It's the same story again, a player can get tired, but the team can't get tired. Make the opposition tired instead, because we're terrorising them. Now the only people who want us to win this title are people who live in Wigan and the people in this room. Nobody else is going to help us to do it, so it's down to you working for each other, working as one.'

If Wigan's power, class and professionalism in defeating Widnes had taken them to the brink of the title, they had to summon some more old-fashioned virtues to rescue an apparently lost cause against Bradford. Right from the kick-off it was obvious that this was going to be a very different game. Bradford's big pack held their own in the forward exchanges and though Wigan dominated territorially, Bradford took the few chances that came their way, while Wigan could not get across the Bradford line. Only a few minutes into the game, Monie's nightmare from the Regal Trophy was repeated, as Pendlebury side-stepped a feeble tackle and broke clear. His pass sent Bradford's captain, David Hobbs, diving in under the posts. A second try to their Kiwi scrum-half, Brett Iti, left them 12–2 ahead at the break, Wigan's only response a Frano Botica penalty.

Wigan's defence had been far from perfect in the first half. The team looked jaded – understandably after their gruelling run-in to the title – and there were ominous signs of injuries. Andy Gregory had injured his groin and was hobbling pain-fully. Andy Platt, Joe Lydon and Shaun Edwards were all struggling as well. John Monie was in no mood to find excuses in the injuries or their tiredness, however. He got them all seated in the dressing room, gave them five minutes to rest and think and then ripped into them. 'We fought all this way to get here, the title is within our grasp and we're going down without a fight. To come all this way and then go out like cowards.

'This is like the Sydney Grand Final, win this game and we've won the Championship, and yet we've got some players that I haven't even rated three out of ten on their first-half showing. Tell me you're tired and I'll take you off the field.'

No-one responded. 'This is a test of character. This is when you find out what's inside you. Squeeze an orange and you get orange-juice out of it, because that's what's inside it. Now you've come to the squeeze and we're finding out what's inside you. I don't want players who are great when we're winning, I want players who'll dig deep into their guts when we're struggling.

'I hope you're angry, you've got a right to be angry, they've got 10 more points than you. Don't worry about scoring the 10 points, you'll score the points, worry about not letting them score any more. It's defence that'll win this title. Stop them scoring this half and we'll win the title. Get into them. The Wembley team will be made up of tacklers; I won't take anybody to Wembley who won't put his neck on the line tonight. There are fifteen of you. Together as a team let's win the title.'

I had never seen Monie as angry, his normally cool, unemotional front had been stripped away to show the raw nerves underneath. When he had finished speaking, Ellery rose to his feet. 'These are our 2 Championship points. We're not going to let them have our 2 points, not in our own backyard.' Despite the words, the atmosphere was flat. There were no 'give me tens' during this interval, the players filed out for the second half in silence.

They started by laying siege to Bradford's line for five minutes, but when Bradford broke out, it was to score another try. Their wing, Gerald Cordle, got free on the right and though a despairing cover tackle stopped him two yards short, the defence was in tatters and centre Darrall Shelford was able to dive over straight from the play-the-ball. A fine conversion left Wigan 18–2 down and apparently out for the count.

Gregory was in obvious pain as he struggled with his groin injury and he would certainly have been substituted if Monie had not reasoned that the departure of Wigan's chief playmaker would have signalled to both sides that the game was up. Gregory stayed on the field, as did Joe Lydon despite a hamstring pull, and Shaun Edwards, who was also feeling the effects of a groin injury, a recurrence of the problem solved in Tuesday's miracle 'cure'. Straight from the re-start after the Bradford try, Ellery showed that he was willing to take on Bradford single-handed if necessary, scattering defenders in an awesome burst. It awoke the crowd, which had been strangely quiet throughout the first half, sensing Wigan's disarray. As they roared Wigan on, Hanley and Skerrett, having a towering game against his former colleagues, lifted Wigan's spirits as they carried the battle to the enemy. Helped by a string of penalties, Wigan piled on the pressure and steadily whittled away the deficit. Denis Betts dived over straight from a tap penalty and Botica's touchline conversion made it 18–8. Two penalties by Botica took the score to 18–12 and then Skerrett roared through for a try, scattering defenders like chaff. Botica's conversion levelled the scores.

Five minutes from the end, Skerrett seemed to have secured the title, plunging over the line, only to be recalled as the referee ruled Gregory's pass forward. Still Wigan could have won it. In the final minute of normal time, Frano Botica's drop-goal attempt faded a yard wide of the posts, and then, as the clock ticked into injury time, they spurned the chance to clinch the game. The forwards drove the ball towards the posts, but under the shadow of the cross-bar, only a yard from the line, Wigan unaccountably ignored the opportunity to drop a goal from the easiest of positions, in favour of an attempt to score a try. Bradford's defence stifled the threat and Wigan had no time for a further attempt.

The supporters' bitter disappointment at the failure to win and clinch the title was outweighed by recognition of the stupendous effort of will required to come back from the dead, overhauling a 16 point deficit, despite the weariness and the injury toll brought about by their incessant programme of fixtures. The crowd acclaimed Wigan's effort as loudly as if their heroes were parading the Championship trophy, but the Wigan players now knew that they would have to climb the mountain once more in the final game at Leeds, to be certain of the title. They would also have to do so without several key men.

The players sat grey-faced with fatigue in the dressing room, completely drained. John Monie sat on the bench with them, too dispirited to speak more than a few words. 'I just can't understand why you didn't go for the field goal when you had the position right under the posts.' No-one was willing or able to enlighten him. What seemed obvious from the crow's nest may have been less so on the pitch, where minds as well as bodies were fogged with fatigue.

Andy Gregory could scarcely walk, the groin trouble that had plagued him for two years having flared again. Shaun Edwards also had his groin packed in ice. Andy Platt had already played two games with pain-killing injections in his injured hip and would require another before taking the field at Headingley. Joe Lydon's hamstring made him a certain non-starter, while Kevin Iro's knee was scarcely healed sufficiently to allow him to return.

The Wigan players had already shown character, resilience, resolve, team-spirit and sheer endurance beyond belief, they now had less than forty-eight hours to recover, before being asked to summon up all those qualities once more in a last desperate effort to clinch the title. The cruellest irony of all, though none referred to it, was that the Bradford game was the one postponed back in January because of the failure to switch on the under-soil heating. At the time, Wigan were fresh and just beginning their winning run, while Bradford could scarcely manage to win against anyone. Had the game been played on schedule, Wigan would almost certainly have taken the two points and the victory over Widnes would then have given them the title. As it was, if they were to lose at Leeds, Wigan might look back on the failure to switch on the under-soil heating as the single thing that had cost them the title.

Champions

WIGAN'S battle-weary players assembled for the coach journey to Leeds knowing that if they could drag one more effort from their exhausted bodies, the title would be theirs. Hardly a player in the side was not carrying some sort of injury. As Joe Lydon remarked, 'At this rate we'll be sponsored by Zimmers at Wembley.'

Several players needed pain-killing jabs before the game. Physiotherapist Denis Wright was far from happy about it, but realised there was no alternative. 'It's ridiculous, playing with pain-killing jabs is just storing up trouble for the future. Some of these injuries may not even be right for next season. Andy Platt is playing with a jab for the third game in a row, Shaun Edwards has one in his groin, Martin Dermott's got one in his ankle, Kevin Iro in his knee.'

Denis was also unimpressed by the remarks of some old-timers, who dismissed Wigan's complaints about the fixture back-log, claiming that they used to play forty games a season without trouble. 'There's no comparison between the old times and now, or between this and other sports. People talk about other physical contact sports, but this isn't a physical contact sport, it's a high-speed collision sport.

'In the old days they used to train by doing a couple of laps of the pitch and then having a game of "tig and pass" and they built team spirit by how many pints they could sup. There's no comparison with the fitness players now have, nor the impacts they have to take.'

The non-playing members of the squad, Andy Gregory, Ged Stazicker, Joe Lydon, Mike Forshaw and Kelvin Skerrett, who was beginning his four-match suspension, had made the trip to Headingley to support their mates. Bart Simpson had also been recruited for Wigan's Wembley campaign. Stazicker, nicknamed 'Bart' by Andy Gregory because of the alleged similarity of hairstyles, was wearing a tee shirt emblazoned 'Wigan at Wembley '91' with Bart Simpson pictured wearing Wigan kit and snarling 'Eat my shorts – it's our cup.'

The players spread out around the capacious Headingley dressing room, Shaun sitting in one corner, listening to his Walkman. In the opposite corner, Bobby Goulding knelt in prayer, facing the wall. Steve Hampson pointed this out to Andy Platt, saying, 'Have you seen Bobby?'

'Don't knock him for it.'

'I'm not, I'm just saying. I've never seen him do that before.'

Shaun disappeared into the showers, where Dr Zaman was running a production line, administering pain-killing jabs. 'That hurt like hell,' said Shaun, emerging wincing a couple of minutes later. 'That's the worst pain I'll have to take today.'

The atmosphere in the dressing room was completely different from that before the Bradford game. This time there was the same kind of quiet confidence, the grim will to succeed, that there had been before the Widnes match. Despite their fatigue, the players looked ready to give whatever was needed to win. As the minutes ticked away towards the kick-off, Monie ordered all the players to sit down and began his last, and most important pre-match address of the Championship season.

'On Thursday night I didn't feel like coaching and you guys didn't look like you felt like playing. You wanted to win, but you weren't prepared to pay the price. Today the atmosphere is better. Today's the day that we put our bodies on the line. For the first fifteen minutes, just rip and tear and bust. Play it by the rules though, no cheap shots, no penalties. Let's be careful, get back from the five yard line by half a step and talk to the referee, "Is this alright, ref, am I back far enough?" that sort of thing.

'Now first of all, advance the ball. Do some of the forward plays and moves that we've practised. But don't do anything in the first fifteen minutes that you aren't prepared to do in the last minute as well. Play this game like it's your last game ever. Play it like this is the game people will remember you for. Play it like it's the last game of your career. Whatever it takes to do, we'll do it to win today.'

Bobby Goulding needed no urging from his coach to give his all. A big game from Goulding might well give him a place in Wigan's Wembley line-up, for Andy Gregory's torn groin made it possible that he would be unfit to play. If Wigan needed a replacement scrum-half at Wembley, Goulding was determined that no-one would be chosen ahead of him.

Wigan began the match with awesome authority. This was once more the controlled, calculated football that they had so often played on the run-in to the title; total professionalism, unyielding, often brutal defence, power running and clinical execution on attack. The forwards, Lucas, Dermott, Platt, Betts, Clarke and Hanley gave the Leeds pack a battering and behind them Bobby Goulding was everywhere. His drop goal gave Wigan an early lead and he continued to torment Leeds, making darting, zig-zagging breaks, hunting alertly for half chances off the runs of his forwards and varying his kicking game superbly. One minute he was kicking deep to the corners, the next he was chipping over the top, threading touch-finders through a forest of legs or sneaking grubber kicks just behind Leeds' defensive line.

Wigan were in complete control, and though it took twenty-five minutes for them to register their first try, there was no sign of alarm. When they had the ball, they were playing out their six tackles, forcing Leeds to bear a heavy defensive workload. By contrast, the home side were error-prone, pressured by Wigan's savage defence into yielding the ball early in the tackle-count through forced passes or handling errors. Their ex-All Black full back, John Gallagher, was having a nightmare game, unable to put a foot right, but it was an error by the wing John Bentley that gave Wigan their first try.

A steepling Bobby Goulding 'bomb' bounced off Bentley's shoulder as he vainly tried to catch it. Shaun Edwards booted the ball against Gallagher's body when he tried to clean up, Phil Clarke collected the rebound and his overhead pass was finger-tipped down by Andy Goodway, playing out of position in the centre, who scored close enough to the posts for Frano Botica to add the conversion.

Goulding's second dropped goal extended Wigan's lead, and though Leeds reduced the arrears with a penalty shortly before half-time, right on the hooter Hanley got in on the drop goal act, his first ever in five years at Wigan, to send them in at the break 9–2 ahead. There was still some way to go, but the title was now firmly within their grasp.

John Monie was waiting for them when they reached the dressing room. 'You've had twenty-four possessions, twenty-four uses of the ball in that half, so they've had to do a hell of a lot of tackles next door.' While Monie was speaking, Shaun was having a further pain-killing injection in his groin. Just as in the Championship decider and the Cup Final of the previous season, it seemed that he was once more fated to play a vital game for Wigan through a haze of pain.

'Now take your shirts and shorts off, all of you,' said Monie. 'You're going back out there in new gear and you're going to start all over again, as if this was the start of the game; a new forty minutes and a new attitude. The biggest mistake we could make is to think we've already got it won.

'What you've got to do for the next forty minutes is to keep fighting one more round. You're never beaten as long as you'll fight one more round. Get up and fight one more round. Drag yourself to your feet and fight one more round. Keep dragging your mate up and fight one more round.' The players filed out for the last forty minutes of the Championship season.

As they left, Graeme West turned to Monie and asked 'Did we really have the ball for twenty-four possessions in the first half?'

'Let's see. Yes, this time we really did.'

Bobby Goulding soon stretched Wigan's lead with his third drop goal of the day, but Ellery Hanley was forced to leave the field after pulling a hamstring during a typically powerful burst downfield. The departure of their captain could have been a morale-shaking blow for Wigan, but instead they merely tightened their grip. Again they were playing out their full six tackles, forcing the tiring Leeds forwards into greater and greater defensive efforts, while Leeds continued to cough up the ball early in their tackle count. Wigan were getting no favours from the referee on this occasion, but they had no need of them. After a relentless period of pressure, Leeds cracked, Martin Dermott throwing a huge dummy and diving over from close-range.

Leeds hit back with a well-worked try after their one fluid passing movement of the game to close the gap to 6 points – one converted try – but Wigan passed this character test, too, with flying colours. A punch thrown in a tackle by a Leeds defender enabled Botica to extend Wigan's lead back to two scores and Denis Betts then guaranteed the victory and the title, picking up and diving over the line for the final try. There could not have been a more appropriate person to score the deciding try, for Betts had played in every single game of the season for Wigan and his contribution to their Championship had been massive.

As the hooter sounded, Hanley limped back on to the field to embrace each of his players, then climbed up to the podium, followed by his team, to collect the trophy and the sponsor's cheque for £44,000. They walked, rather than ran their lap of honour; few of the players could have managed even to break into a trot. They had given their all, but they had the reward.

Their travelling band of supporters, far out-numbering the home fans, gave them a rapturous welcome. Many had dug deep into their own reserves during the hectic closing weeks of the season. The loan-sharks had been doing a brisk trade, enabling some to meet the cost of a game every two or three days. Many Leeds fans also stayed after the final whistle, applauding the worthy champions. It was a generous gesture of recognition, mirrored by one of the Leeds directors, Harry Jepson, also the President of the Rugby League. He went into the Wigan dressing-room to add his own congratulations. 'In the entire history of the game, I don't think a team has ever achieved what you have done. This will go down in the history of the game as the greatest Championship feat ever. It reflects great credit on you and on Wigan. No other team in the world – and I mean in the world – could have done it.'

Maurice Lindsay and his directors popped champagne corks and shook hands with each other, the players and the back-room staff, who had worked as tirelessly as everybody connected with the club to land the game's greatest prize, despite the crippling programme. The reporters flooded in, prodding John Monie to criticise the system that had forced his team into such a fixture pile-up, but he contented himself with a couple of brief remarks.

'I'm just a coach, we have administrators to sort out this kind of thing, but I'm sure they will be reflecting on what we've had to do. The players went through pain barriers galore to win all those games, theirs was the physical endeavour. I sincerely hope that no other club is ever asked to play such a gruelling programme again; I have witnessed an awful lot of suffering over the past few weeks. Rugby league isn't supposed to be a test of endurance.' Immediately afterwards he lightened the mood, saying, 'We've got a week off before the next game. I don't know what I'll do with myself.'

'It'll be like a summer holiday,' said Denis Betts. 'I've had to drag myself through this last week. I could hardly lift my arms after some of the games and I couldn't turn over in bed because of the bruises. I was physically exhausted and mentally drained. In fact I reached the stage on Thursday where I didn't want to play any more. Now we've won the Championship, though, all the aches and pains have vanished.'

Virtually every other member of the squad had a similar tale of fatigue, bruising, sleeplessness and sheer mental and physical exhaustion. The exception was Bobby Goulding, celebrating a key role in the victory on his return to the first team. For the moment he was on top of the world. Whether he would be quite so happy, if Andy Gregory recovered from his injury before the Cup Final, would be revealed in the next fortnight.

For Gregory and the other seriously-injured players, Ellery Hanley, Shaun Edwards and Joe Lydon, the first round of the end-of-season Premiership competition – a knock-out tournament between the top eight sides – would come too soon. All four made the journey to see a London specialist, the best in his field, on the Monday morning, and all had their thoughts and hopes focused on being fit for Wembley in two weeks time.

Wembley

THE OMENS did not look good for at least two of them. The London specialist rang Maurice during Tuesday night's board meeting, to say that in his opinion neither Ellery nor Joe would be fit to play at Wembley. He said that Joe was definitely out and only Ellery's remarkable recovery rate from injury gave him even a slight chance of being fit in time. 'If it was anybody but Ellery, I would say he would definitely not be fit,' said the specialist, 'but I've seen before how quickly his injuries can heal.'

Ellery would stay on in London for the rest of the week and a decision on his fitness for the Cup Final would be left until the last minute. There was better news of the other two, for the specialist was confident that both Andy Gregory and Shaun Edwards would be fit to play.

John Monie had given his entire first-team squad the Tuesday off. After four games in six days, they scarcely needed any fitness training, but most of them still came in to have treatment on their various injuries. The team for the first round of the Premiership against Featherstone was unrecognisable from that used against Leeds. Youngsters Paul Gartland and Steve Blakeley, both making their debuts, joined Graeme West in the squad, West appearing for the second time in a fortnight, after an eighteen-month absence from the first team. There was also a first appearance of the season for the disgruntled hooker Augustine 'Ducky' O'Donnell.

Wigan had been less successful in the Premiership than any other competition; in its fifteen-year history they had won it only once. Part of the reason for that was its timing. The first and second rounds always sandwiched the Challenge Cup Final and players building up to, or coming down from the ultimate trip in rugby league – down Wembley Way – were often understandably off-key in the Premiership. This phenomenon is not confined to Wigan, for no team has ever won both competitions in the same season. With ten first-choice players ruled out through injury and one because of suspension, for Skerrett's appeal against his ban had been unsuccessful, it seemed certain that Wigan would not be bucking the trend this year either.

On his way into the Tuesday board meeting, Maurice Lindsay had been ambushed by the architect of the new stand, who wanted to show him the plans for various additions to the new structure, including a leisure centre, a pub and new changing rooms, which the board had envisaged in more optimistic times. 'We're going to struggle to pay for what we've built already,' said Maurice. 'We're already £300,000 over budget, but if we don't give the players new dressing rooms, or at least a new home dressing room, they'll go mad. So we'll have to have that, but the rest may have to wait until we have the money.'

The main items on the agenda for the board meeting were the arrival of two players at Central Park and the impending departure of another one. The two new ones, 16-year-olds from the Blackbrook club, were being signed as amateurs. The intention, routine in Wigan's junior signings, was to involve the lads with the club as amateurs, before signing them on professional terms as soon as the laws would allow, on their seventeenth birthdays.

While the two boys, their parents, the Wigan scout who had spotted them and the chief scout, who had also vetted them, waited outside, the directors discussed the two players. Maurice, who had gone to watch them play for their amateur side the previous night, gave his opinion on their merits, together with another prospect he had spotted. 'There was another player I saw when I went to watch those two, who could be a sensation,' said Maurice. 'He's a winger. He only got the ball four times and every time, he went straight through the defence, scattering them all over the place. He's coming to training on Thursday.'

The boys and their retinue were ushered into the boardroom. Dressed in their best clothes, the two sat tongue-tied with embarrassment, overawed by their surroundings. Maurice did his best to put them at their ease, without notable success. He gave them his standard 'Welcome to Central Park' speech, stressing the professionalism of the Wigan set-up, the facilities and individual coaching available to them and pointing out the many members of the present Wigan squad, such as Denis Betts and Phil Clarke, who had once come to the boardroom in similar circumstances.

The players signed amateur forms, and posed with Maurice for snaps for their family albums, taken by their proud mothers, then the group reluctantly took their leave as the board awaited the arrival of the disaffected Mark Preston, who was again seeking a meeting about his future at the club.

John Monie came upstairs to brief the board before Mark came in. 'He's going to want to know if I'll pick him in the team next year, but my answer has got to be the same as it would be to any player: "If your form's good enough, I'll pick you – and that isn't going to satisfy him."'

'Well he's turned down the terms we've offered him and we don't feel we can go any higher,' said Maurice. 'So, really the next step is up to him.'

Preston left them in no doubt about his intentions when he appeared a couple of minutes later. 'I'm frustrated that I can't get in the team, especially after playing at Wembley last year.' Preston's frustration was understandable. He had played 41 games the previous season and scored 32 tries, making him Wigan's leading scorer. This season he had played only four games, scoring two tries. The double signing of David Myers and Frano Botica had blocked Preston's route to the first team and in Monie's eyes, he was no longer even the first reserve for the wing positions.

'You know that Wigan was the club I always wanted to play for,' said Preston, 'but I feel now like I want to move, make a fresh start with a new club.' No-one attempted to dissuade him.

'We'll notify the Rugby League,' said Maurice 'and they'll circulate all the clubs to let them know you're available.'

'I'd just like to say that, though you've obviously been frustrated at not getting into the side this season, I've been impressed by your attitude,' said Monie, extending his hand. 'You haven't moaned to the press or the other players about it and you've shown great dignity. I wish you good luck, wherever you finish up.' As Preston shook hands, Monie added: 'And by the way, you're in the team on Saturday, so you've a chance to put yourself in the shop window.'

Wigan's patched-up side lacked eleven of the likely fifteen for Wembley in the Premiership tie against Featherstone.

Despite battling bravely, they went down 31–26, their first defeat since New Year's Day, eighteen matches before. It was a disappointment, but not altogether unexpected. It meant that the Challenge Cup Final on the following Saturday would now be their last game of the season.

Wigan's hopes of ending their year on the highest possible note on British sport's greatest stage, received a great boost the next morning. As the players went through a light-hearted game of 'tig and pass' enjoying themselves greatly in the warm spring sunshine, Ellery Hanley walked out onto the pitch. John Monie's face broke into a huge smile when he saw Hanley walking towards him. The Wigan captain talked to him for ten minutes before disappearing again, without a trace of a limp. It appeared that Hanley's remarkable self-healing powers would once again confound medical opinion. He looked a certain starter at Wembley. He didn't join in the tig and pass game, nor did Martin Dermott who was gingerly jogging round the pitch, trying out his injured leg. Assistant coach Harry Pinner, some years past his prime as a player, was recruited to make up the numbers. When he took a pass close to his own line, a huge gap miraculously opened up for him. He shot through it and ran seventy yards flat-out before grinding to a halt, red-faced and panting heavily. When he turned round it was to see the players rolling with laughter at the success of their practical joke.

Monie and the rest of his coaching team were keen to keep the week's preparation as far as possible 'business as usual'. Bill Hartley had been worried that the players had slump, ' so heavily after their efforts in the final weeks of the Championship season that they might have had difficulty picking themselves up for the Cup Final, but the sight of the players skylarking on the sunlit Monday morning had eased his fears.

If the players were full of the joys of spring on that sunny morning, however, they were far from recovered after their punishing run-in to the Championship. Arguably they would have found it easier to play the Challenge Cup Final a few days after the final League game, rather than come back to it after a two-week break that gave them time to stop and realise just how exhausted they had become, but not sufficient time to recover completely. Many of them were still troubled by injuries, and Dr Zaman's pain-killing injections would once more have a major role to play at Wembley. Both Ellery

Hanley and Joe Lydon had made surprisingly good progress with their hamstring injuries, but neither was anywhere near fit. They had not even jogged since sustaining the injuries.

Wembley is the most unforgiving place for a player carrying an injury. Over the years, many have tried to get through a Cup Final when less than fully fit and most of them have been found out, becoming a liability to their team, often cruelly exploited by their opponents. If any player could be an exception to that rule, however, it had to be Ellery Hanley. Wigan delayed, and then delayed again, a decision on whether to include him in the side, before finally announcing that the decision would only be made after a pre-match fitness test, on the Wembley turf, just thirty minutes before the game. It was an unprecedented step and would be the most public fitness test ever, in front of 75,000 fans.

Throughout Friday, London had been slowly submerging under a tide of shell-suits and Northern accents. Bemused hotel barmen tried vainly to keep pace with the beer orders machine-gunned at them, while simultaneously trying to comprehend complaints about the prices, delivered in pure 'Lanky twang'.

On Saturday, the Wigan and Saints hordes, augmented by fresh phalanxes who had journeyed down that morning, emerged from their hotels in their tribal markings – replica shirts, scarves and hats. The neutrals sported the colours of every club in the country and a good many from all over the world. They converged on Wembley from every point of the compass, a noisy, beery, but good-natured throng, come to teach the capital its annual lesson about their kind of rugby, a game in which the action is fast, fearsome and confined to the pitch, not the terraces.

The Wigan team had followed their normal pre-match routine as far as was possible in a hotel a long way from home. They had a light meal, listened to John Monie's briefing and watched a video, before boarding the coach for the forty-minute journey to Wembley from their hideaway in darkest Essex. Ninety minutes before kick-off the coach turned off Empire Way into the stadium approach and nosed its way through the crowds to the massive double doors guarding the entrance. Wigan fans banged on the sides of the coach and waved to the players, who largely remained lost in their private thoughts.

As the doors thudded shut behind the coach, it stopped in a place the players knew well, the tunnel leading to the pitch. Players and officials immediately walked up the tunnel to sample the atmosphere and walk the Wembley turf, before returning to the dressing room. Alone of the party, Ellery went straight to the dressing room to change for his highly public fitness test.

As the rest of the party came out of the shadow of the tunnel into the bright spring sunlight, the stadium, already two-thirds full, erupted into life. Saints' fans were booing and jeering, Wigan's cheering and brandishing their home-made banners, one the inevitable Bart Simpson with the legend 'Prepare to be Dazzled' another, rather more poetic, 'They may be saints, we may be sinners, but in 1991 we're still the winners'.

The players strolled around the pitch with Wembley debutant Phil Clarke already burning up with nerves, opening up a fifty yard lead on the rest of his team-mates as he hurried through his lap and disappeared back down the tunnel to begin his preparation for the game. Ian Gildart walked more slowly, with the rest of the players. After Ellery's fitness test, Gildart would have a mere thirty minutes warning of whether he would be watching the game from the stands or taking the field.

As the Wigan party disappeared back down the tunnel, Maurice Lindsay told me: 'Ellery's going for his run as soon as the Saints players have left the pitch, in about ten minutes. Ian Gildart's fired-up and ready to go if necessary. He's mentally prepared to play but it may all be for nothing if Ellery's fit, as we hope he will be. We're just keeping our fingers crossed. Don't come into the dressing room for a minute though, Ellery's a bit hot-wired.' Two minutes later I slipped in and was ushered hastily to the far side of the room, opposite the corner where Ellery was changing ready for the test. As he laced his boots, both Lindsay and John Monie stood anxiously over him.

Hanley stood up and strode out of the room, Lindsay hurrying alongside him. I followed, like a Muslim bride, three respectful paces behind. They walked through into the adjoining shower room where Dr Zaman had established his mobile treatment centre. Several of the other players would be having the by-now routine pain-killing jabs, but that would not have worked for Hanley's injury. What was needed was something completely different, which Dr Zaman was about to supply. He gave Hanley an injection, after carefully exploring his injured leg and while Ellery returned to the dressing room to allow it time to take effect, Dr Zaman explained to me what he had done.

'It's a technique I use in my work as a plastic surgeon, but it is very rarely done for sports injuries. It's a nerve-blocking injection and I decided to use it on Ellery after John Monie asked if there was anything I could do. I was his last hope. The technique is a bit difficult to explain, but it involves drawing a diagram which shows the exact location of the injury. It has to be very precise, because you are dealing with nerve ends and if you are not highly-trained, you could easily miss it. The effect of the injection only lasts four hours and obviously he still has the injury, but that will heal in a couple of weeks and there will be no permanent damage. Providing it has worked, the pain should already have eased.'

A few minutes later, Hanley emerged from the dressing room and set off up the tunnel, again with Maurice Lindsay in close attendance. When Ellery reached the top, he broke into a trot, jogging out onto the immaculate Wembley turf as the Wigan fans in the stadium cheered and chanted his name. He began running to and fro behind the goalposts, going at half-pace, not really stretching out and certainly not sprinting. As he ran, a TV crew scampered alongside, frantically trying to keep pace with him. After a couple of widths of the pitch, Hanley abruptly wheeled away and headed back towards the tunnel. He disappeared into the gloom, with Maurice Lindsay again hurrying to keep up. It was not only the most public fitness test ever, it was also the least searching. Hamstrings don't go when players are jogging at half-pace, they go when they are striding out or sprinting.

Lindsay, Monie and Hanley went into huddled conclave with Dr Zaman in the shower room, I expected one of the trio, chairman, coach or captain, to come through and make an announcement to the rest of the team, but the players merely carried on with their pre-match preparations, scarcely glancing as the three quietly filed back in. Perhaps the other players had already guessed the near-inevitable outcome of the 'test'.

John Monie walked over to Ian Gildart and murmured,

'Ellery's going to be OK.' Gildart nodded, hiding what must have been bitter personal disappointment. A moment later he had removed his jacket and was helping the physiotherapy team to rub down the players. Joe Lydon came across to Gildart for a few words, he of all the players knew what Gildart was feeling, for Lydon had voluntarily given up his own chance of playing to ensure that Wigan could afford the risk of playing Hanley. To start a Cup Final with one player carrying a hamstring injury was risky enough, to have done so with two would have been crazy and Joe made it easy for John Monie by withdrawing. As Monie told me after the game, 'Joe sacrificed his own chance so that Ellery could play. He did it for the team and it was an amazingly courageous decision.'

The tension and the Wembley nerves seemed to be affecting everyone. The dressing room was deathly quiet, with even Andy Gregory's incessant flow of chatter reduced to a few sporadic comments. 'Come on,' said Andy, 'we know how to win, they don't. They accept losing because they're a side full of losers; we don't.'

'There's only one thing we accept,' said Andy Goodway. Monie's thought for the day, on a placard fixed to the wall, was a simple one:

Great defence
Ball control
Field position

The pre-match comments from Monie and Hanley emphasised the theme with a familiar litany: defence, good talk, basics, concentration.

'Stick to our game plan,' said Ellery, 'let the generals control things, get them into the corners, do the basics.'

'Our defence is fifty points better than last year,' said Monie. 'That's what'll win this Cup – great defence. Force them into errors, force them into errors.'

Pinned to a locker was a clipping torn from a tabloid newspaper, an interview with St Helens' stand-off Jonathan Griffiths, under a screaming headline *WE'LL WHIP WIGAN*. He could not have chosen a better motivational tool, particularly for Andy Gregory. Griffiths scored two tries in Saints' semi-final victory against Widnes and because of both that and his background in Welsh rugby union, was very much media flavour of the month, to Andy's obvious displeasure. 'He's had one decent game and he's not been out of the papers since – knock him on his arse.'

Dr Zaman came into the room, clutching a collection of used syringes and needles. 'Do you have a box for sharps?' he asked the uncomprehending Wembley employee presiding over the tea urn in the corner. 'Just shove them in a plastic bag, they'll be alright,' said Steve Hampson, winking.

I left the dressing room just as the players began their 'give me ten' pre-match ritual. The sounds of the community singing drifted down the tunnel as I walked up towards the circle of light. The singing is an increasingly anachronistic feature of Cup Final day, conducted by an embarrassing singing comedian in a white suit. The fans sang their own tribal chants with far more gusto than *Delilah* or *Yellow Submarine*, though the traditional Cup Final anthem *Abide with Me* brings a lump to the throat of even the most hard-boiled press-box hack. Ten minutes before the kick-off, with the teams already filing out of the dressing rooms to begin the slow walk up the tunnel, the Wigan team changes were announced to the crowd. The words 'Number thirteen – Ellery Hanley' were greeted by a huge cheer from the Wigan fans.

The two teams made their measured ascent of the tunnel, side by side. Saints were obviously under instructions not to look at Wigan and to ignore any pre-match taunts, but Hanley made sure that they, like the crowd, knew he was there. As he walked up the tunnel, he kept slamming the ball against the concrete floor, shouting 'Defence, defence' to his team-mates. The crowd roar had diminished to an expectant murmur, every fan straining his eyes, peering into the gloomy tunnel for the first sight of the teams. At last they emerged into the light, the crowd's thunderous welcome bouncing off the roof of the stadium to drown everything in waves of noise. Red and white, and blue and white favours in their thousands flashed in the sunlight. Many of Wigan's already hard-pressed fans had dug even deeper into their reserves, or borrowed even more money, to buy replica shirts in the club's reserve strip of blue and white. St Helens had won the toss for choice of colours, held because though the two teams' first choice shirts are different patterns – Saints' chevrons and Wigan hoops – both are red and white, confusing for fans at the ground, let alone the television viewers around the world.

One desperate junior Wigan fan had written to John Monie in the week before the final, saying that he'd been saving for a blue and white strip ever since Wigan had been told they would have to change, but he had not been able to raise enough money. 'Would it be possible to borrow one until Monday morning?' A smiling Monie passed it on to the club shop, saying, 'Maybe they'll give him one.'

The teams lined up opposite the Royal Box for the presentation to the day's dignitaries and the national anthem, then peeled off one by one as their names were announced. Either through nerves or psychological warfare on the part of the players, or a cock-up on the part of the organisers, the announcer read out the wrong team as the players peeled-off, Wigan introduced as St Helens and Saints as Wigan. It was not to be by any means the last mistake that the Saints were to make that afternoon. Despite the confusion, each player was still rewarded by a cheer, that for Hanley the loudest, with a blast of boos from the Saints fans, drowned in a roar from Wigan's supporters. As St Helens kicked off a few moments later, another even greater roar rose from the crowd.

Two years before, an error-prone St Helens had been destroyed by Wigan, crushed 27–0, an unbearable affront to the pride of the team and the town. This was to be their chance for revenge, yet they began as if determined to repeat the experience. They could scarcely string two passes together without spilling the ball and compounded the errors by conceding a rash of penalties, though many errors were forced by the ferocity of the Wigan tackling, with Andy Platt in particular making some juddering hits.

Frano Botica struck a perfect penalty goal from wide out to give Wigan a sixth minute lead and within two minutes a St Helens error gifted them their first try. Full back Phil Vievers began to return a fine Andy Gregory kick deep in Saints' territory, but Shaun Edwards met him with a ferocious hit that jolted the ball loose. Kevin Iro swooped to gather it, popped it over the top to David Myers and he stepped inside a despairing cover tackle to cross for a try just a few minutes into his first Wembley appearance.

Botica's conversion attempt faded just to the left of the posts, but within five minutes he had crossed the line himself. Again a St Helens error gave Wigan possession, Paul Loughlin failing to find touch with a penalty kick. After a couple of drives up the middle, Wigan spun the ball left and Dean Bell made the initial break, off-loading to Denis Betts. He galloped forty yards, deep into Saints' territory and though the supporting Ellery Hanley was held back by Griffiths, preventing Betts from passing to him, Botica was free on the outside. As Betts fell to the full back's tackle, he got the ball away to Botica, who squeezed in at the corner. His touchline conversion sailed high between the posts and Wigan were 12 points ahead in as many minutes.

St Helens played out the remainder of the half under constant pressure, created in equal amounts by their own error rate and their opponents' power and professionalism, but Wigan failed to score again to put the game beyond recall and there were warning signs that their desperate weariness might yet be their undoing.

Twice in the closing stages of the half, Saints caught Wigan napping. Shane Cooper's lobbed kick sat up invitingly for winger Hunte, who knocked-on when it looked infinitely easier to take the ball and score and then, as the half-time hooter sounded and the Wigan players stopped momentarily, Saints' hooker Bernard Dwyer, realising the ball was still 'live', set off upfield. Hanley's lack of fitness was obvious from his failure to set off in pursuit and Dwyer made sixty yards before finding Connolly in support. With the defence closing in, Connolly had to kick optimistically to the posts and Botica, covering back from the opposite wing, was first to the ball, gathering it safely and touching down behind his own line to end the first half. The score remained 12–0, highly flattering to a dismal first-half performance from St Helens, but by no means an irreversible deficit.

The Wigan players slumped around the dressing room, as Monie and Hanley tried to lift them for one last effort. Hanley had been operating well below his peak in the first half, but though very far from fit, the psychological impact of his presence, both on his own side and the opposition was so great that the gamble of playing him was well worth the risk. It was inconceivable that he would leave the field before the result was decided.

'We're falling into the St Helens trap of trying to keep the ball alive when it's not safe to do so,' said Monie. 'Keep it simple, keep it direct, get back to playing our game. Now they've done probably twice as many tackles as you, so they're tired. We don't have to shut up shop, but play our game, not St Helens'.'

While Monie spoke, Shaun Edwards, who had damaged his knee ligaments early in the half, became yet another suitable case for treatment with Dr Zaman's pain-killing needle. Dean Bell was also troubled by an ankle injured in the first five minutes of the game. All the forwards looked weary, but there were still forty minutes to play and the game far from over. Talent and professionalism had put them 12 points ahead but only willpower and sheer guts would keep them there. Just forty minutes more effort and their once turbulent season would end in total triumph.

After a spell of early pressure, a long-range Andy Gregory drop goal gave Wigan another vital point, stretching their lead to three scores, but as Saints sensed their opponents' growing tiredness, they at last began to raise their own game, rousing their fans, who had subsided into silence during the embarrassingly one-sided first half.

Saints' running forwards Mann, Harrison and Ward, began to punch a few holes in Wigan's previously impregnable defensive line and fiery scrum-half Paul Bishop sparked his backline into action. He also kicked superbly and made several darting breaks through midfield. On one of these forays he was flattened by Steve Hampson after kicking the ball past him, an offence which earned 'Hampo' ten minutes in the sin-bin.

Wigan held out in his absence, but within two minutes of his return to the field, Saints finally cracked Wigan's last-line defence.

For once the ultra-professionals were the ones making a basic error, Andy Goodway throwing a loose pass in his own territory. Saints seized the ball, Jonathan Griffiths wriggled away from a tackle and floated a long pass out to the wing, enabling Hunte to cross in the corner. Bishop's superb conversion and his subsequent penalty put Saints within striking distance at 13–8 down, still with ten minutes to go, but a return to their error-prone first-half ways proved fatal to their chances.

The pressure on Wigan eased and with Andy Platt and Denis Betts both tackling like demons and driving the ball up as relentlessly at the heart of the Saints' defence, as they had done throughout the game, Wigan dredged up the last shreds of their reserves of strength and drove St Helens back downfield, out of the danger zone.

For the last five minutes, though their bodies must have been screaming for respite, Wigan battered at Saints, pinning them in their own territory, until the hooter signalled that 'Mission Impossible' was finally over. Wigan had achieved the Championship and Cup double for the second year running and had taken the Cup for an unprecedented fourth year in succession. Maurice Lindsay's remark in the aftermath of the previous year's first ever hat-trick of Wembley successes, 'This record will never be broken . . . or at least the only people to beat it will be this lot next year' had proved to be remarkably prophetic.

Twelve months before, Frano Botica had been a rugby union player, watching on television in New Zealand as Ellery Hanley lifted the cup. Now, 12,000 miles and twelve months later, he had scored the points that had given Wigan victory and was following his captain up the steps to the Royal Box to collect his own winner's medal. Each step bears the outline of a footprint, formed by the heads of nails embedded in the concrete. Some of the Wigan players looked so weary that they were probably grateful for the guidance.

The players took it in turns to raise the cup above their heads, as wave after wave of noise from their ecstatic fans broke over them, then toured the stadium showing the trophy to the crowd, a ritual become almost routine after four successive years. Dave Myers kept one hand on the cup most of the way round. If it was routine for Wigan, for him it was a new and overwhelming experience. As the players walked, limped and hobbled back down the tunnel and into the dressing room, they gave themselves up completely to the fatigue that they had held at bay for so long. I had never been in a winner's dressing room that was so silent and low-key. Only the smiles on the faces of the officials showed that this was not the losers' dressing room.

Andy Gregory's right shoulder was covered in blood from a gash on his head, Andy Platt was battered and bruised, with one eye rapidly closing. 'He looks like he's gone fifteen rounds with Mike Tyson, doesn't he?' said Maurice. 'It bloody feels like it as well,' came a muffled reply. For the second year running Shaun Edwards had carried an injury through the game. 'It's not a lucky dressing room for you, is it Shaun?' said Maurice, 'your face last year and now the knee.'

John Monie came in, having shaken off – for the moment – the pack of TV crews hounding him for interviews. 'With what we've been through, we didn't win the Cup today with talent, we did it with sheer guts and determination. We'll be back next year as well. Great work. Congratulations.'

Ellery followed, praising the back-room team as well as the players and reinforcing the point by giving the match ball to Andrew Pinkerton, the junior member of the physiotherapy triumvirate, working at his first Wembley final. The rest of the players applauded briefly but there were no cheers, they looked simply too exhausted to celebrate. For Kevin Iro there would be no return to Wembley next year, for as he sat on the bench, too tired for the moment even to strip off his kit and take a shower, he confirmed what the rumour mill had been saying for weeks, that he would be leaving Wigan to join his brother Tony and former Wigan coach Graham Lowe at the Sydney club Manly-Warringah.

As the usual media pack swamped the room, Denis Betts, the Lance Todd Trophy winner, was engulfed by the press. His own choice of man of the match would have been Andy Platt, who as ever had done the hard graft, always willing to make the tackle, drive the ball up, 'Fight one more round' in Monie's phrase of two weeks before. Asked for his thoughts, John Monie had a rather more surprising choice. 'The Lance Todd Trophy should have gone to our club doctor for his achievements this week. He was magnificent, I don't think any other doctor could have got Ellery Hanley onto the pitch. I can't thank him enough for what he has done for Hanley and all the other players in the last few weeks, when so many of them have been struggling with injuries. We owe him so much. Hanley was only about 20 per cent fit, but that was enough, because we needed him on the field, I wouldn't have done it for any other player, but Hanley is special – he's our leader and our inspiration.'

I asked John how many of the players had needed pain-killing jabs before the game. 'They were held together by needles and sticking plaster. Denis Betts and David Myers were the only two players who were fully fit, all the others had something wrong with them. Normally during the season you expect to take the field with eleven fit players and two carrying injuries, today we had two fit ones and eleven carrying injuries.'

The pressmen, the television crews and the photographers departed, the players showered, changed and drifted out of the room one by one. As usual Dean Bell was one of the last. He sat wincing on the bench as Keith Mills bandaged his injured ankle. 'You've got to take a bit of pain in this game sometimes, Dean,' said Keith with a smile.

'Have you, Keith? I didn't realise that. Get it down in your quotes for the book, Neil, it's a beauty!' As Ellery came back through from the showers, Keith looked up, winked at us and called out, 'Official training for the new season starts on the first of July, Ellery.' There was a burst of laughter. 'Thanks Keith, that's what I really needed to know right now.'

The stadium approach was already almost deserted, Wigan's army of fans having begun the long journey home. By the next day, 30,000 of them would be lining the streets for the annual Wigan spring party, welcoming home the team as they paraded the Challenge Cup through the town. Only a few stragglers still wandered down the concrete ramp from the stadium, among the empty beer cans and hot-dog wrappers stirring lazily in the breeze.

In the Wigan dressing room, the baskets had already been filled with soiled kit and hauled out to be loaded on the coach for the last time in the season. Dean Bell put on his jacket and limped out of the dressing room. Taffy produced a cigar from an inside pocket and lit it. He picked up the Cup in one hand and took a last look around the room, now deserted save for myself and the master of the Wembley tea-urn, waiting patiently, as usual, to lock up. 'See you next year then,' he called to the departing Taffy.

'As usual,' replied Taffy, strolling out into the tunnel and heading up towards the sunlight, the Challenge Cup still dangling nonchalantly from his hand.

Dramatis Personae

THE AUTHOR

Neil Hanson Writer, broadcaster and rugby league aficionado. With 80 per cent more muscle, 90 per cent more skill and a 100 per cent higher pain threshold, plus a heart transplant, he could almost have become a rugby league player himself.

THE PLAYERS

Ellery Hanley Loose forward/stand-off/centre. Professional footballer. The best. The Wigan and Great Britain captain and the greatest player of his generation. A prolific try-scorer, devastating broken-field runner, relentless tackler, superb tactician and an inspirational leader. Returned early in the season after a groin injury that many thought might end his career, to reach new heights as a player and captain.

Were Hanley less reclusive and more willing to 'play the media game' he would certainly have become much more widely recognised beyond the confines of his own sport as one of the supreme athletes of his generation.

Dean Bell Centre. Professional footballer. 'Mean Dean', a New Zealand Test player, is not the biggest, but certainly one of the toughest three-quarters in the world game. A model professional, consistently playing to the peak of his form, Bell is a ferocious competitor and savage tackler, who could put fire into any team and make even the most durable opponent think hard about trying to run past him.

Denis Betts Second-row forward. Student. Burst on the league scene as an 18-year-old, and at 21, is now a seasoned veteran and established Great Britain star. A powerful running forward, so durable that he played in every one of Wigan's games during their gruelling Championship year. Wigan's fans may complain that he doesn't pass enough, it's not a complaint voiced by his coach.

Frano Botica Wing. Professional footballer. Ex-All Black rugby union star signed in a blaze of publicity during the off-season. A quick learner, who has worked hard to improve his game and ease his coach's reservations about the wisdom of the signing. His originally suspect defence is much-improved and he is a fast and elusive runner, scoring plenty of tries. His immaculate goal-kicking has solved a long-standing Wigan problem.

Phil Clarke Loose forward. Student. Though still only 19, Clarke is undoubtedly destined for the game's highest honours and is many people's idea of Ellery Hanley's successor as both Wigan and Great Britain captain. Always a very skilled footballer, he has bulked-up over the past year to become an even more powerful runner. Gets through a lot of unobtrusive work in defence, topping Wigan's tackle count during the Championship decider.

Martin Dermott Hooker. Professional footballer. Extrovert hooker and midfield organiser. A dangerous dummy-half runner, his quick hands make him an excellent distributor of the ball. A Great Britain international, his only weakness is a tendency to blow hot and cold, often following a 'blinder' with an ordinary game. After losing his place to Bobby Goulding early in the season, fought back to make the number nine shirt his own.

Shaun Edwards Stand-off. Professional footballer. 'Gizz' is a former teenage prodigy, and a perfect foil for Andy Gregory at half-back, their rivalry spurring both to raise their game to new heights. Edwards has blistering pace off the mark, great vision and constant alertness for the half-chance. He has a fine passing and kicking game, demands perfection from himself and expects it from his colleagues. He showed his courage when staying on the field, despite a fractured eye-socket and cheekbone, during a Wembley Cup Final.

Andy Goodway Back-row forward. Professional footballer. Goodway's nickname 'B.A.' stands not for Bachelor of Arts, but Bad Attitude, a frequent complaint from his previous coaches, though John Monie has found the way to bring out the best of him. Goodway is an explosive running forward, at his best wide of the ruck. Often pops up in the centres and is quick enough to play there when injuries require it. A prolific try-scorer, Goodway suffered a badly broken arm in mid-season, but returned to play his part in the Championship bid.

Bobby Goulding Scrum-half. Unemployed. Mercurial half-back, destined for greatness, if he can control his temperament. He has the complete range of scrum-half skills and may even be better than Andy Gregory one day. Andy is Bobby's hero, but Goulding is increasingly reluctant to wait patiently in the great man's shadow for his first-team chance.

Andy Gregory Scrum-half. Scrap-metal dealer. Brilliantly inventive half-back, with more tricks up his sleeve than Paul Daniels. A pugnacious, combative character, the lynch-pin of Wigan's attacking game and the best half-back in the world game.

Ian Gildart Second-row forward. Maintenance engineer. A workaholic forward and tackling machine. If you are looking for a forward to knock out forty tackles a game without complaint, Gildart is the ideal candidate. Not the most subtle or creative footballer with the ball in his hands, but a 100 per cent trier and one-man defensive unit.

Steve Hampson Full back. Publican. The gap-toothed 'Hampo' is popular with players and fans alike. A no-frills full back, brave to the point of foolhardiness, and a supreme defuser of 'bombs' – the steepling kicks known as 'up and unders' in another era. Hampo gathers them to him like a protective mother cradling a child, leaping high into the air to snatch the ball in the teeth of onrushing opponents. His only weakness is a rush of blood to the head that sees him launch himself into last-line tackles like a Cruise missile. If he is on target, the result can be devastating, but he risks decapitation for his opponent or embarrassment for himself as he flies airborne past an opponent who has checked and stepped inside him.

Kevin Iro Centre. Professional footballer. 'The Beast' is a gentle giant off the field, but a brute of a centre on it, almost impossible to knock down and surprisingly quick for a man of his size. His fend could stop a charging rhino in its tracks and his only weakness is his handling, which sometimes lets him down.

Joe Lydon Centre or wing. Graphic designer. Another great of the modern game, so versatile that he has filled every backline position for Great Britain. Has a siege gun boot, sending downtowns from one end of the pitch to the other. Increasingly injury-prone, he may be in the twilight of his career, but is still capable of turning a game with a try or, on one memorable occasion, a sixty-yard drop goal.

Ian Lucas Prop. Antique dealer. 'Mal' is a hard-grafting prop forward who added a touch of 'mongrel' to his play during the season, to cement his first team place at Wigan, claim his first Test cap and make a strong case for being regarded as the best number eight prop in the British game.

David Myers Wing. Professional footballer. Signed from Warrington in the close-season, a fast, determined, jinking runner and strong defender. His weakness is an occasional tendency to take the longest route to the try-line, while his scoring rate is not as high as a winger with Wigan should achieve, but he is young and full of the potential needed to develop into a lethal finisher.

Andy Platt Second row or prop. Professional footballer. The most consistent and the most consistently under-rated forward in the British game. Hits the advantage line earlier, faster and harder than any other player. A relentless tackler, whose work-rate compares with any player in the game. Quiet, un-demonstrative and a good clubman, Platt is a coach's ideal player, and there is not a coach in Britain who would not break the bank to sign him.

Kelvin Skerrett Prop forward. Professional footballer. The rugged prop was signed from Bradford at the end of the previous season, after he had destroyed Wigan's pack in a Premiership game. Bradford mothers used to frighten their children to sleep by threatening that Skerrett would come and get them! Troubled by injuries and asthma during his first few months at Central Park, he battled back to become again one of the best props in the British game, always likely to smash a hole in the dense defensive traffic around the ruck and off-load the ball to a supporting player. His major weakness is a short fuse that saw him sent off twice during the season, the second earning him a suspension that forced him to sit out the Challenge Cup Final.

ALSO APPEARING

Steve Blakeley Stand-off. Student. A late-season debutant against Featherstone, who made a try-scoring start to his senior career.

Russ Bridge Hooker. Came on trial from Second Division Fulham at the start of the season. Played in the Charity Shield, but was not offered a contract.

Ged Byrne Utility back. Window cleaner. One of the most versatile and well-liked players at the club, Ged was transferred to Wakefield Trinity, against his coach's wishes, early in the season.

Mike Forshaw Back-row forward. Council worker. Forshaw's versatility means that he can fill almost any role in the pack. A genuine and wholehearted competitor, so far limited to just a handful of senior appearances.

Paul Gartland Centre. Electrician. Made his first-team debut in the penultimate game of the season, after enduring the frustration of being a non-playing substitute against Wakefield two months before.

John Gilfillan Utility back. Transferred to Salford after just one appearance, in the Charity Shield.

David Marshall Wing. Sales assistant. Promising young player, who suffered an horrendous knee injury early in the season. Despite opinions that he would never play again, has bravely and relentlessly worked to prove those opinions wrong.

Augustine O'Donnell Hooker. Construction worker. 'Ducky' had three substitute outings the previous season but only managed a single first-team game this time, in the Premiership match against Featherstone. His first-team chances were limited by John Monie's preference for Goulding, Goodway and Stazicker as replacements for Martin Dermott, ahead of the specialist, but less experienced O'Donnell.

Mark Preston Wing. Insurance underwriter. Free-scoring winger who was unable to reclaim a first-team place after the summer signings of Botica and Myers. Finished the season on the transfer list.

Ged Stazicker Back-row forward. Student. Versatile and industrious forward who was frequently drafted into the first-team squad as injuries took their toll.

Shaun Wane Prop. Played in the Charity Shield, which turned out to be his last appearance for Wigan. He was transferred to Leeds in September.

Sean Tyrer Full back. Plasterer. Son of a former Wigan player, his first team opportunities were limited by the consistency of Steve Hampson.

THE DIRECTORS

Maurice Lindsay Wigan chairman and the driving force behind the club's rise to greatness over the past decade. May run Wigan from the heart, but his shrewd business brain is never far behind. Part schoolboy enthusiast, part Machiavelli, Lindsay's other occupation as a rails bookmaker has honed his gambler's instinct; not many of his gambles at Wigan have failed.

Jack Robinson Vice-chairman. Joined the board at the same time as Lindsay and is closest to his chairman in both age and approach. Robinson's business interests include antiques shipping.

Jack Hilton By far the longest serving member of the Wigan establishment. A white-haired, old-fashioned businessman, Hilton, alone of the Wigan board, was a professional footballer himself, playing for Wigan in the 1950s.

Tom Rathbone A local bread magnate and acting, honorary, unpaid boardroom telephonist, co-opted onto the board shortly after Lindsay and Robinson.

THE COACHING STAFF

John Monie Wigan coach. A cool, thoughtful, methodical and brilliantly effective coach. Given the daunting task of succeeding the phenomenally successful Graham Lowe at Wigan, Monie has equalled and even surpassed his achievements. He came to Wigan from the Australian club Parramatta, having coached them to Grand Final success in Sydney and has reached even greater heights with Wigan.

Harry Pinner Assistant coach. One of the most skilful, ball-playing loose forwards to play for Great Britain, Pinner spent most of his playing career at St Helens, but now helps to coach their most hated rivals, as John Monie's right-hand man.

Graeme West 'A' team coach. Rangy, craggy New Zealander, one of the first of the wave of overseas imports after Wigan's 're-birth' in the 1980s. Captained them to Wembley triumph as a player, now coaches the reserves. Even at 37, is still fit enough and good enough to turn out for the first team when injuries require it. Also works in the club's Promotions Department.

Bill Hartley Sprint trainer. A former British Olympic athlete, now Wigan's conditioner and sprint trainer, charged with overseeing the general fitness training and working with individual players to iron out deficiencies in their running style and improve their sprint speed.

Bob Lanigan An Australian weight-training expert, 'Lano' was brought over by Monie to work with the players during the summer and the first couple of months of the season, building up their strength and power through relentless weight-training.

THE BACKROOM TEAM

Denis Wright Physiotherapist. Performs a vital role in treating Wigan's injured players, getting them fit and back on the field quicker than at almost any other club.

Keith Mills First-aider and 'strapper'. A former Wigan player, who became first-aider after his own career was terminated by injury. Wigan's most consistent performer; has never missed even one of over 1,500 first team and reserve matches since then. Also acts as messenger-boy between the coach and the players out on the field.

Dr Ansar Zaman Club doctor. Attends every game, giving instant diagnosis and treatment of more serious injuries, stitching cuts and on all-too frequent occasions, administering pain-killing injections, enabling players carrying injuries to take the field for vital matches.

Andrew Pinkerton Masseur and junior member of the physio, first-aid and strapping crew.

Derek 'Taffy' Jones Head groundsman and kit-man.

BACK STAGE

Mary Charnock Club Secretary. One of the few women performing a traditionally male job in rugby league and doing it as well, if not better than any of her male peers.

Mandy Roper Assistant Secretary.

Other Members of the Backstage Team: Anne Ashcroft, Peter Aspinall, Billy Bithell, Billy Blan, Cathy Blan, Paul Bradshaw, Pauline Cahill, Gordon Harrison, Jack Keane, John Martin, John Martindale, Anne Mills, Elaine Mitchinson, Vince Smith, Derek Standish, Mary Stretton, Tom Stretton, Paul Taylor, Billy Unsworth, Sharon Yardley.

APPENDIX II

Results 1990–91

Date	Venue/Result	Attendance
19 August	Widnes (Charity Shield) (Swansea) L 8–24	11,178
26 August	Barrow (Lancashire Cup 1) (H) W 70–8	8,377
2 September	Widnes (Lancashire Cup 2) (A) L 22–24	13,889
9 September	Sheffield Eagles (H) D 18–18	11,808
16 September	Castleford (A) W 38–18	9,477
23 September	Rochdale Hornets (H) W 24–2	11,108
30 September	Bradford Northern (A) L 30–31	9,321
7 October	Hull (A) L 4–24	9,500
14 October	Australia (H) L 6–34	25,101
4 November	Oldham (H) W 38–15	13, 847
13 November	Hull Kingston Rovers (A) W 36–6	5,500
17 November	Featherstone Rovers (H) W 24–4	7,609
27 November	Wakefield Trinity (A) L 12–14	8,000
2 December	Whitehaven (Regal Trophy 1) (A) W 24–6	3,800
9 December	Keighley (Regal Trophy 2) (H) W 36–16	5,972
15 December	Bradford Northern (Regal Trophy 3) (H) L 6–12	5, 296
23 December	Leeds (H) W 22–16	14,354
26 December	St Helens (A) W 28–15	13, 326
1 January	Warrington (H) L 6–14	15,986
6 January	Sheffield Eagles (A) W 46–4	5,500
19 January	Widnes (A) W 22–14	7,205
2 February	Hull Kingston Rovers (H) W 34–4	7,410
12 February	Castleford (Challenge Cup 1) (A) W 28–4	6,644
24 February	Rochdale Hornets (Challenge Cup 2) (A) W 72–4	6,487
3 March	Wakefield Trinity (H) W 16–8	11,688
10 March	Bradford Northern (Challenge Cup 3) (H) W 32–2	17,752
13 March	Hull (H) W 34–12	15,309
17 March	Rochdale Hornets (A) W 44–16	3,849
23 March	Oldham (Challenge Cup Semi-final) (Bolton) W 30–16	19,057
26 March	Warrington (A) W 26–8	7,437
29 March	Featherstone Rovers (A) W 24–16	5,334
1 April	Oldham (A) W 10–4	7,307
4 April	St Helens (H) W 28–14	17,400
7 April	Castleford (H) W 24–4	14,018
9 April	Widnes (H) W 26–6	29,701
11 April	Bradford Northern (H) D 18–18	19,182
13 April	Leeds (A) W 20–8	15,313

| 21 April | Featherstone Rovers (Premiership 1) (H) L 26–31 | 9,132 |
| 27 April | St Helens (Challenge Cup Final) (Wembley) W 13–8 | 75,532 |

Wigan Scorers 1990–91

Tries: 29 – Hanley, 18 – Myers, Botica, 16 – Edwards, Iro, 12 – Betts, 11 – Lydon, Bell, 10 – Goodway, 6 – Dermott, 4 – Gregory, 3 – Goulding, Skerrett, 2 – Hampson, Preston, 1 – Blakeley, Clarke, Forshaw, Gildart, Lucas, Platt, Stazicker, West.

Goals: 129 – Botica, 21 – Lydon, 12 – Hampson, 5 – Goulding, 3 – Tyrer, 1 – Edwards.

Drop-Goals: 3 – Goulding, 1 – Gregory, Hanley.

APPENDIX IV

Stones Bitter Championship
Final Table 1990–91

	P	W	D	L	F	A	Pts
Wigan	26	20	2	4	652	313	42
Widnes	26	20	0	6	635	340	40
Hull	26	17	0	9	513	367	34
Castleford	26	17	0	9	578	442	34
Leeds	26	14	2	10	602	448	30
St Helens	26	14	1	11	628	533	29
Bradford	26	13	1	12	434	492	27
Featherstone	26	12	1	13	533	592	25
Warrington	26	10	2	14	404	436	22
Wakefield	26	10	2	14	356	409	22
Hull K.R.	26	9	3	14	452	615	21
Oldham	26	10	0	16	481	562	20
Sheffield	26	7	2	17	459	583	16
Rochdale	26	1	0	25	310	912	2

APPENDIX V

Glossary of Rugby League Jargon

Advantage Line – imaginary line drawn through the play-the-ball. Coaches expect their players to get across the advantage line in attack and prevent the opposition from doing so in defence.

Bomb – the high kick called a 'Garryowen' in rugby union circles. Known in the League as an 'up and under' during the Eddie Waring era.

Bust – a break, e.g. 'we made a bust up the middle'.

Downtown – kick downfield, usually, though not always, made late in the tackle-count.

Chase – pursuit of downfield kick by a group of players aiming to tackle the opponent collecting the ball close to his own line.

Fend – a hand-off.

Grubber – kick along the ground, usually placed just behind the opposition defensive line or into their in-goal area, forcing defenders to stop and turn and giving attackers an even chance of reaching the ball first.

Hit – a tackle. Bit hit – a crunching tackle intended to intimidate the opponent or jar the ball loose.

Marker – defender guarding the opponent at the play-the-ball.

Money is on – a phrase meaning that an extra large bonus is being offered to the players.

Name-Drop – mention a player by name. Done to put off an opposition danger man. By continually calling out his name to each other, e.g. 'Get McKenzie, watch McKenzie,' the players let him know that they have singled him out and will be in wait for him if he tries to run or make a break.

Talk – a huge amount of talk occurs out on the field. Part of this is 'sledging' – trying to put an opponent off his game by telling him how bad he is, or who his girlfriend is sleeping with – but talk is also the means by which players gee each other up and make sure the defensive line is properly organised. As a general rule, a team still talking late in the game is a team on top.

Offload – pass.

Play-the-ball – means of re-starting play after a tackle has been completed.

Prop – either a prop forward or another word for side-step; e.g. 'he props off his left foot'.

Reefing the ball – stealing the ball in the tackle, which is allowed until the tackle is completed or the referee calls 'held'.

Ruck – play-the-ball or area around the play-the-ball.

Settler – a drive by one of the players, who takes the ball up, while his team-mates organise a move.

Sin-bin – mythical place, actually the bench in the team dug-out, where players guilty of infractions of the rules are sent for five or ten minutes to cool down and repent. More serious offences are punished by a sending-off.

Six tackle rule – in rugby league, the ball is retained by one side until a player has been grounded by a tackle six times. At the end of six tackles the ball is handed over to the opposition.

To avoid this, teams routinely kick downfield or hoist a 'bomb' or a grubber kick before the last tackle.

Spill the ball – drop it.

Step – side-step; e.g. 'he has a left foot step'.

Stiff-arm – illegal tackle in which a defender's stiff arm hits an opponent's head.

Support – often used as a noun describing players backing-up in support of a player making a break.

Unload – pass.